THE BOY FROM BAGHDAD

NADHIM ZAHAWI

THE BOY FROM FROM BAGHDAD

MY JOURNEY FROM WAZIRIYAH TO WESTMINSTER

HarperCollins*Publishers*

HarperCollins*Publishers*
1 London Bridge Street
London SE1 9GF

www.harpercollins.co.uk

HarperCollins*Publishers*
Macken House, 39/40 Mayor Street Upper
Dublin 1, D01 C9W8, Ireland

First published by HarperCollins*Publishers* 2024

1 3 5 7 9 10 8 6 4 2

A catalogue record of this book is
available from the British Library

ISBN 978-0-00-864069-9

Printed and bound in the UK using 100%
renewable electricity at CPI Group (UK) Ltd

To my beautiful wife, Lana

'A woman was the first with whom I fell in love, and desired to live with and talk to ... It is she who was the first one whom I desired to be next to and help ... A woman is the remedy of youth, the beauty of nature, the splendour of life, the garment of pure spring and its purple smiling flowers, and is the poetry which makes men sing ...'

Jamil Sidqi al-Zahawi

CONTENTS

Part Three: To Westminster

PREFACE

Even before it started, the evening of 1 February 2011 looked set to be a pretty important one. I'd spent the previous decade as chief executive of YouGov and had handed over my keys to the building in order to become MP for Stratford-on-Avon in the 2010 election. Face time with the prime minister was a rarity for any new backbencher but, after a mix-up with his wife's diary, David Cameron had found himself stuck at home on babysitting duty one night and decided to use the time to get to know a few of the new recruits. I must have done something right because, at 4 p.m. that day, I got a call to say I was one of them. I put on my best suit and prepared to sell myself to my new boss.

I'd spent fifteen-odd years waiting to become a member of parliament but had never really imagined how heavily my earliest steps might influence later ones. I was not to know that less than ten months in, I'd be faced with the first real test of my moral compass or that the conversation that night would ensure I stayed pinned to the backbenches for the next seven years.

Dinner at the Downing Street flat was the kind where you ate in the kitchen and brought your own wine but, even so, the PM was never wholly off the clock. As we took our places at the table, he made advance apologies for a call he'd have to take from Egypt's then President Mubarak. An hour in, and he excused himself as predicted, returning a while later a lot more flustered than when he'd left. 'You look a bit flushed, Prime Minister,' I ventured. 'What happened?' The answer was an explosive conversation with an enraged dictator whose country was under siege from citizens revolting against 30 years of political oppression. In response to the uprising, the Americans had sent an envoy to talk to Mubarak. Mubarak had assured the envoy that he'd not only announce reforms, but that he wouldn't contest the election results in the autumn either. It was good news all round. It wasn't until the envoy was about to board a plane back to the United States that Mubarak revealed the changes he'd promised wouldn't be coming until September. Cairo was burning; by September there'd be nothing left to reform. His concessions weren't going to appease anyone. In the hours leading up to our dinner it was agreed that the British PM would pick up the baton and call Mubarak himself to squeeze from both sides, hence the interruption to our meal that night.

With diplomatic niceties out the way, the PM pressed Mubarak to reform immediately, not kick the can down the road and hope the problem would go away. His suggestion was met with a sufficiently long silence for Cameron to think the line had been cut, which made Mubarak's response even more disarming when it did come: 'Prime Minister,' he bawled loud enough for Dave to have to hold the phone away from his ear, 'you don't understand! Your people are good people. These people are terrible people!' At least that explained the colour of the PM's face when he returned to the table.

A week or so later and Mubarak was gone, but my dinner that evening served as a reminder that, when your values are challenged, you have to be ready to stand up for what you believe in, no matter how loud or intimidating the voice of your opponent.

It was a lesson that would stand me in good stead, and much sooner than I might have expected.

As we sat around Dave's big kitchen table, the conversation inevitably turned to his forthcoming legislative programme. While I may have been a novice MP, I was already 43 years old with more than two decades of experience as a salesman and entrepreneur under my belt. I was no spring chicken. The open-door policy I'd implemented at my own company was a reflection of my professional bottom line: surround yourself with talent and listen to what they have to say.

I was used to working in an environment where people felt safe to speak their minds so, when the topic of the House of Lords and its proposed abolition came up, I decided to be honest about my feelings. 'I think you're making a mistake, Prime Minister.' Since the ground hadn't immediately opened up beneath me, I carried tentatively on with my argument. Our parliamentary system has two houses but the Commons is supreme. While the Lords can delay a Bill, they can't actually stop it. When it came to the nomination of new peers, what we needed was a truly independent panel to select the best of the best from each and every walk of life, not another elected House that would compete for oxygen with the one we already had. But I knew the moment you created a democratic mandate for the Lords, that's exactly what they'd have to do. The whole point of the Upper House was not to *make* legislation but to improve it, and the diversity of its civilian membership and the range and breadth of their experience made it uniquely qualified to scrutinise the work of the Commons. I did not believe this was something we should be dismantling any time soon.

Dave was not in agreement with my position and argued that the 'senate' he had in mind would not be the same as that of the

US – mired in pork-barrel politics and routinely gridlocked. That only 10 or 20 per cent would be elected to avoid the same pitfalls. Even so, I said, our constitution is largely unwritten; while early participants of a reformed house might be compliant with its etiquette, one day you'll get a charismatic senator latching onto the idea that because his constituency is technically bigger than any MP's in the Commons, he's also that much more powerful. When a person like that decides to steamroll ahead with their priorities, there won't be much we can do to stop them. This, I argued, would be the moment when his proposed reforms threatened to create a dysfunctional democracy.

Visibly irritated by my comments, Dave quickly shut the conversation down. I may not have been powerful enough to press the point but my gut told me this Bill would set a dangerous precedent and concluded with a simple, 'We should be careful what we wish for, Prime Minister,' a line he clearly liked even less than my opening gambit. I left that evening aware I'd probably not made the best first impression on my new boss but slept soundly in the knowledge that I'd at least said my piece.

Three months later, a first draft of the Reform Bill was published and I wasn't the only one with concerns about its contents. I came from a country where the decimation of national institutions went completely unchallenged. My family had fled Iraq and the regime of Saddam Hussein more than thirty years before. I felt strongly about the need to maintain the checks and balances our democratic institutions provided over *any* one leader or *any* one regime because I'd lived under the alternative. A key tenet of conservatism is that things are difficult to create and maintain but very easy to destroy. Our parliamentary system has evolved organically over hundreds and hundreds of years and is admired the world over for its stability. It wasn't perfect but it was the best we were going to get – perhaps the best anywhere – and I had no intention of helping pull it down now.

Over the following weeks, my friend and fellow new MP, Jesse Norman, began talking about mounting a backbench rebellion against the Bill. In July 2011, a year before it reached the Commons, his intention was to present a private letter of dissent to the chief whip signed by as many Conservative backbenchers as he could get his hands on. It would be a clear but courteous shot across the bows to say there'd be serious trouble to come if the Bill were not dropped.

As my dad always said, the best way to lead an army is from the front. When your values come under threat, don't wait for others to defend them. Stand up and be counted even if it means you're the first to be shot down. I'd already put my head well and truly above the parapet that night in Dave's kitchen so there was no point turning back now. I knew Jesse to be one of the brightest, most principled men in Westminster; only an issue of the deepest constitutional importance could have persuaded him to organise a rebellion, and I felt exactly the same way. When the time came, I had no hesitation in signing that letter. Along with a few other like-minded MPs, I took my place by Jesse's side and led the charge against my own government.

The Queen's Speech at the 2012 state opening of parliament included the declaration that 'A Bill will be brought forward to reform the composition of the House of Lords,' which meant I was quite an odd choice of candidate to make the responding Humble Address, given my well-known opposition to the Bill. Ordinarily, the Address is given by one rising star and one veteran, and the list of MPs who've made it in the past is formidable. Since you're responding to the monarch, your speech isn't meant to be overly political. It should ideally deliver a serious point but with enough humour to hold the whole house, which is invariably packed for the occasion. With no heckling or interruptions, as a new backbencher, it's a unique opportunity to demonstrate your prowess as an orator in front of an audience that's not baying for your blood. For someone not long elected, it was an enormous honour and an equally daunting prospect.

While I'd like to think I was an objectively good candidate in my own right, when I was asked to deliver the Address that May, I knew it was a last-ditch attempt to lure me away from the rebel ranks rather than any sign of favouritism. My response, therefore, was to make clear that, while I was hugely grateful to the prime minister for the opportunity, my acceptance had no bearing on my attitude to the Bill. I would still be going against the party line. But the government had one last nugget with which to try and tempt me. As I walked back to my office that day in Norman Shaw North I was stopped by Nick Boles, MP for Grantham and Stamford and one-time director of Policy Exchange, a think tank that shaped much of Cameron's political persona. Nick had a message for me from the chancellor: 'George says if you pull away from the rebellion now, you'll be a minister next week.' Early preferment was something every new MP dreamed of: your rising star being noticed by the 'right' people and a shortcut through the back corridors of Whitehall to cabinet. Of course I wanted to be a minister. Who didn't? Having a hand in the way your country was run was the reason most people came to parliament, but I didn't want it at this price. 'I'm really sorry,' I said, 'but I can't do this. However much I'd love to be a minister, I can't go against my conscience.'

In those early months of my career, it is fair to say I wasn't making friends or influencing anyone – at least not anyone who could give me a leg-up – but I was happy with my lot. The backbenches, I would learn, were just as comfortable as the ones at the front and sometimes the conversation there was even more interesting.

In June 2012, the House of Lords Reform Bill was introduced to the Commons by Nick Clegg, who made clear that if it was opposed by the Lords, the government would use the Parliament Act to push it through. The press speculated that 30 to 40 Tories would be enough to defeat it, which meant that when we published a letter of opposition backed by 69 rebels, all hell broke out in the House. When it transpired Jesse had sent an email trying to persuade anyone wavering to back us hours before the vote, it turned the heat up even further. In the event, 91 Conservative MPs voted against the government; the biggest rebellion against a Bill at second reading since the Second World War, and a resounding victory for our alliance. Cameron was furious and demonstrated his displeasure by prodding Jesse repeatedly in the chest in the lobby after the vote for what he saw as his part in the defeat. Despite this, my conscience told me Jesse and I were on the right side of history.

What I'd learn over time was that, provided government has a reasonable majority, it has so many levers to pull that very few rebellions ever work. If you put your hand into the big wheel, you're likely to get your arm broken trying to stop the thing from turning. But this time round, we did it. The Bill was abandoned and formally withdrawn on 3 September. We'd stopped the wheel but the grease it left on my hands would be a black mark against my name for a very long time. I languished on the backbenches for the duration of the Dave and George show, and the message to the flock came loud and clear: if you misbehave, you don't get treats like all the other good children.

Had Cameron known me better he'd have realised a rebellion was quite out of character. For all my enthusiasm, I'm normally a very measured, cool-headed person. But I'd also been the naughtiest kid in school and, though I shied away from confrontation, I was pretty used to getting into trouble and never afraid to stand up for what I really believed in. The fact our rebellion had helped shape parliament in line with my own beliefs meant more to me than its negative effect on my career, and it would not be the last time I put country above both myself and my party. What's best for your career and what's best for your conscience were not always the same thing, and occasionally you'd be forced to choose between the two.

I'd come a long way since fleeing Iraq but my respect for democracy had not weakened in the interim. I knew first hand what it meant to live in a place where men who valued power above people tore down anything that stood in their path to get to the top; where institutions were only valuable until they became an obstacle. Britain might have been my home for nearly thirty-five years but my past was the reason I felt so strongly about protecting everything she stood for now.

Life in Westminster could be complicated. There'd always be more than one voice in an argument and knowing which one to listen to was not always clear-cut. Sometimes you had to trust your gut, even if that meant being unpopular. Events in the months after Dave's dinner told me I had a lot to learn about politics. In time, I'd go on to hold some of the most powerful roles in cabinet but, wherever I landed, the same principles guided me: the ones I'd acquired over my years in business and from trusted friends and family. Those things were what made me the person I was, not Westminster. I was 'Nadhim Zahawi' long before I arrived at No. 10; the same Nadhim Zahawi I'd been all those years before in Iraq …

PART ONE

FROM WAZIRIYAH

CHAPTER 1

THE HOUSE ON
THE CORNER

HOME

The only house I'd ever lived in was the one that had belonged to my paternal grandfather on Al-Tabari Street in the Waziriyah district of Baghdad – a detached, flat-roofed, yellow-brick building on a large corner plot. A covered porch stretched the width of the house for the days when it was too hot to step out into the sun. In the 1970s the numbering system became quite complicated, but it never mattered because the postman knew the house anyway and all anyone need say was 'Nadhim Zahawi' and any passer-by could point it out. By the time I was born, Nadhim senior had been dead for three years but everyone still knew who he was.

The garden sat at the front rather than the back of the house. There was no artificial grass or the sort of fancy watering systems that make Dubai look like Finland, so although the gardener did his best to create something that resembled a lawn, it was really mostly just mud. The smell of the water from the hosepipe when it hit the parched earth was something I'll always associate with Baghdad. My mum called it 'mixed water', but I think this was just to try and stop me drinking it straight from the pipe. In any case, I didn't dare because for the first couple of minutes it was scalding hot, having sat baking for hours in the coiled-up tube.

In every town, in every city, in every country of the world, there's a handful of boys who refuse to wear long trousers, and I was one of them. Had I lived in England, I'd have been the child with the mottled milk-bottle legs and grey shorts, trudging to school in the snow. As it was, the temperature rarely dropped below 15 degrees Celcius in Baghdad, even in winter. When it hit 45 or 50 degrees – as it routinely did in summer – the government dealt with these life-threatening extremes by simply not announcing the temperature. That way everyone would think it was okay to keep going to work and school, even though it was hot enough to cook a full English breakfast on the pavement. They weren't fooling me. My allegiance to the shorts was totally justified.

I was very small for my age, with a huge head of coiffed hair that looked like my mother blow-dried it daily. The downside of this was that I was constantly mistaken for a girl. The upside was that I was not too heavy to hide among the branches of our narenj tree, where I'd sit for hours at a time, my thin little legs dangling down like two pieces of brown cotton. The mass of waxy leaves provided the perfect camouflage if I didn't want to be found, but all my mum need do was shake the tree and that would be enough to smoke me out. I loved to hide. Although I had a tendency to get into trouble, it was less about trying to avoid punishment than wanting time alone to think. Even now when I'm sad or troubled I like to be by myself.

ANISSA AND SAADIDEEN

When the shade of the tree was not enough I'd play poker on the porch instead with my maternal grandma, Anissa, or 51 if we could persuade my sister and a friend to make up a four. Anissa made no secret of her love of gambling or thought anything of passing on her passion to her eight-year-old grandson, though she stopped short of taking me with her to the casino. As a little boy I promised her that when I grew up I'd buy her her own casino so she could play roulette all day long. For a woman born in 1901 she had an incredibly liberal, modern outlook on life. After my grandfather died in the 1970s, she came to live with us in London, where there were two things she grew to love even more than gambling. The first was Steve Davis, whose matches we recorded for her on our VHS top-loader. It was not snooker in general she liked, just Steve Davis. When 18 million people watched him in the 1985 World Snooker final against Dennis Taylor, she was one of them. But the thing she loved even more than Steve was the wedding of Charles and Diana, which she watched on a loop every single day until her death. Even after years living with us in the UK she didn't speak a word of English, which made her love of both these things even funnier to me. I understood what she saw in Diana and why she was so furious when Charles got back together with Camilla, but Steve Davis? Even by his own admission he was the most boring man in snooker. But perhaps that's where her not speaking English worked to his advantage. She did have a slightly naughty streak though, so maybe it was straight-up physical attraction. Her husband – my maternal grandfather, Saadideen al Isa – had the same wiry frame. He was one of the earliest Syrian GPs in Basra and the first time she laid eyes on him was the day she turned up in his surgery with an eye infection. She came from a huge, well-respected family in Basra in southern Iraq – the Al Zuhairs – and was very used to fighting for what she wanted. Having taken a fancy to her doctor she went straight home to tell her mother she'd met the man she was going to marry and could she manufacture an excuse to invite him over? The poor guy didn't stand a chance.

My grandmother was a very determined lady but *I* could always get round her. At five years old I somehow persuaded her to give me the key to the safe in her bedroom. It was where she kept the money she'd periodically ask me to fetch so she could pay a tradesman or go to the market. One day I decided to take a little for myself and went off to the corner shop with 20 of her dinars – approximately £100 in today's money. At the counter I handed over the whole lot in return for a single bottle of Pepsi Cola. Fortunately, my parents knew the owner, who came round that evening to give my grandma what amounted to her c. £99.90 change, and the safe key was duly removed from my pocket. Even years later when I was sixteen and my mum refused to give me a house key on account of my ongoing misbehaviour, my grandmother would wait for me at her bedroom window at the front of the house and throw one down so I could let myself in. I was spoiled by both grandmothers and I loved them unconditionally for it.

SUAAD AND NADHIM

I was very close to my paternal grandma and hers was a love story I'd heard many, many times growing up. Like all good romances, it started with a beautiful woman. She came from a very tight-knit orthodox Armenian community in Baghdad, who had no interest in their Christian women marrying into Muslim families. And so, just as with many great love stories, happiness came at a price, and that price was that, after she married, she never spoke to her family again. She cut herself off from them for the sake of her husband. Not only that, but because *he* came from a very well-to-do Sunni Muslim family, they didn't accept her either. They point-blank refused to recognise her as his wife, meaning to this day I've never met a single person from my grandmother's family. The only time my dad ever did was on a flight from Baghdad to Basra when he happened to bump into his aunt and she recognised him from a photograph. For those sixty minutes in neutral territory they experienced what it might have been like if things had been different for their families. It was sort of romantic and devastating at the same time.

THE ZAHAWI LEGACY

My grandfather's house was not especially grand but it was absolutely huge and full of large airy rooms befitting an 'important' man in Baghdad. The neighbourhood was one largely inhabited by what we called the professional classes: people who worked in government or as high-ranking civil servants. In Arabic, Waziriyah – named after the Ottoman grand vizier, or head of government – translated to 'Where ministers live'. Though it was a very different atmosphere, the closest comparison in terms of environment would have been Westminster. My grandfather was a government official and lived accordingly close to his work: the Finance Ministry in the Sarai, the Ministry of Trade at the far end of Baghdad's most famous thoroughfare, Al Rashid Street, and the newly formed Ministry of Oil on Sadoon Street. All these ministries have now moved but, at the time, he was right smack in the political heart of Baghdad and so were we.

If there were such a thing as an aristocracy in Iraq, the Zahawis historically would have been part of it. They were originally a core wing of the Baban family, who were princes of the Baban principality and built Sulaymaniyah, a city known for its creative, artistic and progressive origins. But their standing in the community wasn't about money; it was about education. They were not so much recognised for their wealth as for their minds, and between them they had intellectualism well and truly covered. My great-great-grandfather – Mohammed Fedhi

Zahawi – was the grand mufti of Baghdad. For Sunni Muslims, the mufti was akin to the pope, the most senior theologian in the country. His son, my great uncle Jamil Sidqi al-Zahawi, was both an unapologetic atheist and one of the most well-known poets in the Middle East. Not quite on a footing with Shakespeare or Chaucer, but almost. His work became part of the curriculum in many Arab countries – not bad for someone whose first language was Kurdish. On top of this he was largely self-taught, an early advocate of women's rights and a fan of Western-influenced socio-political reform. One of the most famous cafes in Baghdad was the Al Zahawi Coffee House, named in his honour, where he'd sit for hours and hold court. When he died in 1936 he was buried with full military honours and his coffin carried through the streets of Baghdad. He was a true progressive but equally someone who sought to move forward with harmony. This was hardly standard practice in early twentieth-century Iraq, though not out of the ordinary for a Kurd. They always were a forward-thinking people.

In the 1800s my great-great-grandfather was gifted hundreds of thousands of acres of land by the Ottoman sultan. By anyone's measure, the Zahawis were rich. His youngest son, my great-grandfather, Abdul Jalil Zahawi, ran the whole estate – a vast area of agricultural land farmed for export. When the mufti died in the 1920s, the estate was divided up among the beneficiaries, which included not only thirteen children, but four wives as well. By the time I was born, the wealth had dissipated but the Zahawi reputation had not. My grandfather's house was a local landmark but, for me, it was just the home I grew up in and the only one I ever knew in Iraq.

My father's father was the 'original' Nadhim Zahawi, grandson of the mufti, and his was quite the name to live up to. He was regarded as the most honest politician in Baghdad. He was also hugely accomplished and those accomplishments much mentioned in our house. After graduating with a law degree, he taught himself to speak fluent English before moving onto the board of directors of the Iraq Petroleum Company in the 1950s in London. From there he became governor of the Central Bank of Iraq and for many years his signature was on the Iraqi dinar. In the 1960s he became minister for trade and acting minister for oil, and presided over the creation of OPEC, which was signed and sealed in Baghdad in 1962. With all that under his belt, when the Ba'athists took power in a bloody coup in 1968, he decamped to Saudi Arabia at the invitation of the crown prince and helped set up the Saudi Central Bank. Not only was this an enormous amount to achieve in one lifetime, but even more so given he was dead at fifty-two.

My grandfather's income and standing meant they lived very comfortably and he taught my father to enjoy the finer things in life: classical music, literature, theatre and gastronomy. At lunch with a friend at Wheeler's in Old Compton Street one day he famously ordered oysters for both starter and main course. You could never, apparently, have enough of a good thing, which is presumably why he was also a chain smoker.

For everyone left behind, death only really falls into two categories – sudden, unexpected and traumatic, or long, drawn out and painful to watch. My grandfather's end was very much in the first category and the hole he left in our family was huge. A generation on, and retelling and repetition mean events can lose their impact and it's easy to become detached from what it must have been like to experience things first hand. My grandmother was a widow at fifty – a situation I'm sure neither she nor my grandfather ever once contemplated or planned for. Why would they? They were in the prime of life. He was four years younger than I am now but had achieved ten times as much. By anyone's measure it was a life cut short. At fifty-six, I sometimes contemplate my own death. I can come to terms with the notion that one day I will simply no longer exist, but the idea of leaving my children is painful in a way I could never have imagined before becoming a father myself.

Like an unwanted guest, a brain aneurysm typically bursts in with no notice or warning when you least expect it, and you've only got a 50/50 chance of saving someone even if you do get to them in time. All the while it sits, undetected, like a car bomb, the driver completely unaware it's there, ticking away. I often wonder what it must have been like for my grandfather to have been alone when he collapsed. No one was sitting by his side, holding his hand, whispering comforting thoughts. My parents were living with my grandparents in Saudi Arabia when he died. My dad was still in bed when Mum got up to find my grand-father pale and cold on the hallway floor. It must have been sudden but I wonder if there was a moment when he realised, 'This is it, I'm off.' Death must be pretty frightening when you look it directly in the eye. It seems a terribly lonely way to leave the world.

NAJDA AND HARETH

My own parents were not quite on my grandfather's level, though we'd still have been regarded as middle or upper middle class. Like many women in her sphere, my mum had a job. In Waziriyah, she was the famous lady dentist. In the mornings she worked for the state and in the evenings at her own private surgery. Professional wives wanted to practise the profession for which they'd studied and most of her contemporaries sought to work. An income separate to that of their husbands was both desired and necessary if they had the kind of lifestyle my parents did.

My dad had his own construction company but, as time went on, I realised he was an entrepreneur who just so happened to be invested in construction. His focus would change many times over my lifetime but his approach remained the same. He was a risk-taker, in every sense of the word. Several times in our lives he rolled the dice. Sometimes he won, sometimes he lost. And when he did, so did we. But he always, always got back up. If you're going to gamble I suppose you've got to know you have it in you to roll with the punches otherwise you're just a failed, fair-weather player. He knew how to live life well and how to enjoy it.

Not only was my mum educated and successful in her career but she was a seriously beautiful woman. On her wedding day everyone said she looked like Sophia Loren. It wasn't an empty compliment either – I really think she did. But my dad was hand-some too; they were a very good-looking couple, an even match. Dad, however, brought an extra ingredient to the mix. He was a player, a charmer. My mum was warned about it before their marriage but I guess she thought she'd be the one to tame him. Life with my dad could be something of a rollercoaster ride. Those kinds of people can be dangerous and intoxicating in equal measure and, while I loved him very much, I didn't like the stress of those ups and downs. As a boy, I was more like Mum: the steadying hand.

I idolised my mother and even now would describe her accom-modation of his behaviour as angelic. She was an extraordinary human being and that's how Dad felt about her too. He sees in her the things he lacks in himself: where she is calm and thought-ful he is rash and loud, but he is also dynamic and able to envisage the future before anyone else, which is why she fell in love with him. Marriages are more than just black-and-white equations, and what a child wants in his parents is not always the same as what those parents look for in one another. I get that now. Nevertheless, I can tell you for sure my wife would never put up with even a tenth of what my dad did. I'd be mincemeat.

As a husband and father now, I'm not sure if I'd rather my mum had dealt with things differently – chucked him out or put her foot down. Would that have pulled him into line? I'm not sure, to be honest. It was a gamble. In time my dad took risks I considered selfish and I didn't like the way Mum was left to clear up the mess. She had her own income, so could have left had she chosen to, but it wasn't just about money – particularly in a society like ours. There was a shame attached to a woman leaving a man that did not apply to the reverse. That was just how things were.

As a child there was one film I'd seen on the big screen that really stayed with me. Like a lot of movies we watched it hailed from Egypt, and this one was an out-and-out tear jerker. *Areedoo Halaan* centred around a woman whose husband refused to release her from a desperately unhappy marriage. Since he wouldn't consent to her leaving, her own family couldn't support her either because that would bring shame on them too. As a ten-year-old boy I was hardly the target audience, but it haunted me. I hated that guy. For me the lady was the heroine and his behaviour towards her, disgusting. I didn't think this was the norm, but I knew that in the part of the world I came from this stuff happened. It wasn't just a story. My own parents prided themselves on being incredibly liberal and my dad doted on my mum, but even so, she was still a woman living under a patriarchy and I guess I didn't like that either. It never occurred to me before now that it was a funny film for a little boy to be so moved by.

I grew up in the shadow of the men who'd come before me, but my father's work took him away from home often and that left me with a houseful of women to shape my outlook. My mum and sister were joined in time by both my grandmothers, and it was these ladies who raised me. It was kind of a lucky break.

CHAPTER 2

HOW WE USED TO LIVE

LIFE BEFORE ENGLAND

My primary school, Al Mansour, was based on the English system and had once been private under the British mandate. By 1973, not long after I started kindergarten, it had been completely nationalised. The Ba'athists might have been bloodthirsty terrorists but they were also socialists. Every government official, including Saddam Hussein, sent their kids there. The rest of us were terrified of them, particularly if they wanted to be friends with you or, worse still, if they fancied your sister. No one wanted to get too close. When the teacher asked the class what we'd done at the weekend or what we'd discussed the night before over supper, we all knew what it meant. Any child who inadvertently said the wrong thing would mark out their family as traitors and the teacher would write a report about them to the government. Then their dads would be arrested and imprisoned or murdered. Sometimes the children themselves were forced to write their own reports on their parents. Primary school was no less barbaric than anywhere else in Iraq.

Up until a few years before I started, Al Mansour had been known as 'Miss Saunders' – a quaint leftover from what was effectively a period of colonial rule. All the teachers had been English, the wives of military officers or even ex-military themselves. In my day, there were none left and we were taught exclusively in Arabic. My father was Kurdish but at home we spoke Arabic too. Most people did in Baghdad. During my time at school, the Ba'athists were making their presence felt in every walk of life and eventually closed Al Mansour down, calling it an imperialist institution.

Our head teacher was Miss M'barak, a Lebanese Christian who'd educated a huge section of Iraq. She was legendary in Baghdad. She never married or had children herself but was perfectly in tune with us all. She was also big on discipline, which was important for a boy like me. I traded 100 per cent on being naughty. It's what I got up for in the mornings. When you put me with my best friend Omar, that was a recipe for disaster. Ultimately, it would prove to be my undoing one day as we played tag in the playground and he attempted to get away by running round a large hedge. Never one to be outwit-ted, I decided to go *over* rather than *around* the obstacle, like a steeplechaser, unaware it housed a large lead pipe in the middle of its leaves. As I dived at Omar across the top of the bush, I was impaled, mid-flight, like a taxidermied dog and held momentarily in the air. With the bone in my leg now totally exposed, a call from the teacher to my mum was unavoidable. Luckily her dentistry surgery in Baghdad was not far from school. Calls like this were frequent enough for them to know my mum's secretary by her first name. Though I'd promised Mum I'd do my best not to get into trouble, I liter-ally couldn't help myself and spent much of my time trying to wrangle out of whatever tight spot I'd worked myself into. Often this meant weathering something worse than whatever punishment she might have given for the original offence, but I think letting her down was ultimately the thing I couldn't bear.

The perfect example of this was the day my sister Jihan was off sick and I'd persuaded Mum to let me stay home too. I spent the morning rummaging round the large piece of land opposite our house where Dad kept the heavy machinery that belonged to his construction company. Concrete mixers and flat-bed trucks were a treasure trove for an inquisitive kid, and I managed to locate a length of steel rod among the detritus that would make the perfect indoor javelin. Jihan was three years older than me with a radar so finely tuned to my misbehaviour she could pick it up a mile off. My sister was the person most likely to get me out of a scrape and it didn't take much to see that a nine-year-old with a five-foot metal pole was a lethal combination, and she immediately threatened to tell Mum what I was up to. I was absolutely livid and did my best to convey this in a loud argument on the pavement outside the house. With every action there is an equal and opposite reaction, so when I threw the rod to the floor in a fit of fury it bounced back up off the concrete to return to my face with some considerable force. The hole it left in my face was big enough to see my teeth through and the volume of blood was really quite impressive. My plan was to pinch what remained of my top lip between my thumb and forefinger and hope for the best. As luck would have it, the incident coincided with a visit from my dad's dispatch manager, Abu, looking for some paperwork. Instead, he found a boy with a lip split to the base of his nose and a scene that looked like an outtake from *Carrie*. It was off to the hospital, where the doctor told Abu I'd need five stitches and prepared to fetch the anaesthetist. 'Oh, no thank you,' I told him in a muffled voice through a blood-soaked hand, 'you can do it without the anaesthetic. I need to get home quickly or my mum will know I've been in trouble.' I don't know whether he too had a naughty son, but he understood instantly and put the sutures in Rambo-style. I did indeed get home before Mum but, needless to say, my promptness was not the focus of our conversation on her return. The scar on my top lip is now covered by my moustache but serves as an eternal reminder that there's nothing so mind-blowingly stupid a small boy won't do if he thinks there's a chance he'll get away with it.

Al Mansour wasn't the only thing left over from a bygone era. Ask any middle-class Iraqi of my generation who grew up in Baghdad and they'll know about the Alwiyah – the old country club under British occupation, now staffed almost exclusively by ex-military levies. It was an outpost of the old regime under the king; an oasis in the middle of an increasingly violent world outside. When you walked through the doors it was like stepping into Oz; the strictures of the East dimmed and the lights of the West were turned on. It was the only place any educated, professional Iraqi socialised. Somehow, despite its clearly stated imperialist leanings, the Alwiyah managed to survive the Ba'athists. Perhaps it was that they felt safer knowing where we were at the weekends. At least they could keep an eye on us all.

As the British trickled out of Iraq after the fall of the monarchy, more and more locals took their place at the club. Many had studied or worked in the West but some were the old revolutionaries. It turned out even sociopaths liked nice things too. The Ba'athists had their spies inside and monitored the more progressive Iraqis smoking and drinking but, within the walls of its landscaped gardens, we knew we were safe. My father had been a member and his father before him. For the Zahawis, the Alwiyah was a home away from home.

The dining menu at the club looked like it had been lifted directly from a British boarding school: puddings were something stodgy with custard, curries were English and the roast beef came with gravy and Yorkshire puddings. The activities mirrored those of a British resort on the Costa del Sol too: karate, bingo and draught beer on tap. In the evenings we'd have kebabs on the grass and watch a film on the outdoor screen in the gardens. The Alwiyah prided itself on showing British subtitled films, though most came from Egypt, which was considered the Hollywood of the Middle East. The influence of the West was not limited to the entertainment, though; it strayed into the moral values of the Alwiyah too. I never once saw a woman with a covering on her hair and the swimming pool was totally mixed. Outside of the club this would have been as good as nudity in some circles. In fact, you wouldn't see a woman swimming in public full stop.

We never stayed at the club but it did cater for overnight guests. There were several houses you could rent if you wanted longer-term accommodation and I still remember the story of one old Englishman who lived there permanently. He'd been in Baghdad as part of the British occupation when his son had drowned in the Tigris. His body was never recovered and the man always believed his son had been kidnapped by the government and would one day return. The old man continued to live at the Alwiyah until the day he died but his son never did come home.

Supposedly there was no class divide in Iraq, but the description above will tell you otherwise. The Alwiyah was undoubtedly an elitist retreat but it was also a non-political safe haven. Most of its members shared the same opinion about the Ba'athists, and it was not favourable. The club was a sanctuary for the silent liberal class of which my parents were card-carrying members. There *was* a divide in Iraq but it was defined more by education than wealth. While my mother and aunt wore up-to-the-minute fashions and lunched at the club, in more rural parts of the country there were still people sitting on the floor, eating with their hands. And the division came down to education. If you could read and write, you were part of the 'elite'. It had very little to do with money.

Other than the Alwiyah, socialising was mainly done in private homes. I don't remember ever going to a restaurant as a child. It was never so cold that lunch couldn't be eaten outside, even in winter. If my parents were entertaining, our cook Abid would prepare the meal under the watchful eye of my grandmother, who was something of a perfectionist in the kitchen. Often it was meat or fish with Basrawi spices, or dolma, which was an Ottoman favourite of vine leaves, stuffed tomatoes, courgettes and sweet red peppers. For something special we'd have a leg of lamb with saffron rice. Iraqi lamb was regarded as the most delicious in the region because of the type of grass the sheep ate and the soil it grew on. Abid always put the tail into the mince when he made kebabs because that was where all the fat and flavour was. The men drank beer and the women helped the kids assemble plates of salads and kebabs from long tables placed in the shade of the trees. Pudding was fruits, with strong tea to follow and Turkish delight if I'd not been too naughty during the week. But at Christmas it was usually my dad who'd cook the turkey.

My parents loved to host and held big parties for other like-minded liberals. Whatever the regime and consequential climate, the one thing that united the Middle Eastern people was music, but at our house it was never Western. My father's friend was a scholar of music and had a beautiful voice. Sometimes he'd come and sing at these parties. Everyone would sit around him and join in with the chorus. These were the songs we all knew – folk music from southern Iraq that told tales of fisherman and seafarers. Whatever the agenda, the glue that held the evening together was Johnnie Walker Black Label for the adults and Pepsi if you were too young to get drunk.

Whoever the guests, whatever the occasion, the one thing you knew to avoid talking about was politics. Everyone in my parent's circle hated the status quo but, unless you were about to do something really drastic, it was a cross you just had to bear. We were all trapped. I have friends in China now and I see the same behaviour. Even when they're in England, politics is a topic they avoid at all costs. It's a mindset. You become conditioned to being cautious and it takes real bravery to break the cycle.

Religion wasn't part of my family's life. It was something people did privately in their own homes but it played no part in Iraqi politics at that time. The country was completely secular. You could accuse Saddam of being a psychopath but he didn't care whether you were a Sunni, Shia or Christian, he'd kill you anyway. His motivation was all political. Nevertheless, when you said you were a liberal, what that often meant was that you were also agnostic. There was an inherent overlap between the professional classes and the belief that much of the trouble in the region stemmed from religion. The liberal elite shied away from it because of the destruction wrought in its name in the history of the Middle East.

My parents, like their friends, were Muslim but everyone drank and no one covered up. When I was little, my abiding memory is of my aunties' mini skirts and beehives if I looked up. The women modelled themselves on Liz Taylor and Doris Day, just like all the other women in the world; fashion was where the influence of the West was most keenly felt. If you were to look at any photograph of the country prior to 1979, you'd be surprised how Westernised we all looked. In fact, one of the only telltale signs you were in the Middle East would be all the hats.

CHAPTER 3

YOU CAN TELL A LOT ABOUT A MAN FROM HIS HAT

THE HISTORY OF IRAQ

The fez wasn't just a favourite of Tommy Cooper, it was also the official hat of the Ottoman Empire. Originally it hailed from Prague, but, under occupation, the Ottomans appropriated it and made it their own. If you were a student or an official in an office in Egypt up until 1952, the fez was mandatory. Anyone who couldn't read and write wore a turban or headdress of some sort, so the fez became a status symbol that meant you were either part of the administration or being educated to join it. You were the *effendi* – the educated, intellectual class – and everyone instantly knew this by your hat. It was a very simple way of telling the outside world just how clever or important you were. Tommy Cooper nicked his fez from an Egyptian waiter before a gig during the Second World War. Just like that.

Jump over the Red Sea and take a few steps east and we're now in Iraq where, on 23 August 1921, King Faisal I was installed to rule over the (relatively) new country. In order to distinguish his modern kingdom from the fez-wearing Ottomans who'd ruled over the domain for the previous four hundred years, King Faisal adopted several things – one of which was a new hat as part of a drive to create a form of national identity. The sidara was a fabric cap that could be folded flat when you took it off, like the ones worn by American GIs and the RAF in the Second World War. In time, the Iraqi version of the hat became known as the Faisaliah, after the king, and, from 1921, it was mandatory, including in schools. It was distributed to ministers and anyone of note, and was most prominent in Baghdad because that was the centre of learning, governance and civility. In much the same way you'd be faced with a sea of bowler hats on any London street in the early twentieth century, the sidara was what you'd see on the streets of Baghdad. It became symbolic of a particular kind of governance and political bias, and continued to be worn until the 1958 coup, when the British-backed monarchy was kicked out of Iraq and the republic began. When the monarchy went, so did anything that looked like it might belong to it. Or to the British. So the hat was really much more than just a hat. For many it was a symbol of a time when Iraq's political and cultural infrastructure was more closely aligned with the values of the West. Which is exactly why no one wore it under Saddam Hussein; the Faisaliah was no more.

I wasn't born until 1967 and all this pre-dates me, so why bother telling you? The thing is, it's difficult to comprehend the Iraq I grew up in without really understanding its history. It's one mired in tradition, symbolism and quite a bit of superstition, and to understand the mentality and collective fear of the people I grew up with, you have to see how and why they got there. A childhood in Baghdad was not like one in London or Paris. It was like one in East Germany or Russia. The playbook for Saddam's Iraq was the East German Stasi. As his power increased, so did his confidence and he added more and more appalling extras to the template.

Before the British came along, there never *was* an Iraq. For four hundred years the Ottoman Empire ruled over many provinces in the Middle East, of which Mesopotamia was the one most closely geographically in line with what we now know as Iraq. The new country was a post-First World War invention, created by the Allies – principally France, Russia and the UK – who were fighting the Central Powers – Germany, Austria-Hungary and the Ottoman Empire. As the victors, the Allies had to decide how to divvy up what had once belonged to the Ottomans. In 1916, a secret agreement had been drafted between France and the UK to define their future spheres of influence in the event of an Allied victory. In 1921, their plan came to fruition and British MP Mark Sykes and the French foreign minister, François George Picot, sat down to enact the Sykes–Picot Agreement in which the parameters of modern day Iraq were plotted. New boundaries for a new nation. This is a huge topic but, broadly speaking, many felt these outsiders did not understand the landscape or demographics of the Middle East and that their delineations did not take account of thousands of years of tribal history.

In order to decide these boundaries, the Allies consulted a lady known by the Iraqis as Miss Bell. Gertrude Bell was a wealthy, educated adventurer and archaeologist who travelled the Middle East extensively in the early twentieth century. She became friends with T. E. Lawrence and, with him, tried to help the Allies understand the complexities of the region. She was hugely influential with the British government on account of her local network and expertise, and she worked closely with Sir Percy Cox, the high commissioner for Mesopotamia (Iraq) – the de facto ruler at the time. She and Lawrence were mindful of the strength of feeling about Arab independence in the Middle East and believed the British should work with, rather than against, the Arab nationalists who wanted autonomy.

What to do with the Kurds – i.e. my paternal ancestors – was central to the discussion. Like many other provinces under the Ottoman Empire, in the eyes of the Ottoman rulers, Kurdistan was an area rather than a country in its own right and the Kurds were a conglomeration of tribes, rather than a single nationality. The Kurds would tell you otherwise, and vehemently so. They were native to the mountainous regions in the part of Western Asia that spanned what is now south-east Turkey, north-west Iran, northern Iraq and northern Syria. During the war, the Allies promised Kurdistan would be formally recognised as a country if the Kurds fought with the British. When the war ended, however, and the Ottomans were defeated, they were still strong enough to tell the Allies, if you try to carve out a Kurdish country, we'll fight again. They would never, ever have accepted a defeat in which the Kurdish territories of Turkey were annexed. So the Brits had to tell the Kurds, 'Sorry, we can't deliver on our promise. Oh and also, we're going to divide you up between four nations: Iraq, Syria, Turkey and a bit in Iran.' The Kurds were left as a minority in each of their adoptive countries, despite the fact they had their own language and national identity. All of a sudden, the Kurds in Iraq were told, 'You're Iraqi now.' 'Okay,' they say, 'so we're Kurdish Iraqis?' 'Well, actually no,' said the Brits, 'you're just Iraqis.' And this was where the Kurds took real umbrage.

So, while not all Kurds are Iraqi and not all Iraqis are Kurds, their histories – my history – are inextricably linked in a way that's impossible to untangle. Despite all this, it was in the Kurds' DNA to want to embrace the West. To *be* Western. They'd always been a very progressive people. Unlike Iraq, their history was not one of progression through violence. Power wasn't taken by the sword. It was always an intellectual fight. It is no surprise to me that Mahsa Amini, who controversially died while in police custody in Iran in 2022 after being arrested for not wearing a hijab, was a Kurdish girl.

So this (heavily truncated) tangle leads us to the fact that the Middle East now had Iraq. Once the Allies had drawn their lines in the sand, they then decided a kingdom needed a king and drafted one in from Saudi Arabia. All this tells you how Iraq got a monarchy but we still have a way to go before they traded it in for Saddam.

Faisal I went on to rule until 1933 before dying of a heart attack at forty-eight. Next up was his son, Ghazi, who ruled until 1939. Ghazi was a Pan-Arabist and opposed to British interference in the country. His reign was more turbulent than his father's and this was partly Ghazi's own fault. In 1936, he backed what was considered to be the first modern military coup in the Arab world because of tensions between himself and leaders in his own government. Over the next five years there would be a further six coups, and the violent transfer of power from leader to leader became the norm in Iraq.

This first coup was led by General Bakr Sidqi, who succeeded in overthrowing the then prime minister in 1936. A year later, Sidqi himself was dead: shot while having tea in the garden. King Ghazi hung on to the throne a while longer before meeting his own abrupt end crashing his car into a lamppost.

Next up was Ghazi's son, Faisal II. The 'Boy King' was only three when he came to the throne and his uncle ruled as prince regent until he came of age. The Regent was pretty brutal and very Westernised, and generally unpopular as a result. In 1941, he was overthrown and briefly exiled before being reinstated by the British. In 1953, he handed the crown over to Faisal II, who'd just turned eighteen.

Now we take a sideways step into Egypt, where President Nasser had recently toppled *their* monarchy after a huge, but peaceful, revolution. Nasser wanted Egypt to be the central player in a Pan-Arab state and Britain's close relationship with Iraq was a potential threat to these plans. He worried the British were trying to create an Arab state in which *Iraq* was front and centre, which they'd control from behind. To prevent this, he set about trying to undermine the British influence in the region and this culminated in the Suez Crisis of 1956. The Suez Canal was hugely important practically and symbolically and, until 1956, owned and operated by Britain and France. It was a sign of their strength and sway in the Middle East and, when Nasser took it back by nationalising it, it was a massive embarrassment for Britain – ultimately forcing the resignation of the then prime minister, Anthony Eden.

The 1950s and 60s were a turbulent time in the Middle East. Nasser was a hugely influential figure who'd successfully challenged the old imperialist status quo, and in the wake of that, the Arab world was somewhat unified in its political outlook and desire for autonomy. Egypt's revolution was the beginning of decolonisation and it wasn't long before similar feelings crept in to Iraq. It was only a matter of time before the crown would be knocked off whoever happened to be wearing it at the time. So poor old Faisal II only got five years in the hot seat before the really big coup on 14 July 1958, which toppled the monarchy in Iraq for good.

The details of this coup were, as always, pretty gruesome. The new leader, Abd al-Karim Qasim ordered the royal family to evacuate the palace and congregate outside the courtyard, with a view to unseating the monarchy. Unfortunately, his plans were derailed by a rogue officer, who decided to shoot every single one of them at point-blank range. Just to make sure everyone got the memo, the prince regent's body was then dragged through the streets, cut into pieces and burned. But that wasn't the end of things. The day after the coup, the former prime minister, Nuri Pasha al-Said, was captured trying to escape disguised as a woman. After they killed and buried him, he was subsequently dug up, hanged, burned and thrown into the streets, where his corpse was run over repeatedly by traffic until it was unrecognisable. Motor vehicles aside, it was the sort of scene you'd expect to see in the Middle Ages, not 1958. As endings go, it doesn't get much more grisly.

It was impossible to separate the monarchy from the concept of Western imperialistic control in the region, and the coup was designed to cut the apron strings once and for all. This brutal dispatch of the monarch and his family was a pretty clear demonstration of this plan. Much of the Middle East had had enough of the West. Qasim seized power and installed himself as prime minister. It was the beginning of a new era and a new republic, but this was no democracy.

Unfortunately, the bloody coup that brought Qasim to power set a precedent for how leaders would go on to deal with their enemies and, five years later, Qasim was on the receiving end of it himself. On 8 February 1963, his right-hand man, Abdul Salam Arif, led the Ramadan Revolution in another coup. For three days, they surrounded Qasim and his army in his office at the Ministry of Defence. The insurgents took control of government-controlled television and radio and announced Qasim's death even though he was still alive inside the building. Though some knew this to be a lie, it was obvious to anyone in power that if you didn't back the new guy, it would be your head on the block next, and if that meant switching allegiance at short notice, then so be it. Congratulations were sent to the new leader before the old one was even dead. Three days later Qasim was shot in the radio station. His dead body was displayed slumped in a chair on television as further evidence of Arif's newly held power. A soldier lifted his lifeless head and spat in his face for good measure. The signals could not have been clearer: there was a new sheriff in town.

So Qasim was out and Arif was in. Arif was a totalitarian like all the others, but additionally a bit unhinged. Tragically, but thankfully for the people, he didn't last long either and died in a helicopter crash in 1966.

Now it was the turn of Arif's brother, Abdul Rahman Arif. But not for long. Two years later in 1968, under the leadership of Ahmed Hassan al-Bakr, the Ba'ath Party mounted a successful coup against Arif No. 2. This one was actually quite civilised. Al-Bakr simply took control of the radio station and phoned Arif to say his services were no longer required since he was now taking over as president. Arif toddled off to exile in Turkey, no doubt grateful to be alive.

Al-Bakr faired a bit better and clocked up eleven years in power, appointing his relative, Saddam Hussein, vice president. When Saddam was put in charge of Iraq's security services, that's where things really began to go wrong. Actually, there were some good things that happened under al-Bakr in the early days: high oil prices enabled the Ba'athists to invest in the infrastructure of the country, which improved people's standard of living and strengthened Iraq's position on the world stage. Like a lot of socialist systems, it began with honourable intentions, and there was an on-paper fairer distribution of wealth and land under the Ba'athists. However, all this came at a price. Gradually, Saddam's security services infiltrated every single institution in the country. Iraq may have had autonomy from a colonial power but its citizens were considerably less free. Al-Bakr eventually 'retired' in 1979 and died a few years later, though there was probably more to that story than meets the eye. In the meantime, Saddam became president and continued to gather speed. Power in Iraq had moved from civil to military hands and the way the government controlled its people now was through sheer brutality.

Saddam turned a country in which two-thirds of the population were peasants into one where people in villages could read and write for the first time, and profits from rising oil prices meant he was able to invest heavily in industrial expansion. So what went wrong? The short answer is power, and too much of it, mixed with a large dose of paranoia. If you run a country through fear, you live every day knowing you're a sitting target. Saddam's response to this was to make sure he had eyes on everything and everyone, which made life utterly unbearable for anyone else involved.

Iraq's history is a seriously violent one and you'd struggle to meet an Iraqi whose family has not been affected by its horrors. When a society is brutalised in this way, you tend to get people who become even more brutal, who think the only way to gain power is to take it by force. The abused become the abusers and the cycle begins again. This was the Iraq of my youth.

CHAPTER 4

THE PLAYBOOK

SADDAM & HIS BA'ATHISTS

The Department of General Intelligence – or the Mukhabarat – was well known for its use of torture and was run by Saddam's half-brother, Barzan al-Tikriti. Barzan's mission was to find and eliminate anyone who might be perceived as a threat. His definition of 'threat' was pretty wide ranging. If you represented a British or American company in Baghdad, you were a threat, an agent of the West, and it was a crime punishable by death if the wrong person chose to pursue you. If you listened to foreign radio, you were a threat. If you were a Kurd or a communist, you were a threat. The list of things considered threatening was long and diverse. Not too dissimilar from Iran today.

I grew up in a single-party police state. That meant no voting, no democracy and next to no contact with the West for the vast majority of people. Access to the outside world in all its forms was a major factor in retarding Iraq in many ways. There was a strict ban on the import of foreign publications of all types. Subscriptions to any printed matter were confiscated. Even private letters were routinely opened and read by security. TV satellite antennas were strictly banned and owning one was punishable by law. Iraq under Saddam became the Arab world's Iron Curtain. For this reason, it's hard to convey the value I put on the freedoms I gained in moving to the UK. When you tell people you grew up in a single-party state it's almost meaningless unless you've experienced it yourself. It might have more impact if I told you my wife's uncle hid his own extracted teeth in the pocket of his trousers that he sent home to be laundered as a way of telling them he was being tortured in prison. That a man I met in Kurdistan whom I'd known as a boy told me the men in his village were all dissolved in a bath of acid after they'd been removed from their homes as part of Saddam's ethnic cleansing drive. That on virtually every page of my wife's family albums there's a man who had been shot or hanged – usually by someone else in the same photograph. That is what it meant to grow up under a dictator.

After the 1968 coup, most of the Ba'athists my parents knew – the ones with a moral code – were out of government, and we were all united against a common enemy: Saddam Hussein. His party took power a year after I was born and, by the time I was at school, they were everywhere. I have no memories of life before him. Just like East Germany or Russia at that time, Iraq became a socialist, nationalist movement. Actually, there was very little ideology involved because it very quickly became about one person, and his version of the Ba'ath Party thought that democracy was some sort of Western trick. The degree of power he had went hand in hand with paranoia about his position. As head of the security services, Saddam systematically hollowed out every institution in the country. In the army, security service personnel were promoted to commanders and generals, and within the civil service security guards were promoted to the highest positions of seniority. This pattern was repeated in every organisation until everything was run by Saddam from the inside out. In the end, rather than being governed by politicians, Iraq was run by its security services, with a side order of fear and paranoia. If you need a metaphor for this style of government, I'd offer up Vladimir Putin's twenty-foot-long meeting table.

If you were a teacher or nurse, working in government or belonged to any kind of public body, you had to join the party, no matter what your political beliefs. It was a criminal offence to take commission from a foreign company, punishable by hanging. It was not illegal to work for a foreign company but you were advised to keep it on the down-low. There should be no advertising the fact or promoting your products. You'd also be well advised not to talk to your colleagues abroad in their native language since this was a sure sign you were a spy. The frequency and ease with which people were labelled an imperialist or a spy would have been funny had it not been so frightening. The resulting atmosphere was what I'd imagine Salem must have been like in the late 1600s.

In 1969, my auntie Samira was working as the head librarian at the Mustansiriyah University in Baghdad. This was a year or so after al-Bakr and Saddam came to power. Both men were very keen on self-publicity and sent their portraits far and wide to be displayed in the halls and corridors of Iraq's public institutions; the library was one such lucky recipient. My aunt was a good-humoured lady and, on seeing the picture of the two men dressed all in white, quipped to the janitor, 'Hang these two doves on the wall, would you,' unaware he was a Mukhabarat operative working undercover. The following week she'd scheduled time off to have a mastectomy. The day she returned she was arrested for her comment. She was taken to an unknown location and kept in total darkness in a tiny cell without any post-surgery medication. Ten days later she was released, a totally changed person. She became a loner, afraid to talk to anyone, including her own family. Months passed before she was even able to mention the event at home. To this day, I don't know what happened to my aunt during those ten days in solitary confinement, but I can imagine. The Ba'athist government used the Mukhabarat to carry out a long and barbaric witch hunt, and everyone knew to be on their guard.

INDOCTRINATION

Religion and superstition merged fairly seamlessly in the Iraq of my childhood and were used to both frighten and manipulate a society isolated from external rational checks and balances. There were two principal methods these dictators used to control their citizens: one was indoctrination, the other was fear. Everything we were told in Iraq came modified by one or the other. While I now know the lies we were told as children, when they were fed to you by people you were supposed to trust or by people of whom you were terrified, what choice did you have but to believe them?

The creation of a skewed past to justify a particular bias had been going on for as long as the Middle East had existed. After the 1958 revolution, a new school curriculum was set and the textbooks redrafted with a new version of events. Students were obliged to study and sit an exam for something that roughly translated as 'patriotic upbringing', which was the Ba'athist's account of why we supposedly needed them. Common sense told me these things must be lies but, at the same time, when it's drilled into you, it starts messing with your mind. Israel and the Six-Day War, for example, was taught to us as a conspiracy by the West to take Arab Muslim land. 'These nasty Zionists; they all want to kill you!' I grew up thinking Jews were evil invaders who had fabricated the Holocaust and would one day be thrown into the sea. Literally. And I believed it. Even today, there are still those in the Middle East who believe in the conspiracy that the reason Jews control so many of the world's most profitable institutions comes down to the existence of a blood-sucking cabal able to manipulate the world's economy.

It was indoctrination pure and simple, in a place that should have been a safe, neutral space for children. The history books we studied described a past that suited the ideology of the current regime. Richard the Lionheart was a case in point. In our school books he was portrayed as a blood-sucking thief. His portrait was drawn like something from a Grimms' fairy tale; the witch or villain, designed to haunt our dreams. And it did. For years. Richard had led the Third Crusade in 1191 to take back Jerusalem from the Muslims led by Saladin, who had himself taken it back from the Christians four years earlier. By the time Richard reached the Holy City, he was exhausted, as was Saladin. Instead of fighting, the two men agreed to a truce. The Treaty of Ramla left Muslims in control of Jerusalem but gave Christian pilgrims the right to visit without persecution. When Saladin died a year later, we were told the first thing Richard did was stamp on his headstone as a mark of disrespect. In fact, the two men had huge mutual admiration and were known to have treated one another with great respect. The first thing Richard actually did on Saladin's death was to go and pay his respects, but you would not have known that in Iraq because it didn't suit the narrative. They needed Richard to be a bloodthirsty, imperialist satanist in order to justify their own actions.

The pattern of forceful, often bloody, transfer of power in Iraq meant that with every new dictator came a new version of history. The authority of each new leader depended on his ability to discredit and undermine all that had gone before him. I grew up in a place where each new tyrant destroyed the world created by the last, and historical accuracy and truth were as susceptible to manipulation as everything else. It was a vicious cycle of terror.

The US and the UK were known simply as Big Satan and Little Satan respectively, and the fusing of politics and religion in those phrases was no accident; they were targeted at a people who were controlled by a fear of both. The thought of what might happen to them at the hands of the government or God if they stepped out of line is exactly what kept them in line. I was sad but not surprised to hear the same tropes in Putin's recent speech on the forced annexation of Ukrainian lands. Western countries, in their greedy desire to colonise his country, 'have abandoned religion and embraced Satanism' and the retribution would be biblical in scale. A plague might not rain down upon us but nuclear weapons were a good substitute. The language used harks back to a time when a lack of widespread education, together with stringent restrictions on communication with the outside world, made it very easy to control the masses. It was a horrible, triggering thing to hear from the leader of a world power in 2022. 'The dictatorship of the Western elites is directed against all societies ... the suppression of freedom itself has taken on the features of a religion: outright Satanism.' Putin's is a statement that could have come straight from the mouth of Saddam Hussein.

As a teenager arriving in the UK, I started asking the obvious question: if the ideals of Iraq were so great, why was there such freedom in the West? As soon as I started school in England, I came to realise that most of what we'd learned in Baghdad was lies. That the Jews in the state of Israel had been demonised for political gain. That what we'd been taught was a horrific, twisted version of reality. That there was a kind of person and a kind of regime that believed just by saying something enough times, they could make it true. That by framing a version of reality that plays to people's fears and vulnerabilities, you can manipulate them to support your personal goals. That lying was absorbed into the fabric of the regime when it suited a particular end. I have to tell you now, my friend, this is a spectacularly dangerous route to go down. One of the things that scares me most about the extreme polarisation of global politics now is the tendency to rely on this technique to win votes. A lie is a lie, however you dress it up or whoever you are told it might be helping. The really frightening thing was, the school I attended was considered to be very liberal. God knows what was being taught elsewhere.

STATEMENT NO. 1

Alongside school, the other principal method of control was television. Just like in the West it had huge power because it came directly into our homes and aimed to influence what we thought, said and did. Unlike in the West, the one channel and two radio stations were wholly state owned and controlled. When I was a child, television transmission began at 6 p.m. with the Iraqi national anthem. Although it was still a secular society, Saddam soon realised he could use religion as a way of controlling the masses and TV helped facilitate this plan. The anthem was followed by a seemingly never-ending diatribe from some cleric or other offering up religious recitals from the Quran, normally sung, like the call to prayer. Then we moved on to the 7.30 p.m. 'news', which was really just hours and hours of ego massaging. 'Today the president visited a carpet factory in Basra and then a local shop where he bought a bottle of Pepsi Cola.' It was never Coke, because that was banned in Iraq on account of their having a bottling plant in Israel. Iraq was a socialist country where everything was owned by the government, so all these presidential tours were just one piece of propaganda after another. They filled hour upon hour of television in this way. They had to, because there *was* no news.

How could there be when anything from the outside world was blocked and considered a threat to the status quo?

For me, entertainment consisted of the same cartoon in Russian week after week – a Soviet animation about a lazy boy called Antoshka. Sometimes this was interspersed with an episode of *Kojak*, whose subtitles gave the government a degree of control over the subject matter. They were fairly relaxed about anything sexual, but when it came to the promotion of Western ideologies they were resolute; should Telly Savalas happen to praise 'the FBI and their fantastic work' on the case he'd just solved, the subtitles would be tweaked to read, 'Get me a hamburger with mustard and ketchup,' instead. Just like with the history books, they expunged anything that didn't suit their narrative. It was Censorship 101.

The most significant version of this sort of bias was '*Bayan raqim wahid*', or Statement No. 1, and its delivery always meant something sinister. When the government wanted change, they acted first and announced it second. When one regime overthrew another, Statement No. 1 would deliver the news on television, a tirade denouncing the colonialist traitors and infidels with whom they'd just dispensed. There was no recourse if you didn't like it. During a coup you might hear gunshots or aircraft overhead before Statement No. 1 would tell you whether the attack was successful and the nature and identity of your new leaders. Everyone fell silent; the doors of homes would be closed as their inhabitants waited to see what the rest of their lives were going to look like. Some would rejoice, while others made preparations to be arrested or to get the hell out. In Iraq in the late 70s, the only place to hear the truth was Western media, which is precisely why you could be arrested for listening to the BBC World Service. It's easy to argue about the impartiality of the BBC now, but you might feel differently if you'd lived under a dictatorship. In my experience, the BBC was the closest thing we had to a trusted adult.

FEAR & LOATHING

If you really want to control a body of people through fear, there have to be serious consequences to any perceived rule-breaking. You must be able to illustrate the repercussions with shock and awe if you want your authority to be genuinely feared. The Ba'athists were all over this. I don't know a single family unaffected by the terror of Saddam's regime. The Zahawis were quite lucky, relatively speaking. My wife's family, however, were repeatedly targeted by his men. Her mother's cousin, Yusif, was arrested by the Ba'athists on a charge of espionage. He was a deputy minister in the government at the time, picked randomly on spurious charges to keep people on their toes. After his arrest they shaved his head, put him on television, made him admit to being 'an imperialist, colonialist spy' and sentenced him to death. Her uncle was finance minister at the time and appealed directly to al-Bakr for Yusif's release. Al-Bakr very 'kindly' agreed to commute his death sentence to life imprisonment, which was an improvement on execution. By this time, however, they'd broken his jaw and removed his teeth; he was the one who sent them home in his laundry to communicate his predicament to his family. After seven years of this, his wife decided to see whether she'd fare any better with Saddam after he'd risen to power. As vice president, Saddam installed a dedicated help line, direct to his desk, with which to liaise with his subjects. Through this she was able to organise an audience with the dictator and took their young son along with her on the day. As soon as Saddam referred to Yusif as a spy, the boy burst into tears. Saddam evidently had a soft side to his character, because he beckoned the boy over and put his arm around his shoulder: 'Wipe away your tears,' he said. 'Daddy will be home next week.' Sure enough, he was. Saddam had proved he was not only brutal and powerful but fickle too. A truly heady mix. I'm not sure if you could describe what happened to Uncle Yusif as a happy ending but it was what passed for one under the Ba'athists. Taking all this into consideration, her other uncle got off quite lightly. On his last day as Iraqi ambassador to Afghanistan, he was shot seven times by his First Secretary as he sat at his desk in the embassy one afternoon in June.

I tell you all this to illustrate how closely we lived to fear. These weren't things that happened to 'other people'. They happened to 'our' people, all the time, and the legacy for many was a lifetime of paranoia. A knock at the door or a strange look in the street: all these things were a potential trigger. When people move in and out of favour with no notice or rationale, it's easy to see how switching sides became a national way of life. The tendency was born out of self-preservation rather than caprice. In the UK, people easily understand the difference between an acquaintance and a friend, but in Iraq it was different. Everyone was your friend, until they weren't. It was a horribly unnerving way to grow up.

Even on coming to England, the paranoia didn't stop. Moving country wasn't enough to protect you. This was clearly demonstrated when Iraq's ex-prime minister, Abdul Razzak al-Naif, was shot and killed on the orders of the Iraqi government outside the Intercontinental Hotel on Hyde Park Corner, in broad daylight, six months before we arrived. At this stage in Saddam's career, it wasn't about mass murder; it was about sending a message. You were never truly safe while he was alive, and this bred a certain kind of mentality: the way you kept a secret, the insecurities you felt. It was an ethos based on a foundation of terror.

THE PLAYBOOK

THE LONG VIEW

We were not the norm in fleeing Iraq. Far more of our friends and family chose to stay, believing they had too much to lose. From a distance we still lived with the fear of Saddam, but their lives continued to be ruled by his oppression. My entire generation, as well as that of my parents and grandparents, lived under the shadow of political tyranny. Ultimately, I believe dictators fail, but that failure may take decades. The issue is one of timescales and the fact we tend to judge them to fit our own lifetime. On average we're on this earth for seventy to eighty years. If we don't see positive change in that time, we consider it a failure, right? But if you were to step back and take the long view, things may look different.

If an alien landed on these shores anytime between the Magna Carta and 1928, they'd think our democracy was lacking because, until then, women weren't fully enfranchised. Democracy as an exercise had failed. There were 713 years between those two historical events and many, many significant social upheavals in the interim to get us to where we are today. Europe didn't progress until after the Thirty Years' War, when Church and state were separated in the seventeenth century. The difficulty is, democracy is a process. We've been through civil wars in the West and had nearly a millennium to get to a place where people's rights are protected.

When you remove a dictator who's hollowed out all the institutions in his country, it's not an overnight fix. It's been forty-five years since the Iranian people toppled theirs, but it's taken until now for the theocracy that took his place to be seriously challenged. These things rarely happen in one take. So when people question whether the West should encourage these countries to rise up against their oppressors or whether we're intruding on a different set of values, you have to appreciate that desire for freedom is a universal one. That these people want the same things as you and me: to work hard, do well and for their children to prosper too. They're not a different species.

As unpopular as this may make me, if we were to look back in 200 years at what Tony Blair and George W Bush did in Iraq, I don't think we'll consider it a mistake. Their actions allowed the country to free itself from the tyranny of Saddam and the Ba'ath Party. The Iraqis muddled through and struggled initially, and some bad people rose to the top, but eventually they began their journey towards a place in which people had some of the freedoms we've taken for granted for many years in Britain. If I were to say this in parliament, I'd be vilified from left and right, and I'm sure Tony Blair is still living with the weight of the invasion on his shoulders because we judge everything in the moment. People rarely step back to look at the bigger picture, but we must. Progress comes with time, but it may be that *that* time is not during *our* time.

CHAPTER 5

GOODBYE TO BAGHDAD

'THEY'RE COMING FOR YOUR NECK'

I was eleven years old when the chain of events leading to our departure from Iraq began with my aunt. It was a Monday, but we were having lunch with family because it was Boxing Day. Despite the fact we were Muslims, we'd celebrated Christmas since my grandfather's era. My parents' circle of friends all did. Christmas pudding from Marks & Spencer was one of the highlights of the year. On this occasion, lunch was hosted by my maternal grandparents. Mum was one of seven children. Her parents lived in the Jameela district of Baghdad, where two houses sat back to back, linked by a communal garden in the middle. One belonged to my grandparents and the other to my Auntie Samira – my mother's eldest sister. Her husband Ali was very well connected to the Ba'athists via *his* brother. Through them, my father had learned that their nephew, Adnan, was looking for work and gave him a job at his company. This quickly proved to be a mistake. Adnan saw from the inside how well my dad's business was doing and decided he'd be the perfect person to blackmail. Six months earlier he'd walked into Dad's office and threatened to write a report on my father and send it to the party if he didn't agree to give him 100,000 dinars – approximately half a million dollars in today's money. My dad responded to the threat by setting a trap via a friend in the security services, who caught Adnan red-handed trying to extort cash from my dad. Ever the optimist, Dad convinced the security services to let Adnan go. People caught by the security services tended not to fare well in Baghdad, but this kindness was Dad's biggest mistake.

Six months later, Adnan was at it again. Here we were, about to tuck in to my dad's home-cooked turkey, when my aunt pulled my mother aside. Adnan had indeed been as good as his word and written a report. My father, he said, was an agent of the British and the construction business he ran was a cover for his 'real' career as an informant. News of my father's supposedly treasonous activities had now reached the highest level of government and he was to be arrested the next day.

We left my grandmother's immediately. I remember the urgency of my mum rounding up my sister and me; the hurried goodbyes to aunties and uncles. I knew there must be something wrong. Our favourite part of these big lunches was gossiping about family on the way home or deciding whose side of the story we were on. Today we rode in silence. Jihan and I were dropped at home and my parents went on to visit their friend Shabaan Jassim. Shabaan was a Ba'athist but a fair one, and a very senior official at the central bank. If anyone could confirm or deny the rumours it would be him. It was, by now, late afternoon and Shabaan was having his nap, but seeing the panic in my father's face, his wife agreed to wake him. When Dad told Shabaan the rumours of his arrest, Shabaan told him to come back in three hours. He'd see what he could find out. On my father's return Shabaan confirmed the worst: 'Get the hell out now,' he said. 'They're coming for your neck.'

I don't know whether it was shock or denial but at first my mum didn't take it that seriously, but Dad was in no doubt about the gravity of the situation. He knew many people who'd been killed and that the party liked to make an example of anyone with a 'name', which is exactly what the Zahawis were. Because of his own father, Dad was a prime target. The choices were leave or die. They left Shabaan and drove straight to the travel agent, where they bought a first-class, round-the-world plane ticket for £1,000. It was far more than he needed but the only safe way to get cash out of the country unnoticed. Once he was in England he could get a refund on the unused leg of the journey. Mum gave him the diamond and sapphire necklace he'd bought her and told him to sell it if push came to shove.

The minute my parents walked back through the door of our house, Mum began packing a bag and Dad got on the telephone to anyone who might be able to help. I don't remember being told what was happening but it quickly became obvious. The atmosphere in the house was sharp and black. It was more than forty years ago and, while I've forgotten many of the details, what I do remember is the panic around me. It's always been my way to respond to sadness or stress with silence. Nowadays, it's my wife who has to deal with it, but in this instance there was no time for anyone to even notice. It was like being sucked into the centre of a silent vortex while everything around me was swept up in a tornado. I felt totally paralysed. I desperately wanted to go out into the night and sit among the branches of the narenj tree but instinctively felt I shouldn't. This was a moment when my presence in the room was a show of solidarity, even if there was nothing else I could do to help. I just stood there watching the end of my childhood unravel in front of me. If there ever were a God, this seemed like as good a time as any to ask for his help. My grandma picked a phrase from the Quran and told my dad to write it on the kitchen wall. 'Allah is my suffice, and the best deputy.' Given that neither of my parents were openly religious, this was a fairly transparent mark of their increasing desperation.

The next morning I heard Dad on the phone to his secretary, Fatin. 'If they come looking for me, tell them I've gone to Mosul and I'll be back tonight.' When they did come looking, that's exactly what Fatin told them. She knew that by lying for my father she was putting herself at great risk too, but she was more afraid for him than for herself.

Finally, it was time to go. Fatin had already sent my father's driver and his car to Mosul as a decoy, and now it was time for Dad to leave too. As we reached the front door he must have noticed how quiet I'd been. He stopped and turned. 'Come with me,' he said. It was the first time he'd looked or spoken to me properly since lunch the day before. There'd been no time. I followed him into the kitchen. I saw the note on the wall. I'd never read the Quran and asked him what it meant. He told me it was seeking help from the divine and revenge on our enemies. I was very small for my age, a tiny boy really, but suddenly I felt a surge of courage rush through me. I wanted to protect him from whoever he was running from. 'If they get you, Baba, I'll get them too.' He picked up a pen from the table and began writing across the wall in large letters. In all the chaos and turmoil this seemed like the most bizarre thing to stop and do. Sort of childlike but defiant at the same time. 'My name is Hareth Zahawi. This is my home where I one day hope to return.' When he turned back round, I could see he was crying. Somehow in that moment I was more frightened than at any time during the last twelve hours. It was an admission of my father's own fears. If he didn't know what the future held, who the hell did?

We drove to the airport without a word. Halfway there we stopped at the office of the Public Notary for my dad to sign over power of attorney to my mum. She was to sell everything we owned. Dad had one small bag, and we stood at a distance as he checked it in. So many things contributed to the weight of this moment, it was impossible to carry it all out in the open so we just stood there in silence. When you know your father is leaving but you don't know when or where you'll see him next or whether you'll see him at all, the feelings are too big to articulate or contain. You want to scream everything you never knew you wanted to say because tomorrow might be too late. But there were eyes everywhere in Baghdad so instead we made do with a wave and a small 'Goodbye Baba', as if he were off to a conference in a neighbouring city. We could not afford to do more.

As he walked through the gate, the countdown began. He'd booked the Swiss Air flight to London via Geneva, even though it was two hours later than the first available plane out. We all knew the story of his friend who'd sat next to an ex-minister on an Iraqi Airways flight. After take-off the plane had been brought back down to allow the security services to board and arrest the former official. But even Saddam couldn't call back a Swiss Air flight. The minute the wheels were up, Dad would be out of the country. All we had to do was bide our time. This did nothing to allay my fears as we stood waiting for the bus to appear from the terminal. I knew he wasn't safe until take-off. Five minutes passed, then ten. After fifteen it felt like fifteen years and he finally appeared among the crowd of passengers, squinting into the sun as they crossed the tarmac. He didn't turn round and we did nothing that might suggest we were connected to this man.

The observation deck at Baghdad International Airport was a pretty basic affair in 1978. Airports were not the human tidal wave they are today. We stood in silence behind the thick grubby glass staring at the Swiss Air 737 parked on the runway; me to one side of my mother, Jihan on the other, each of us holding one hand. We all knew what we were waiting for. Two lights on the departure board flashed red, obstinately refusing to turn green to signal they were cleared for take-off. An interminable wait for the stewardess to close the door was followed by the ominous appearance of a dark green armoured truck in the distance, sweeping predictably round and pulling up next to the portable steps of the aircraft. The stewardess appeared at the top, framed by the open door, like an advert in the back of a glossy magazine for international travel. Two armed guards got out of the truck and climbed the stairs as if she'd been expecting them. No one said a word. The air around me was still but my mother's hand felt damp. Like most mornings in Baghdad, it was fine and sunny, an odd contradiction to our collective mood. I'm sure it can't have taken much more than a few minutes but it seemed like an eternity before the guards reappeared at the top of the steps. I felt an instant urge to be sick. They were empty-handed. My dad was still on the plane. He was free. The guards descended the steps and drove away in search of another plane. We learned later they'd got the wrong flight, but all this meant was that, for another family, there'd be an entirely different end to the day. Had they been there too on the viewing platform? If they were, I hadn't seen anyone falling apart. Not that I would have. I know that if it had been my father, we'd have left to go home without a word. Without a fuss. Yes, one of our pack might have been taken but there'd be no sense in attracting attention and getting ourselves arrested too. Like all sensible citizens we'd have gone back to our homes and kept our heads down, as if we were characters in an Orwell novel.

An hour later, a travel ban was formally imposed on my dad.

There were no mobiles or text messages and no way to communicate until my father eventually found himself somewhere with a phone. That could take hours, days, weeks perhaps. Even then the conversations would be rudimentary. Every call from a different number, and never the place he was living. Coded messages in case the authorities were listening in. So it would be a while before we learned that, by the time his flight crossed over Cyprus, Dad had polished off a full bottle of Dimple Haig whisky. When armed police board your plane on the hunt for traitors and you think, 'This is it, boy, your time is up,' I suppose that's a pretty reasonable reaction. The adrenalin was enough to ensure he wasn't even drunk when he landed in Geneva.

That evening the mukhtar came to visit my mum. The mukhtar was the closest thing Iraq had to an elected government official; chosen by the residents to see to their local affairs. Just like an MP here, he had to live in the area he represented and was usually an old timer who knew everyone's face. Ours was a long-time friend, Nadim Hilmi, and he had come to warn Mum that the authorities were on their way. In those days, the police or security personnel couldn't enter your home without the presence of the mukhtar, and an hour later, just before sundown, five shadows appeared on the porch – Nadim and four security officers. Mum opened the door as I watched from behind the sofa. When they asked her where Dad was, she told them he'd left the country on business – just like they discussed – but that he'd be back soon. The police in Baghdad could be a bit yakety-yak, not too much to worry about, but the security services were another matter. They were vicious. It was a test of who could hold their nerve longest. Eventually my mother prevailed. I'm sure they didn't believe her, but there was not much they could do to prove it so they reluctantly left for the night.

In the years since, I've met many people whose stories didn't end the way ours did that day. Families whose fathers were tortured. Wives who were raped. Children who were murdered. Our neighbour whose uncle no longer talks on account of the fact the party cut out his tongue. I knew we weren't just watching my father leave for England that day. We were waiting to see whether he'd escape under the wire or whether he'd be taken away to be kicked like a dog or shot in prison, his body returned to us with a bill for the bullets used to kill him. It was a gamble but one he had no choice but to take. It was the least worst choice and, in 1978, under the Ba'ath regime, just another day in Baghdad.

In the end, there'd been no big conversation about whether or not to leave Iraq. The alternatives were the imprisonment or death of my father, so there wasn't much to discuss. Me, Mum and Jihan were not in the same sort of danger for one simple reason: women and children were not seen as a threat. They apparently did not congregate, collaborate, plot or plan; they were powerless and unimportant. They were not considered a threat because they were not considered equals. Had you seen my mother in the eight months after my dad left, you would not have described her as powerless, unimportant or incapable. She was a force to be reckoned with. The idea that the capabilities of a whole swathe of society should be swept aside on the basis of gender is something I've never understood. Whether you liked her or not, I'd argue our most powerful British leader was a woman. Likewise two of our most enduring, productive and well-respected monarchs. Though perhaps it has never really been about underestimating them but actually about fear. The efforts to silence and control women in the Middle East would suggest an underlying cognisance of their potential collective weight were they to mobilise, and there's no greater modern example of this than events in recent times in Iran. Throughout history, women have put themselves second, as mothers and carers. This lack of ego is possibly one of the greatest advantages they have over men. The desire to be top dog has been the downfall of many powerful men and many regimes. While women are looking at the bigger picture and what's best for the many, men are arguing over who's in charge.

With two children and a full-time job already, my mother became responsible for liquidating my father's company and its assets in a fire sale, and managing the backlash in the wake of his departure. The moment he chose to leave, Dad branded himself a criminal, never mind that the charges were bogus. When people think the head of your household is a traitor, they very quickly turn against you in an environment that thrives on fear and manipulation. If he hadn't done anything wrong, why had he left? All those people used to switching sides at a moment's notice did exactly that. Anyone who stuck by us was in danger of being tarred with the same brush so the vast majority simply backed away.

News travels fast in a place like Baghdad. At school, I was thrust into exile overnight. Unofficially sent to Coventry. No one had to 'agree' to do this; it was second nature. They all knew the drill. My dad was a criminal and probably an imperialist spy – the very thing we'd been warned about repeatedly on the television. No one wanted to risk being seen with me: the children of party officials in my class might see us together and then what would happen to *their* fathers? When you live under a tyrant, people get used to keeping their heads down. There was one person, however, who did stand up for me and that was my best friend Omar, the one I'd been playing tag with when I'd impaled myself on the bush the previous summer. He was the only one who risked talking to me and it was he who told me what people were saying behind my back. 'Your father's being chased by Interpol. He'll be tried and executed for treason when they find him.' As frightened as I was, Omar's selflessness in my time of need was the high point of our friendship as far as I was concerned. Omar wasn't just fun, he was kind and loyal. When my parents told me we were leaving Iraq to escape the tyranny of a dictatorship to enjoy the life and freedoms of the West, I was devastated. Omar was my best friend and I couldn't bear the idea of that friendship coming to an end. Oddly, in the face of all that was happening, this was the hardest thing to swallow.

No one in my immediate family was killed or tortured by the Ba'athists so you could say we got away lightly, but the really traumatic thing for me about leaving was the lack of preparation. Most people I knew who'd left had done it in a much more orderly way. They'd had time to process the transition. At eleven, life was turned on its head and there was no real space for my parents to comfort me or make it okay because the same thing was happening to them. We were in the eye of a storm, just trying to strap everything down in the hope we'd come out the other side with something to hang onto once the winds dropped.

In spite of the turbulence, when Dad left, in some respects the house was calmer without him. I looked up to him, but I worried about the risks he took. In the eight months he was away, that particular stress was removed from the equation at home. For the first time too, I saw how good Mum was in a crisis. In a funny way, she blossomed in his absence. Fat contractors came to look at lorries and trucks parked across the road from our house, and she negotiated their sale. What drove her was me and Jihan; every sale she made now went some way further to creating a better start for us in the UK and she threw herself in headfirst. She was Amazonian.

My father was fortunate in that his work meant he'd always had a UK re-entry visa so London was the natural place for him to go, but this time he'd be starting again from scratch. While Mum collapsed our old life, he rented a small flat on the Gloucester Road, took out his Rolodex and put down the roots of a new one. Eight months later, it was time for the rest of us to join him. It's fair to say the move was traumatic for the whole family but, as the youngest child, I had no concept of the bigger picture. I didn't understand what was happening or why it was happening to me, and my overriding emotion was anger – at being taken away from my circle of friends and my childhood home. To this day, I don't remember a single thing about the journey or arrival but, in the summer of 1979, I landed with my mum and sister at Heathrow Airport to begin a new life in England. Things were about to get interesting.

PART TWO
VIA LONDON

CHAPTER 6
'JERUSALEM'

WELCOME TO ENGLAND

A friend once said that if you saw my parents at a party you'd instantly know they were immigrants, but not so me. That's a funny divide to have open up between you and your own mum and dad; to be at once their child and at the same time operating on a completely different level to them in your adoptive country. What was it about my parents that distinguished them from me? It was a difference between us that would never have arisen had we not moved country, but one I'd venture most first-generation immigrants notice in their own family dynamic. Language certainly played a part, but a British education was probably the bigger factor. At the time this comment was made I was in my thirties. I had twenty years of English under my belt. My dad spoke good English, but still heavily accented. My mother's was not so good that she'd choose it as a first option and I still speak Arabic with her to this day. I recently met someone who told me I 'sounded like an actor not a politician'. I'm not sure if she meant it as a dig or a compliment, but in essence she was right. English is not my mother tongue. I didn't pick it up subconsciously like you would as a baby. I pieced it together from sounds I found in adverts on TV, conductors on buses and cashiers behind tills, not cooed or sung to me by my mother. Perhaps this did have a bearing on what I absorbed and how I regurgitated it.

The roots of England went back a long way in my dad. Summer in the UK was quite common practice for the affluent Iraqis we mixed with; a well-loved touchstone. Any access we had to the popular culture of the West was brought back with us from these trips. Every summer my grandfather rented a house in Barnes, and Dad and his siblings would ride along the footpaths by the river through what must have seemed like lush countryside compared with Baghdad. He never stopped loving the place.

My parents are still probably the most patriotic people I know. Even now, having moved to Jordan, they live like Brits abroad; they love the sunshine but refuse to watch anything other than British television. Should you quiz them on their top choice of shows it would be an unequivocal vote for *The Repair Shop*, followed by *Dad's Army* and anything starring Charlie Dimmock. If you asked them now whether they consider themselves Iraqi or British they would say British, and I feel exactly the same. There's a historical bond between the two countries that I think would surprise a lot of people. The mandate lasted nearly forty years and many Iraqis regarded the British as more sophisticated than their Middle Eastern brethren. My brother-in-law will happily tell you, 'Everything I know, I was taught by an Englishman' and hums 'Jerusalem' every time he flies over London to land. For us, England was the promised land. Even the smell of it meant safety.

In the first instance, it took me and my sister time to adapt to living in the UK. It was a huge change in atmosphere but London was not unfamiliar to us. We'd often spent school holidays here, typically at the Hilton on Park Lane – London's first hotel skyscraper and still very new at the time. When it arrived on the scene with its mid-century décor and modernist vibe, it spoke to the changing times. Apparently nothing described the 'fashionable and exciting international mood of the Park Lane scene' more than the London Hilton. My parents certainly thought so. If they weren't drinking whisky and soda highballs and Bloody Marys in its basement tiki bar, they were dinner dancing on the rooftop – my dad in his suit from Simpsons of Piccadilly and Mum in her floor-length evening gown from Harrods.

The bottom line was, in the 1970s, the Hilton was the hotel of choice not just for the well-heeled businessman and his family, but celebrities too, which was something I found out first hand one morning over breakfast in the restaurant with my dad. As I sat, idly dipping my toast into my fried egg, I noticed a handsome man smiling at us from the table next door but one. If you're eating with kids in a nice restaurant, there are typically two types of response from diners without them: horror or a concerted effort to engage. This man did the latter and began trying to coax me over to his table. Rather than be alarmed by this, my dad was positively egging him on because the man in question was Muhammad Ali. It was the summer of 1976 – only a year since he'd beaten Joe Frazier in the 'Thrilla in Manila', so I knew exactly who Ali was. Everyone did. I don't know whether it was shyness or arrogance that stopped me but for some reason I point-blank refused to go and sit with him. He was so insistent and I so adamant that in the end I shouted across the tables, 'You come here instead!' which, to his credit, he took with immense good humour. My dad, however, was not about to miss out on the chance to meet Ali and, on the way out, we stopped at his table and chatted a while. Evidently I'd got over whatever it was that had been bothering me because I climbed onto his lap and sat there while they talked about Islam and the Middle East. He was like a real-life gentle giant; his hands the size of plates and his voice like maple syrup. Up close it was like meeting a character from a fairy tale.

In the early days, it was much easier to pick up the language from the written word than anything being said. In class, I'd latch onto sentences here and there but the fact I didn't have a firm grasp of the language had a knock-on effect in other subjects, causing teachers to tell my parents I might have learning difficulties. In reality, I'd just needed more time to crack the code but school alone wasn't going to get me there fast enough. Every day after classes finished, I started stopping at the newsagents on Shepherd's Bush Green near our house on Aynhoe Road to pick up a paper. Most Kurdish Iraqi dissidents, including my dad, read the *Guardian*, but I had no idea about the political leanings of different papers. When I bought the *Telegraph* I didn't know it was the most right-wing one going. It just looked like the sort of newspaper a clever man might read. At this point, I'd had about six months of English lessons in Baghdad so I could tell you the blue house was on the left and the boy liked holidays by the sea, but I was in no way prepared to tackle the nuances of a broadsheet. I couldn't understand a word, and the same proved true of *The Times* and the *Observer*, and I quickly moved on to the ones that looked like comics. The genius of the journalists in the Red Tops was that they could write a column that delivered a message and a story that was easy to read, which, for someone whose English was weak, was a godsend. It gave me huge confidence because I could actually read the bloody thing. I'd found a way in.

There was an extra silver lining to the *Sun* though and that was the early love of my life, Linda Lusardi. And not just Linda. Page 3 more broadly was pretty key to my interest in the paper. That you could open one and find a picture of a nearly nude lady came as quite the pleasant surprise. But more important even than Page 3 – the really big turn-on – was Dear Deidre and her infamous Photo Casebook. Deidre was a sort of agony aunt mixed with an Ann Summers' sales lady, which, for a somewhat naive but increasingly randy twelve-year-old boy from the Middle East, was extraordinary. Her speciality was suburban sexual fantasies and I absolutely loved it. I was there at the newsagent counter every day like clockwork for my copy of the paper and nothing was going to get in my way. Anything I couldn't understand from the words I could usually guess from the pictures, so it really was a very effective learning aid.

The Middle East was too far ingrained in my parents by the time we left to ever completely disappear but I was gradually moving further and further away from it. London was becoming my home. I don't know what life might have been like had we stayed in Iraq, but I was in no doubt what it meant to be in Britain. As my mother told me repeatedly, 'Son, the daughter of a grocer has just become prime minister; anything can happen here.' Standing here now, I can tell you she was spot on.

BROWN IN BRITAIN

I've often felt a tinge of guilt describing myself as a refugee – as if I'm an imposter. It's an odd feeling because, while I know my parents landed more comfortably than many, the trauma I felt in leaving my country as a child is an integral part of who I am; it's too far entangled to say who I'd be without it. But am I really a political refugee? Somehow I feel like it's a label that should be reserved – protected – for people who haven't been as lucky as me. It would be ridiculous of me to pretend I don't know the good fortune I have now in life, but I think it's this that prevents me from seeing myself in those terms. Can a person be both? A refugee and a 'rich man'? Does being one exclude you from being the other? Does power or success remove your claim over the events of your past? It's a complicated question.

The 1951 Refugee Convention defines a refugee as 'someone who is unable or unwilling to return to their country of origin owing to a well-founded fear of being persecuted for reasons of race, religion, nationality, membership of a particular social group, or political opinion'. Yep. That summed us up. My sister always called us 'runaways', but if my dad had returned to Iraq in 1979 I was in no doubt he'd be imprisoned or executed, so why do I feel an awkwardness around the term? I've been interviewed and questioned about it to the extent that it's started to sound like something from a book – almost fictional – as if I'm separated from my own story. Sometimes I worry it's in danger of being leant on as a prop or that I'm making too much of it, or cheating. But when I stop and think about my daughter, who's roughly the age I was when we fled Iraq, I'm in no doubt how horrendous it would be to put her through anything like the same thing. I want to wrap her in cotton wool and tell her these things don't happen anymore. But of course they still do.

Part of the complication is that we're talking about two different people when I ask the question, 'Am I a refugee?' – the boy I was then and the man I am now. I can't separate myself from the former even though he no longer exists, but how did he feel? How did he cope? On one hand, not well; it was a catastrophic rift at a time when I was at my most impressionable. On another, I'd say it was the making of me, and that's true of many people I've met who've experienced trauma early in their lives. It makes or breaks you. In the Middle East, Kurdish women are famous for their strength. You don't trek up a mountain in treacherous conditions with a brace of young children and survive without some serious inner strength. When you're an oppressed community, you get used to fighting your corner.

In the UK, it's not uncommon to meet people who've fled politically or physically dangerous situations and made huge sacrifices for the sake of their family. Get in an Uber and you could lay money on meeting one. We take for granted these people will mop our floors and take care of our sick, but when you think they were the ones brave enough to leave, it woefully underestimates their capabilities. How many times have you spoken to somebody who said the job that they did in their own country hugely outranked the one they do here? Many people in this country suffer great economic hardship, but it's unusual to find a born-and-bred British person who's had to move abroad to work in order to support their family at home. A commute to Swindon, maybe, but emigration? It's pretty rare. You begin to think, surely people with this strength of character are the kind you want in your country? As an employer, that 'can do' attitude is the first thing I look for in any new member of staff. I've never minded if people need training or support, but attitude is key for me. You can get a long way in life with the right mindset. Make the most of what you've got in front of you. It could be worse. Much worse. There's a saying that being a refugee is not a profession: it stays with you but you move on, and I think that's how I like to see it. Harnessing that energy is just one of the reasons we need safe and legal routes for those fleeing persecution and tyranny.

Originally my name was pronounced 'Nathim' like my grandfather before me, and this was what my father called me: my 'proper' name. At home, Mum called me 'Doo Doo'. In the UK, it seemed easier to simplify the 't' to a 'd', and I quietly became Nadhim. At one point in the 90s, I flirted with the idea of changing it to Nathan in the belief that would make me seem both cooler and more British, but thankfully thought better of it. Even so, no one at school could pronounce 'Nadhim' properly, so everyone just called me Noddy. The world's now heard of Rishi, Kemi, Sajid and Barack, but in 1979 it was a much, much narrower place.

It took me a little over twelve months to speak English fluently, but by then I'd missed out on properly integrating at a crucial time for a teenager. After my father left, things had been so turbulent that I'd not finished my final months of schooling in Baghdad. Added to that, because of the differences between the Iraqi and UK education systems, when I arrived in London I'd missed out on my first year at senior school here as well. In the space of two years, I then moved between Holland Park School and Sheen Comp, and in all that time I don't remember having a single friend at either. Had I been a fly on the wall in the playground, I think I'd probably have felt quite sorry for the boy I was then. Small and skinny, brown and friendless, walking home alone before his English was good enough to be able to properly connect with the other kids. In Iraq, I'd been popular at school – largely because I was so often in trouble. I was always the one standing outside Miss M'barak's office at lunch time because I'd covered the board in chalk dust or split my head open on the steel frame of the window dangling out to throw spit balls at the teachers below.

My memories of those early days in England are patchy but tiny slithers poke through, like walking on the pavements in the snow with Jihan or slipping on the ice in the first bitter-cold winter after we arrived. Predictably, it's largely the bad stuff that sticks: the day Jihan was tripped up by bullies or when I was dunked head first in the pond by some older kids at Holland Park. The time I was pitted to fight against a Bangladeshi kid at Sheen Comp was a particular stand-out. He'd been picking on me for no reason – flicking my ear in class or something equally stupid – and I knew he was being goaded to do it. At first I ignored him but there was only so long I could go before I had to stand up for myself, and I was bloody livid. 'What's wrong with you?!' I wanted to say. 'We're both BROWN! We're clearly being played here!' But he kept on flicking, egged on by a group of popular kids at the back of the class. All I could think was how stupid it was that we were obviously going to be that lunch time's entertainment. Sure enough, the minute the bell went, a circle formed in the playground and we were prodded and jostled to its centre. The chants began quietly at first and then with more confidence once they realised no teachers were lurking nearby. 'Fight, fight, fight.' I felt horrible, like a performing monkey dancing for the pleasure of some stupid kids who couldn't pronounce our names. Neither of us were what you'd call fighters, and in the end I wrestled the boy to the ground and sat on him, which seemed to satisfy the crowd. It was a pyrrhic victory. I wasn't big but he was even smaller, and we must have looked ridiculous. Pathetic even, I expect. These two tiny boys with brown faces waiting for the other kids to tell us when it was okay to get up and leave. As I sat there, my overriding feeling was what an idiot this boy was for allowing himself to be used like that, but more to the point, how annoyed I was he'd roped me in to it.

I had no choice but to fight back. I knew exactly what my dad would say if I came home with a black eye; he'd made his feelings about bullying very clear one holiday when the son of another couple started picking on me. I'd ignored it. That was my way. Turn the other cheek and hope the other kid gives up and goes away. I hated confrontation. When we got back to the hotel, however, my dad had other ideas about how to handle these kinds of situations and called me over to where he sat on the bed. Blithely unaware of what was coming I lolloped over with a casual 'Yeah, Dad?' His response was a hard slap across the face. Hard enough for me to burst into tears. 'The next time someone hits you, you hit him straight back.' My first reaction was that this was completely unfair – I wasn't the one who'd started the fight. When I saw how serious my dad was, this was quickly followed by a full-blown burst of anxiety because I knew then I'd have to do something about it. To face up to it. I can't not see these people. We're on bloody holiday with them.

The next morning at breakfast it was a toss-up who I was more worried about: the boy or my dad. I settled for the latter, and as soon as the boy started on me again, I jumped straight up and wrestled him to the ground. The adrenalin surge was huge and I doubt I'd have won any medals for technique, but it was definitely enough to shut the boy up. To my surprise, it did feel good to have stood up for myself. In an odd way, I now see the way my dad behaved as quite selfless. He wasn't afraid of not being liked by me if he thought it was for my benefit. He saw the dangers in the world and felt like the best way to protect me was to prepare me. 'Don't allow yourself to be bullied, Nadhim.' Mum was quite different. I remember once climbing a tree that protruded dangerously out over a cliff edge on holiday one year. My mum was beside herself but my dad insisted, 'Let him climb, Naj! Keep going. Don't be scared.' He was the same when I started riding horses. When I was thrown to the ground in a showjumping competition and dragged underneath my horse as she hurtled towards a pile of rusty reinforcement bars, it was Dad who told me to get straight back on. My mum was practically prostrate with worry but Dad was firm about the need to face my fears. He wasn't afraid to be the bad guy.

In every one of those scenarios I'd go through the same series of emotions: stress and anxiety at the thought of facing it but then the feeling that, you know what, maybe Dad was right. There's no better way to get over your fears than to face them head on.

During my childhood, the way men communicated their thoughts to one another was fairly primitive. Had my dad and I been less afraid to share our feelings, we might have found we had the same fears. If you asked him now, I expect he'd tell you I can be quite guarded and I'd say I can find him difficult to approach, but I feel sure that had we been born thirty years later, things might have been different. Perhaps we could have been a comfort to one another. It's not that I didn't want to open up to my dad, I just didn't know how, and I think the same was probably true for him too.

While I don't recall much about those very early days in London, what I do remember is the anxiety that underscored the first couple of years. Until I learned to speak English properly I was very isolated. I couldn't connect to anyone. In Iraq, I'd traded on being naughty; showing off, making the other kids laugh. That was more difficult to do when you didn't speak a common language, and my currency disappeared overnight. I was no longer that troublemaker Nadhim whose granddad was a minister. No one knew him here. I was just 'that new kid from the Middle East'. My identity was wiped out in an instant.

The thing that's easy to skirt over when 'normal' people look at immigrants is that once upon a time these people were not minorities. In one place at one time, they were the majority. Their otherness was not the thing that defined them. They were not strangers or foreigners. The sounds they heard around them were familiar, the smells of the cooking were comforting and their faces were probably the same colour as everyone else's. They had networks and families and a history, but the act of leaving meant their status as a human being was forever changed. No matter how bright, funny, kind or clever, these people are often treated as somehow less important; less than a person, even. For many they cease to have the dimensions or nuance they did at home. They are put in a box and judged on different terms. They're no longer Mohammad or Fatima, Pritesh or Yelda, and instead they're just 'the refugees' or 'the immigrants,' lumped together, defined by one act. It's the thin end of the wedge. The thick end is wholescale persecution: the Jews by the Nazis; the blacks by the whites; the Kurds by the Arabs. When you class people as a single entity, it's much easier to ignore their individuality and convince yourself their feelings don't matter. If you live in the host country, it can seem every persecuted person in the world wants to settle where you live. In 'your' country. But this is a gross misconception. In fact, the people that choose to come away from those situations are in the minority. The numbers that stay behind far, far outweigh those who flee. In fact, it's a tiny percentage. In reality, most people would prefer to stay at home in the place they know. To stick with what they know. The alternative for most is just too overwhelming. Leaving the place where you grew up and the culture that raised you is no walk in the park.

When I arrived in the UK in 1979, it was not the best time to be a different colour. Right-wing extremism and the accompanying widespread casual racism were enjoying a surge in popularity not seen since the 1930s. While the National Front still exists now, it has no representatives in parliament but, for a time in the mid-1970s, it was Britain's fourth-largest party in terms of vote share. All in all, it was not the most welcoming climate for an immigrant. Especially a brown one.

Although I'd like to believe things have improved greatly since, the colour of your skin is still seen as an indicator even when people don't realise they're making those subliminal judgements. For most it's not malicious or purposeful but a symptom of how far ingrained views of ethnicity are in the collective DNA. It's the times someone like me is mistaken for another Kurd because we 'all look the same' or when someone tells you their daughter's boyfriend is black before telling you he's also a doctor. This sort of 'benign' racism is different to being attacked or taunted in the street, but on another level it's just a more subtle form of the same thing. In my days as a rookie councillor, Jeffrey Archer, one-time deputy chairman of the Conservative Party, took me with him on many of his outings to introduce me to people who might be useful to know. One evening we were off to the home of Bernard Jenkin. Bernard was then MP for Colchester North but primarily known as a long-standing critic of the EU. As we entered his house, he shook hands warmly with Jeffrey and asked whether he'd like a drink. Yes please, said Jeffrey, explaining that he'd brought his driver so was free to have a tipple. 'Wonderful,' says Bernard, turning instinctively to me, 'you can park round the back.' What followed was a painfully awkward and falsely jocular few minutes in which Jeffrey explained *I* was not his driver but in fact the newly appointed councillor for Wandsworth and Bernard did a little dance around his cock-up. Bernard was actually a very sweet guy and I wasn't offended – there was nothing wrong in being a driver after all – but it told you all you needed to know about race and perception in the UK at that time. And that time was 1994.

CHAPTER 7

BAGGY TROUSERS

A LITTLE LEARNING

One of the greatest changes I experienced coming to the UK was that there was a world designed specifically for people like me: the young. In Baghdad, the films we watched and the music we listened to were largely dictated by what our parents liked, watched and listened to. I could still sing you the Arabic songs I loved even now. The party controlled our access to the West, and this included popular culture. That's why I was one of the few twelve-year-old boys in the world without a poster of Olivia Newton-John or Farah Fawcett on their bedroom wall. And I'd lay money on the fact I'm the only kid you'll meet who had one of Demis Roussos. My mum liked him, my aunties liked him, and so it followed my sister and I did too.

The confines of my world in 70s Baghdad were quite narrow. When I came to London those boundaries were blown apart. I was bombarded with a kind of music I'd never really heard before. Music designed to trigger hormonal teens – to make them cry or want to have a fumble. Duran Duran, Spandau Ballet, Human League: men who looked like women; women who looked like men. It was mind-blowing for a boy who'd been brought up on music largely performed on a lute. But the band I loved best had nothing to do with sex and everything to do with rule breaking. Suggs, Chas, Lee and Woody and the rest of a seemingly endless line-up were Madness, and I was devoted. My way into the band was via a girl and her name was Stella. Stella was in my class but, like most girls my age, not interested in me or anyone in her own year and had an older boyfriend outside school. In his DMs, turned-up jeans and braces he was the archetypal Madness fan. The skinhead uniform was designed for fighting in the dancehalls and outside football grounds, material that wouldn't rip in a scuffle and steel-toed boots that were eventually banned from matches. What I didn't know was that Stella's boyfriend was a National Front sympathiser and self-proclaimed fascist – at least as much of one as you can be at 15. I don't remember his name but I do remember he and his mates laughing when Stella told them I liked their favourite band too. Didn't I know what it meant? Didn't I get it? No, I didn't. I liked the music. I just happened to be brown. The fascist fans were an unwelcome appendage Madness struggled to shake off for years and the Nazi salutes at their gigs were as abhorrent to them as they were to any other sane person. At heart, the band were working-class boys from Camden who grew up on football and fighting, but they weren't racists. I carried on listening to my records and went a bit off Stella.

What I really loved about Madness was the anarchy. The nutty boys spoke to my inner nature. In 1983, anarchy was exactly what I wanted. I didn't know I was about to meet a boy who knew exactly how to make it and just where to find it …

Although we'd come to England to start a new life, Dad never really worked here. While Mum, Jihan and I stayed in Sheen, he was now living between Kuala Lumpur and Sabah in the Kinabalu region of Malaysia, running a big communications project. He'd be with us for a week or so out of every two months, which was a huge change from the dynamic we'd had in Iraq. His work meant he went where the opportunities took him, which was great for business but not for my mum, who was left alone to deal with my increasingly bad behaviour. Dad employed an ex-policeman called Bill as a company driver, whom Mum eventually commandeered to take me to school every day. It was only a fifteen-minute walk but she quite rightly didn't trust I'd actually go if left to my own devices or that I wouldn't be distracted by drugs or some other nefarious activity on the way. Monitoring my behaviour became a full-time job.

Dad had always been a larger-than-life character. He lived in the moment and spent money like someone who'd just inherited a fortune. By anyone's measure we were well off, but somehow I never felt we were financially secure. Something about his attitude made me feel anxious. Mum's approach to life was very different. She was a worrier and more cautious than my dad. And for good reason. It was normally her who had to pick up the pieces when things went wrong. Sometimes this meant telling Jihan and I to be careful with money or that we needed to juggle our priorities. When Dad came home he'd simply counter her concerns with a breezy, 'Don't worry, Naj. Everything will be fine.' This did nothing whatsoever to settle my nerves. He was a risk-taker, and it bothered me. It was like being in a car that someone else was driving remotely. I wasn't in control and was never sure whether we were in a good or a bad place, and that insecurity manifested itself in rebellion. My parents were very liberal but I grew up in a patriarchal society and there was no mistaking my dad's word was law, and the fact he was rarely home created a power vacuum that became a green light for my misbehaviour. At fifteen, the streak in me that at seven or eight was classed as naughtiness was in danger of becoming something closer to delinquency. I'd reached the event horizon and there seemed to be no one strong enough to stop me falling in.

I suspect this was part of the reason they decided to take me out of Sheen Comp and put me into a private school in Roehampton in the belief it would pull me into line. Unfortunately, my parents weren't experts on the English education system. They knew *why* they wanted me to be a part of it – it was the greatest system in the world – but they didn't understand its nuances. To them a private school – no matter which one – seemed like a better class of education, which is why they inadvertently made matters worse in choosing Ibstock Place, a fee-paying school just around the corner.

THE FROEBEL SYSTEM

By the time I moved I was a year off sitting my O-levels and the culture shock was huge. Ibstock Place was a school that billed itself as 'different', and its beating heart was the Froebel System. Friedrich Froebel was a nineteenth-century educationalist who wanted to teach children to think for themselves; who believed they should be central to their own education. Forget the passive student and the didactic teacher; you decide what you want to work on and what you want to do, and that's how you progress. In practice, what this liberal approach translated to was a total lack of boundaries at a time when routine and structure were exactly what I was missing.

Back then, Ibstock's reputation attracted a very particular sort of crowd. It was the kind of place where musicians and artists sent their kids – a lot of whom came in after a weekend of partying with their parents, drinking and taking drugs. Nobody wanted to learn, and I was the type of kid who needed very little encouragement to slack off.

The problem was, I'd always been naughty. It was my currency. I had a lot of energy, which I spent messing around. Sometimes I had trouble pinned on me, but mostly it was my own fault and it went back much further than Ibstock. Miss M'barak at Al Mansour had an innate ability to see through a person and she definitely had my number. 'He's talented,' she would tell my parents, 'because he's able to learn without concentrating.' This sounds like a compliment but really wasn't. She knew this 'skill' could be dangerous if misused. It was great for picking things up quickly but could equally make you take things for granted. If you weren't careful, it made you lazy as well. This was exactly the situation in which I now found myself. My 'talent' had come back to bite me on the arse.

At Ibstock, I was a little bit in love with my biology teacher, Miss Carey, mainly because I got the feeling she saw a spark in me. 'You have to remember, Nadhim, you might be able to concentrate in class while you're distracting your neighbour, but can they?' 'No,' was nearly always the answer. As an adult I still have the same ability, which comes in handy if I want to tap into a conversation on the other side of the room at a summit or if I'm stuck next to someone a bit boring at a state dinner. I guess that's what Miss M'barak meant about harnessing my abilities, but it took me a while to get there.

THE DUDE

Ibstock brought many changes to my day-to-day life but the most notable was Max Johnson. Max was a boy who could have been anything, and my friendship with him was one of the greatest, most exciting but ultimately heartbreaking times of my life.

Max was the first person I'd met whose home life was complete chaos. It was a place without boundaries and one in which no one even pretended to maintain their dignity or give a passing nod to social etiquette. Things at the Johnson house were too far gone. Max couldn't control or cover up for his father's erratic behaviour and it was a mark of our friendship that he didn't even try. For any child – which is what we both were – it's a turning point in life to see an adult totally out of control; one who's ceased to pretend everything is alright because they're just as scared and overwhelmed as the children. No one was in charge at Max's house. It was like *Lord of the Flies*.

Max's mother had been a model in the 60s – a Christine Keeler type. Her beautiful brown eyes stared out from her photograph in the pages of a society magazine that hung on the front-room wall. It was obvious she'd been a great beauty, but she'd long ago lost the vitality of someone with a carefree life. I'll never forget watching her one day after school as I walked down their road. Her face was tense and drawn as she left the flat, dragging an old-fashioned shopping trolley behind her. There was a terrible sense of sadness about her. I don't know what had led them to this point, but the disparity between the flea-bitten flat and the photographs on the walls of better days told me that, somewhere along the line, something had gone very wrong for the Johnson family.

Thomas Johnson had been a major in the army. At the time I thought he was a schizophrenic, though I now think it more likely he had dementia. Even so, he still had the voice of a man used to controlling a troop of men and it was no less intimidating to hear it in the confines of their two-bedroom flat. There was something pretty terrifying about seeing a six-foot-four grown man rage against a fourteen-year-old boy. I don't know what triggered these episodes but I felt unequivocally that Max was in danger just by being there. It was no wonder he never wanted to stay home. Usually, we'd go straight to his room in an effort to avoid a blow-up. When we tried to leave, the heavy presence of his father loomed over us: 'You're not going anywhere!' I'd freeze on the spot, as if no one would notice or turn their attention to me if I didn't speak. Sometimes things had escalated, and I'd arrive to find Major Johnson standing in his string vest and underpants screaming at Max in the front room or outside on the balcony. My entrance wasn't enough to cause a ripple of inhibition in the man and they carried on their usual dance: the Major ran at Max, who ducked out the way or did a little Ali shuffle. A derogatory 'Fuck you' and a slammed door followed by an easy laugh was his normal response. 'The Major's off again,' he'd say with the forced nonchalance of someone on the receiving end of repeated abuse. That's how things were dealt with in the Johnson house. The best-case scenario was that Max would survive unscathed until it was time for him to leave home.

I've no idea how Mr and Mrs Johnson afforded the fees at Ibstock, but somehow Max and I found ourselves together in the same game of five-a-side in the playground one lunch time in June. I was never brilliant at football but I loved it. Max played like Dimitar Berbatov. Some players can just slow the game down; when they're on the ball, they just have an extra second or two. It looks effortless – slightly lazy – but you can never get the ball off them. That was Max.

As relaxed as he was with his peers, in front of other people's parents he behaved like the son of a major. 'Hello, sir, how are you?' If you knew him well you couldn't miss the sensation of a smile under the surface. As soon as we were out of earshot it was back to his south London Estuary – a few dropped letters, an 'f' instead of a 'th' now and then. To this day, I don't know which version of things was real.

The bottom line was, I was totally in awe of Max. He was by far the coolest guy at school. Handsome, funny, charming and fearless. Long blond hair, with an infectious smile, and laid back in a way I envied. He was The Dude. I was never a leader, but I always gravitated to the one who was. I liked being in their orbit and this was never truer than in my relationship with Max. I would have done anything for him. The irony – or heartbreak – of the whole thing was that Max could have been one of the masters of the universe, but life had other plans for him.

For the first time since leaving Baghdad, I'd regained my 'position' in the classroom. All in all, a complete lack of structure at school, combined with a mercurial friend I doted on, was a lethal cocktail. We were making trouble and loving it. It didn't help that the Johnsons lived in close proximity to a pub. The night my friend Daniel had come over when my parents were away and we'd made a big dent in Dad's bottle of Johnnie Walker Black, and I'd been sick in their bed, had been enough to put me off neat whisky for life. As a consequence, my tipple of choice now was Southern Comfort and lemonade, which should tell you I was no Oliver Reed. But it was the freedom the pub introduced that was totally intoxicating, and it quickly became the centre of my universe.

In the days before landlords bothered with ID, a typical afternoon saw me coming home long enough to change and turning straight back round to meet Max for an evening at his local. When the doors closed at 11 p.m. we went wherever else would have us. Whether it was a dingy lockup belonging to a slightly dubious Irish builder or a bench on the high street, it wasn't uncommon for me to be out until two o'clock in the morning. Even at home I'd find a way of staying up into the early hours, and there wasn't a great deal Mum could do about it. That didn't stop it upsetting her. She'd always been the one to encourage me in my studies. For her, academic achievement was the key to whether you'd have a 'good' or a 'bad' life. 'You can have everything in this country,' she'd often tell me, but I wasn't listening. As much as I loved her, at fifteen I wanted to be out with people I considered glamorous and exciting. Boys acting like big men. At the time I didn't recognise the reason they were probably behaving this way was because there were no adults in their own lives filling the position. It fell to them to play the grown-ups. I gathered friends from Max, and he in turn gathered them from a largely working-class crowd invested in drink or drugs with a passion for violence on the streets and football terraces. Max may have been the one who guided me onto the wrong track, but I needed little persuasion to go with him.

Eventually, Mum got the inevitable call from school to say I'd finally outwitted the Froebel System. A fight with two other boys resulted in a broken right hand still visible to this day, and I was now predicted a total of zero O-levels that coming summer. Had I not been so bright, the head said, they'd be having a conversation about my expulsion. I'm not sure if Mum realised quite how serious things had become, but this was a wake-up call for us both. For the first time ever, she admitted defeat. 'I don't know what to do,' she told me. 'I don't know how to help you.' Fortunately, there was someone else who did.

Auntie Farida was Dad's older sister. She'd never had children herself so had more time and energy than Mum to take up the fight. Mum was so brow-beaten by my relentless mischief she'd finally run out of steam. She was also very easy to outwit and was as trusting as I was sneaky. It didn't take much to slip out the backdoor unnoticed. But she was out of her depth on a broader level. Just as with many immigrants whose first language wasn't English, the nuances of the British education system went over her head, which made it easy for me to manipulate her when I needed. It didn't help that Dad was not closer to hand. He had very big, broad expectations for me, but in the day-to-day running of things he was pretty hands off, which now strikes me as a bit incongruous. The man who a few years before had slapped me round the face for not standing up for myself in a fight was now nowhere to be seen. If ever I needed guidance, surely this was the time. Why did he never feel the need to be involved or to come home? Was it because he knew he had a strong wife he could rely on to handle things? I honestly don't know because it was never discussed. At least not with me. To this day, I have no idea how either of them felt about it all. I do wonder, though, whether that question mark was part of what drove my behaviour. That perhaps it was just attention-seeking. Whatever the reason, the fact was Dad didn't have to come back because he had a woman at home whom he knew he could rely on to take care of things. In fact, now he had two ...

Auntie Farida lived quite nearby and made Mum an offer she couldn't refuse. 'Let him come and live with me, Naj; let's try and get him some O-levels.' And so, in 1983, that's what we did. For ten months I lived with Auntie Farida and Uncle Gani. The dire O-level prediction was a seemingly insurmountable barrier to moving forward and the idea of turning things round in the short time left seemed like a joke. But Auntie Farida did what nobody had been able to do before: she helped me find a way in. We were quite close already but, on living with her and Gani, I found I could talk to her on my wavelength. It was easier than with my own parents, although I'm sure this had as much to do with the fact I was their teenage son as it did their actual behaviour. Raising a teen is a notoriously ball-breaking task and, if you're the parent, you need a thick skin to survive. Nevertheless, it took someone outside our triangle to break the spell, and for me that was Auntie Farida. 'Tell me about it,' she'd say. And I would. I wasn't worried she'd be judgemental or that my confidences would be used against me. She gave me room to breathe. It was like wriggling free of a net I'd got tangled up in. Everything I'd been mixed up with that was holding me back seemed to fall away and the energy I'd been using on it all was redirected somewhere more important: my future. Auntie Farida was my 'trusted adult' and could not have turned up at a better time.

We took things day by day, bit by bit. She told me to ignore the overall amount of work that needed doing and to tackle it in bite-sized chunks. Not to let the fear of the scale of a problem paralyse me into inaction. It was something I've come back to time and time again in life. Hold on to fear, take it by the horns and don't let it get the better of you. When something seems too big, start at the bottom and work your way up. Even the largest tree will topple eventually if you destabilise it at the base.

I don't think anyone had ever bothered to explain to me how to revise before then, and it was like a stalemate had been broken. She sat with me every day. It was like having a one-on-one tutor and an incredible sacrifice to make for a child that wasn't her own. We'd do a couple of hours' work, then go for a walk or, better still, put a bet on the horses. My grasp of electromagnetic forces and mathematical probability grew hand in hand with my understanding of racing form at Newmarket and Epsom. My standout win was 13–1 on the 1983 Grand National when I put fifty quid on Corbiere – the first Grand National winner to be trained by a woman, Jenny Pitman. Auntie came with me to collect my £650 winnings on account of the fact I was still underage.

I'm relatively unusual for a politician in that I found English language and literature more challenging subjects. My area of expertise was the sciences. They had a logic to them that doesn't exist in the arts. Once you get the fundamentals right you begin to understand how to build on them. That's what Gani and my aunt really helped me to understand: the foundations. Gani had come to the UK to complete a PhD in physics at Aston University in Birmingham in the late 70s. He should have been a teacher. He had such an easy way with him. I was taking all the STEM subjects and he was brilliant at bringing complex theories to life; turning facts into stories in a way I could understand and remember. He and Auntie Farida helped me find the door. What I did on the other side would be down to me.

Those ten months were a turning point, not just in my studies but my overall behaviour. My aunt did what Froebel hadn't managed to do: treat me like an adult and get me to respond in kind. What's more she made me *believe* I could do it, and that was the real pivot point. I didn't stop going out or give up my friends, but something had shifted. I'd finally realised there was life beyond the upcoming Saturday night, and that if I wanted it to be rewarding, I'd have to invest in it now, before it was too late.

CIVIL DISOBEDIENCE

The thing that really united Max and me was our love of football, and when we weren't playing, we were watching other people. When I arrived in Britain, hooliganism was in its heyday, and stadiums were the perfect place to meet and stage – or at least threaten – a fight. The topic dominated the UK press and getting your picture on the front page of the *Sun*, brawling on the streets, was a badge of honour for die-hard fans, and the media attention in turn fuelled the violence. It was the perfect, emotive circle. These stand-offs weren't accidental; you went to the football in order to fight. It was tribal. There are many convincing arguments about why men like to brawl at a match but my theory was, most blokes did it because they didn't know how to express their feelings or manage their frustrations. Max and I had plenty of problems we didn't know how to articulate and, at fifteen, we joined the ranks of troublemakers on the terraces. He was a Liverpool devotee but my heart belonged to Man U.

Historically, match dress code was warm and dry, together with a nod to your club in the colour of your scarf or T-shirt. By the time I was old enough to go to a game, a change had crept in and a new subculture had emerged – the Casual. Max and I were all-in, and there was nothing accidental about the way we looked. It was a uniform born out of practicality: in your club colours you were easy pickings for the police on the lookout for trouble-makers fresh from the terraces. Anyone wanting to duck under the radar found the best way to blend in to a crowd was to do away with the old kit. Fans swept the streets in expensive designer leisurewear and hid in plain sight.

In the 70s, Liverpool were Britain's most successful team and, towards the end of the decade, dominated European competitions too. Italy, France or Spain – where the team went, the fans followed and, just like intrepid explorers of old, when they returned they brought treats from their travels. Raleigh may have given us tobacco and the potato, but Liverpool fans brought us Fila, Lacoste and Sergio Tacchini. The beautiful game got a glow-up. Ours was a display culture, not that different from the Georgians in their ruffled shirts and coat tails or the Teddy Boys in their drapes and brothel creepers, and for Max and me, the velour Fila tracksuit was the centrepiece of both our wardrobes. We were paid-up members of the tribe.

Max was slim and slight, and moved in a fight just like he did on the pitch. I watched him many times as he danced with an opponent in the streets outside a match. Liverpool had a big, big posse of fighters, and the battles were predetermined by their 'leaders'. When Liverpool came to London, the time, place and nature of the fight would already have been agreed. There were no mobile phones or social media so it was all word of mouth and an extraordinary piece of engineering. The two sides would square up and wait for their orders to 'Stand

and turn!' Their allegiance to their leader and their cause was binding.

The date 5 April 1986, however, would stick in my mind forever. Liverpool were playing Southampton in the FA Cup semi-final at White Hart Lane and 44,000 fans crammed into the stands to watch The Reds beat their opponents 2–0. Adrenalin surged through the crowds as we left the stadium that day and, like all forms of energy, it had to go somewhere. Standing among the Liverpool fans on Tottenham High Street later that afternoon, it was easy to see where.

Hundreds of us lined up, shoulder to shoulder, ready to take on the defeated Southampton fans. Residents watched from behind their net curtains or had the good sense to go out for the day. Crowds heaved back and forth like an amorphous mass, breathing as one. Somehow Southampton managed to come round behind us and advanced from the rear, but we stood our ground. A tangle of bodies blurred the line between the two sides as we began to seep into one another's space. I looked behind me; hundreds more jostled for position. There was no way out. I looked for Max but he was up ahead, closer to the front. I was alone, surrounded by a deafening wall of noise: chants, taunts and incessant booing like a low growl. It was totally primal, exciting and terrifying in equal measure. It had only been a year since the Heysel disaster where thirty-nine fans were crushed to death. There was no room to turn or breathe and I started to panic.

And then they came, towering above us. Their coats glistened and the air was thick with the smell of sweat. The horses bristled at the edge of the crowd, held back by their riders. They were taught not to be frightened of anything and to withstand most things – beer cans, bins, bottles – but no one knows how an animal will respond in a moment of fear. Suddenly, the crowd heaved and the horses drove a wedge between the two tribes.

A wall of flesh and the sound of the metal on concrete, sparks flying as they slipped and stumbled. Part thoroughbred, part draught, the temperament and size of these animals meant they were well suited to the task. Heavy work was in their DNA and this is what they came to do. Each one six feet to the wither and close to a tonne in weight. Head on, they rose another three feet in the air, snorting and frothing through a mouth full of silver. They were meant to intimidate and, as they rode through the crowd, prying us apart, they did exactly what it said on the tin.

There was nowhere to go, but trying was better than standing still. As I turned, I was knocked aside by the flank of a huge gelding, slamming me into the glass of a shop window. The wind was knocked out of me and it was all I could do to stay upright. As I stood pressed against the wall, a moment of clarity passed over me. I looked around at everyone there and suddenly saw us for what we were: animals fighting in a cage. There was no point to this; no higher moral code of honour at stake. The only people we were impressing were ourselves and we were too self-absorbed to notice how stupid we looked. When the command came to run, I filtered into the masses and moved with them towards the station.

I've no memory of how we got home that afternoon or whether we even talked about it afterwards, but it was a watershed moment for me. Three years later, crushing in the stands at Hillsborough caused the deaths of ninety-seven Liverpool fans. Max and I had been lucky. Others had not. From then on I'd watch the game in the pub or leave as soon as it was over if I went to a match. I didn't have the stomach for it anymore.

We've come a long way in terms of behaviour. Nowadays, it's only a minority of fans who intimidate unsuspecting civilians in Leicester Square or behave like animals abroad, and when I see them, I am ashamed. But as a teenager, when I was in the middle looking out, things seemed quite different. It had a hold over me. I was an observer, utterly fascinated by what I saw, and there was a glamour to it I found completely intoxicating. I never did hard drugs or drank a huge amount, but for a time I was easily pulled into excitement: especially the kind you couldn't tell your mum or dad about. The change in my direction was a combination of chance and fear: the chance of finding myself in that crowd and the consequential distillation of fear triggered a momentary flash of common sense. But it was luck too, because had it not occurred, I might never have stopped to look up and realise what was happening to my life. When I finally did, I had a family standing in the wings waiting to help. They weren't experts in dealing with a teen who'd veered off the tracks, who they could no longer control, but they cared enough to want to try and had the space, time and mental capacity to do it. Not everyone was in that situation. Max definitely wasn't. He and I were at the same crossroads but no one came to rescue him, and our outcomes as a consequence could not have been more different.

KID, YOU WON'T BELIEVE IT, BUT ...

In 2018, I would become the parliamentary under secretary of state for children and families in the Department of Education under Theresa May. Anyone with ambitions to be in the cabinet would do well to spend time in this department because it's the clearest illustration you'll get of the realities of life for many people in this country. It was eye-opening in a way I've never been able to shake off. It was clear that the way things began for children was often the same way they ended and the issue was in trying to iron out those inequalities. One of the greatest challenges in our education system is that schools work on the 80/20 rule, which means that if 80 per cent of your kids are achieving the right grades, you're classed as outstanding. But what about the 20 per cent? Who helps them? In many instances the answer is no one. I'd once been in that 20 per cent myself, which meant I had a genuine understanding of what it felt like. Staying in that 20 per cent could dictate the terms of the rest of your life. I was incredibly lucky to have a caring, competent aunt willing to set aside a part of her own life to help me better mine, but not everyone has the benefit of an Auntie Farida.

The thin end of the wedge was students who'd been off-rolled or permanently excluded, who struggled to get back into normal schooling because of the lack of time or skills to cope with the additional bandwidth their education demanded. Or those whose inability to read or write properly on graduation had a knock-on effect on their ability to go into higher education and, consequently, their ability to get skilled work. These were often kids whose parents couldn't read to them because English was a second language or had never owned a book themselves. Children who failed in maths because they couldn't read the question. The repercussions of poor literacy are huge and the aftershocks long-lasting. Helping kids find a way out is one of government's biggest ongoing challenges.

The thick end of the wedge was secure homes. This is where government places children deemed too vulnerable to stay at home; whose co-morbidities in behavioural terms have created a situation in which they are now a threat to society. Or themselves. A secure home is not a proposition you would ever want a child or a family to be faced with. Gangs, drugs, violence, exploitation, poverty and despair: these are the reasons we have secure homes. In 2019, I toured one such place and met a boy I'll call Benny. Both sides of Benny's head were badly fractured. To look at, he was not the kind of teen you'd cross the street to avoid. A lanky, stringy kid from a one-parent family, he got into his first gang at twelve. At fifteen, he got cocky and thought maybe *he* could make the money at the top, so he started dealing himself. The gang didn't like that so they smashed in one side of his head. Social services intervened and moved him 200 miles away from home. He just wanted to be with his mum and didn't understand why they wouldn't let him go back. Lonely and arguably more vulnerable than before, he got into another gang, who fractured the other side of his skull. So now he finds himself here, in front of the families minister, telling this stranger his story. The thing was he was smart. Too smart. Articulate, with a beautiful turn of phrase; funny and erudite. I absolutely loved him. I knew exactly who this boy reminded me of, and in a moment of impulse told him: 'Kid, you won't believe it, but if I were looking in a mirror, you are me and I am you.' It sounded absurd – like a soapy storyline from an episode of *Juliet Bravo* – but it was true. It could easily have been Max standing there and, had it not been for Auntie Farida, me too.

In the summer of 1983, I confounded the critics and passed six of my eight O-levels. It wasn't the greatest academic grand slam of all time but it was a far cry from the predicted 'nul points'. And it was enough to get me a place at King's College in Wimbledon. Max did not come with me. In fact, he didn't go anywhere. It was the end of the road for him academically and he left school with the zero qualifications he'd also been predicted.

By the time I was doing my A-levels, Max was heavily into heroin. While my mum had reminded me daily of the dangers of drugs, he had no one to pull him back from the edge. There are definitely worse things that happen to people every day, and Max was not the most badly treated child in the world, but from where I was standing it was the closest thing I'd seen to a genuine tragedy because no one did anything about it. No one intervened.

The thing is, taking Class A drugs isn't just about what it might do to you mentally and physically, it's about the environment it puts you in. Max was hanging out with a lot of pretty edgy guys, a lot of very unsavoury characters. It was easier to continue down the same path as them than resist, especially if you didn't feel you had anything to stop you.

Max was a hugely bright and capable boy. The only thing that separated him from me was the support of a stable family.

CHAPTER 8
AUBREY C. BRIGGS

THE CON ARTIST

Aubrey C. Briggs was as large a character as his name suggests, a six-foot-four American with swept-over grey hair, red face and booming Texan drawl. I'm not sure he ever wore a pocket watch but I felt like he should. He could have been a character in an early-nineteenth-century novel or an old Hollywood movie, a salesman who blows in from out of town. Nobody knows this guy and there's no real way to check his credentials but the family in the story end up inviting him to stay for dinner anyway – he's intriguing, with an old Southern charm. He's passing through town on his way to meet with some savvy investors who want to get in on the ground floor. 'Oh yes?' asks the father as they sit round the table eating their supper. 'What project's this?' There's a little bit of the Wild West about Aubrey C. Briggs and eventually the father says, 'Why not stay the night? The spare room's all made up.' One night leads to a week, and before you know it the father has sold the hay cart and persuaded the neighbours to sell their farm equipment too. No one wants to miss out on the opportunity of a lifetime. Everyone wants to invest in Mr Briggs's new scheme. But from the music alone you can tell it's not going to end well for the family or their neighbours.

Sadly though, this wasn't a story. Aubrey C. Briggs was real, and it was our table he sat at and my father who sold the proverbial hay cart. Ours was the family for whom it did not end well.

It had been seven years since we'd come to England and during that time my dad had worked hard to rebuild a business. He could turn his hand to anything but he'd been lucky too; he had contacts over here to cushion the blow. My dad was a grafter but he was also what you'd class as a more affluent immigrant. On arrival in England, there were networks he could call on to give him a foot up. He found his way to Roehampton, where friends of friends put him up in a flat. He paid rent, but it was hassle-free. He didn't need to pass checks or be approved by anyone because he already had a re-entry visa courtesy of his old company. On top of that, he spoke reasonable English. A big plus.

You'd be surprised how many displaced Iraqis there were in the UK even then. In the mid 80s, there was a huge community in south-west London. The legacy of Saddam's regime is that if you go to any hospital anywhere in the United Kingdom, you'll find at least one consultant of Iraqi origin. The brain drain from the country was extraordinary. Tragic, in fact. Largely speaking, this was the pool of people with whom my parents mixed. Educated and affluent enough to be of interest to a chancer like Aubrey C. Briggs.

By 1985, when I was eighteen, we were living in Clare Lawn Avenue in Sheen Gate near Richmond Park. It was a beautiful double-fronted, red-brick house with bay windows and a horse-shoe drive that took you up to the dark mahogany front door. But the jewel in the crown at Clare Lawn Avenue was the heated swimming pool round the back. My dad loved gadgets and insisted on installing one of the first ever inflatable covers so we could swim in all weathers – like Center Parcs minus the wave machine. For obvious reasons, there were no end of friends wanting to come to my house at the weekends, but things were about to change.

Dad had always been an avid reader and researcher. He'd hear about the next big thing in technology before anyone else I knew. When he read about a piece of equipment that could accelerate air to supersonic speed and be used on a grand scale to cut into the ground, he was sold. This was Aubrey C. Briggs's Air Knife and it was going to change the world. On one level, I fully understand why my dad was so taken with the Air Knife; it was an incredible concept. James Dyson built a business around the same sort of mad idea – the power of the movement of air – but Aubrey C. Briggs was no James Dyson. What's worse, he clearly believed he *was*, and that faith in himself could be quite intoxicating.

The first and only time I met Mr Briggs was when he came to England to talk shop. Dad rolled out the red carpet and took us all to the Hurlingham Club in Fulham for Sunday lunch. We were in England now and he was going to show Aubrey the best of everything. This was a celebration; a back-patting exercise to which the whole family was invited. I felt horribly uneasy throughout. With his comb-over and three-piece suit, Aubrey bulldozed through the club and devoured his Sunday roast like Henry VIII at a feast in his honour. He had an arrogance that made me feel uncomfortable and I instinctively knew there was something not quite right; as if he were pretending to be a scientist. In fairness, I'd not met any other scientists at this point in my life, but my gut told me he didn't *feel* like an inventor. There was not enough academic rigour in him. To me, he just felt like a salesman.

I've since met many inventors and all of them have one thing in common: they're passionate about the science behind the product. During my time as a minister, I ended up meeting James

Dyson, who'd spent £20 million of his own money trying to make a usable ventilator during the pandemic. It wasn't just about profit, it was about the engineering; and when James talks, you can't help but be infected by his passion. Research always drives the product, not the other way round, and that was the problem with Aubrey C. Briggs: for him, it *was* the other way round. Aubrey C. Briggs was a snake-oil salesman and I smelt a rat.

Things start so well. Dad takes the product licence for the Middle East and tours the territory with his prototype. Orders for a trial product roll in nicely. Had he stuck to that he might have been okay but my dad was hugely ambitious – a risk-taker – and decides that this is not enough. He's going to go to America to see where the magic happens. He's completely taken in by the world of Aubrey C. Briggs and announces he's going to invest everything we have in the mothership. Aubrey's positivity is infectious and more money starts coming in from other investors, including ones brought in by my dad. Things are looking great and Dad starts behaving accordingly. He buys a boat and a big car, and one for my sister too. He rides that wave like it's never going to meet the shore. But then the big orders simply never come in. It's always tomorrow or tomorrow, until all the tomorrows run out and Aubrey C. Briggs's Air Knife is no more. The ride is over.

I feel like my dad and I had many discussions around this topic; that I questioned him about why a utility company in the USA that could hire people for next to nothing to dig up roads with shovels would shell out $30,000 for a piece of equipment to do the same job. Or why they'd spend that much on a machine that could only cut through porous earth, not concrete or tarmac. I *feel* like he had an answer for everything. 'No, no, Nadhim; you don't understand. They're going to place an order for 10,000 the moment the pilot's over. It's gonna be bigger than PepsiCo.' On reflection, I honestly don't know how many of those questions I actually verbalised and how many I just ran over in my head in bed at night. The thing is, despite the fact this project failed, my dad was right: at some stage it probably *would* happen but Briggs was never going to be the man to do it. He could sell it, sure; but he just didn't have the credentials to make it work.

I suppose I must have been about seventeen when the house of cards started to wobble. I had no idea how much my dad had invested nor how much of that he'd borrowed. In the early days, I don't think Mum had a handle on it either. Perhaps she did but didn't want to face it. Who knows what really goes on behind closed doors in a marriage? At seventeen I certainly didn't, but it wouldn't be long before I had a clearer idea. The house was in both my parents' names, so I have to presume she knew he'd re-mortgaged, but knowing is quite different to questioning, which I very much doubt she did. I know she trusted him but think that trust was mixed with a tolerance too. It was very hard to say no to my dad. My mum was a well-educated, bright woman in her own right but my dad was – and is – persuasive. And he sells the dream beautifully. And because he'd got it right many times in the past, it was difficult not to back him now. He's not a guy with a track record of failure. He'd demonstrated he could succeed and his passion was hard to resist.

All in all, my dad must have invested a few million in the business as well as a few hundred thousand borrowed from good friends; so, when the mothership went down, we went down with it – and so did our family's reputation.

Oddly, there's never a big bang with this sort of situation. It didn't happen overnight. These things are like a slow train crash because human beings try, right? They start moving cash around, start borrowing from Peter to try and pay Paul. When the post was opened at the breakfast table every morning and the red bills were coming in thick and fast, part of me just ignored it. Someone's going to fix it, right? My sister took a different view of things. 'Stop living in cloud cuckoo land, Nadhim,' she'd say. 'We've got a huge problem.' In my defence, she was three years older than me. I knew things weren't right, but I was busy with A-levels. Going out with friends and dating. My mum still did my washing and cooked my dinners. I didn't know anything about running a house or paying a mortgage, so time moved on and I stuck my head in the sand.

When I'd turned seventeen I'd got my driving licence, and when I turned eighteen Dad bought me a brand new red Ford Escort, complete with boy-racer spoiler. I never bothered to ask how he paid for it. I wanted the car. Now I had a steady girl-friend too and was out every weekend, my head well and truly buried in the ground. And then it came. Finally, something from Mum that resonated with me. 'Nadhim, we have to get rid of your car.' Dad hadn't bought it after all. It was on HP and now we couldn't pay the instalments. Now I was worried too. That admission from my mum seemed to open the floodgates. Everything she'd been bottling up came pouring out. The next day when I came home from school, there was a man in the kitchen with a clipboard. Cheap grey suit, black brogues. He seemed very confident, opening cupboards, making notes. Later that night Mum finally broke down in tears. 'I don't know how big of a problem it is, but your dad's not sending us any money and I don't know what's going to happen. We might need to sell the house.' It was like an avalanche had hit me in the back and knocked me flying. The house of cards was well and truly down.

I can't say it came as a surprise, but I think we were all living in denial. As a teenager my world revolved round what I was going to wear to go out and how I was going to get there. I never thought things were serious enough that we might lose our home.

Mum said she might be able to sell the house, pay off the mortgage and have something left at the end, but it was clearly far, far too late for that. We were beyond controlling our own destiny, and the bank took the house together with anything else that could be considered an asset. The crash had been slow, but when we finally made impact, there was nothing to cushion the blow. Everything was ripped away. Not just physically but psychologically too. The house we lived in, the life we lived; they were built on a lie. On a bet. My dad had gambled everything and our lives were the collateral. If events around the bankruptcy were a montage in a movie, you'd see the glitzy furniture from Harrods being taken away, the keys being handed over for the cars in the drive and the bank putting up the 'For Sale by Auction' sign in front of the house. Me, Mum and Jihan would form the closing sequence as we packed our remaining cardboard boxes into the one thing we managed to salvage from the wreckage because it was in Mum's name: the metallic-brown Vauxhall Senator. Our life was gone in a second.

It took Dad about two weeks to come out of the bedroom. He'd done his best to keep all the balls in the air for as long as he could, but in the end there were just too many. He couldn't make it stand up and when he was finally forced to give in, he just collapsed.

If you were to ask me now how I feel about what he'd done, I still find it nearly impossible to answer. I can't bring myself to say I'm angry with him out loud, but I know that I am. I'm angry that he didn't involve Mum in decisions that affected us and that he didn't fill her in on the gravity of the situation until it was too late. That it wasn't until he crashed that he came to her for help. I'm angry that he behaved like a single man making choices in isolation and that, if he had his time over, he'd probably do it all again. The bottom line was, my dad was a risk-taker and a gambler – and that's where I become conflicted. As a grown man, I admire him enormously for his business acumen, drive and ambition. His ability to envisage success where most people see obstacles is incredible. He's a forward thinker and a true entrepreneur. There are many people in life prepared to follow but very few prepared to lead; to make a decision and take responsibility for its possible failure. It takes a dreamer to think on that scale and my dad is one such man. In this instance he failed, but he put himself out there for something he believed would work. Now, you might say he was an idiot for investing in a company that was clearly not going to change the world, but I don't believe he was a bad person for trying. Business is a long game and, looking at his career as a whole, you'd have to say he came out on top. Aubrey C. Briggs was just one of the experiences along the way.

Fear of failure undoubtedly had something to do with why he kept the full situation from Mum. It's not a subject many people want to discuss. I do know he couldn't live with himself until he'd paid back what he'd borrowed and that the weight of it dragged him to the very bottom. He was also very aware of Mum's part in holding things together and that ultimately, it was she who encouraged him to go back out there and try again. But all that's the man in me talking. The kid? I guess he was more ambivalent about what happened. There's a difference between what a child wants in a father and what an adult looks for in another adult, and the Aubrey C. Briggs debacle was a very good example of this dichotomy.

Dad always rose again like a phoenix from the ashes, and I learned you have to be a bold character and a big dreamer to do that. But with all this came an element of chaos, and he relied on the fact there'd be someone to tidy up the mess in the wake of the storm. Dad might have been the first person I knew like that, but he certainly wouldn't be the last.

I never really rowed with Mum during this time, but we had our moments. Anyone who knows me would tell you my affection for her borders on idolisation, but that doesn't mean I didn't have my issues with how she'd dealt with the problem. I never meant to be nasty, but I'm sure some of what I said must have been hurtful. Why didn't she question Dad? Why didn't she pull him up when he made a mistake? The answer was for the same reasons as me: Dad was such a big, overpowering figure, it was hard to say anything.

Although there was never a question mark over their marriage, Mum lived like a single parent for much of our childhood in England. She, Jihan and I were a little team. Dad went round the world like an adventurer or an old-fashioned sailor, sent money, checked in and took us to dinner when he was back in town, but it was Mum who ran the show. She wasn't as loud as he was but she was strong in her own quiet way. When things went horribly wrong, as they had now, she was the one that pawned the jewellery or sold the furniture to make sure we kept going. If I was happy, it was because she made everything okay. I imagine a lot of women would have walked away, but she stuck it out. I know this was because she adored my dad, but it was mainly for us. That children take priority over everything is something I learned from her.

When faced with the crash I felt completely impotent. Dad's response was, covers over the head, door closed, down and out; so when it came to putting food on the table, I convinced myself it fell to me. The one thing we still owned was the car, and the only way I could think to make something like a proper living was to drive it as a cab. The fly in the ointment was university. After all the years of trouble around school, I was finally on track and due to take up a place at UCL that autumn. I honestly didn't care about going but my mum did. She'd always been the one to push me academically and wasn't about to let all that trickle through my fingers now. She point-blank refused my offer to work, and that was that. I knew I'd never persuade her. She's a pretty formidable woman. By this time my sister and I were old enough to leave home but it never crossed our minds that we would. It was instinctive that we deal with the crisis together and this, I think, was down to Mum. She was the reason we didn't fragment or splinter apart. As terrible a time as it was, in many ways it was really wonderful. You can get through more than you might think you're capable of as long as there's a bond of love.

When you have a financial crisis like the one we had, you find out pretty quickly who your friends are. In an effort to keep the dream afloat, Dad had borrowed cash from friends, which he couldn't pay back. When news like that spreads, pretty soon you start getting a reputation for being someone who's not good for a loan. Our integrity was called into question and that, more than anything, was what bothered me. I knew we were decent people. I knew my dad hadn't meant to hurt anyone. He wasn't a bad person. During my time in government I've met many constituents under huge financial stress. When you're under that kind of pressure, it affects not just the practicalities of life but your emotional and mental wellbeing too, and it can be a hugely destructive force on a family. So when I reflect on what happened, the thing I feel most grateful for is that it did the opposite to us. In fact, if anything it brought us much closer together – literally and figuratively.

When the bank took the house, the most pressing issue was where were we going to live. While most of the friends who'd happily spent their time in our nice big home with the swimming pool disappeared overnight, the silver lining was that we gained others, and one family in particular did more than just support us; they changed the course of our lives. I didn't know it at the time, but I was at another fork in the road.

CHAPTER 9

MEET THE SAIBS

STARTING OVER

Like us, the Saibs were Kurds who'd come to the UK from Iraq. Fawzi was much older than his wife Buthaina and had done well for himself financially. Together with their family home, they owned a small flat in Putney that they rented out. I wouldn't have described them as anything like close friends at the time, but when the bank took our house they offered us a lifeline. 'Take the flat,' they said. 'Pay whenever you can. And if you can't pay, that's okay too.' It was unbelievably generous and there was no reason for them to have done it other than kindness. And so it was, in January 1986, Mum, Dad, Jihan and I moved into Ross Court with the remnants of our lives in a handful of cardboard boxes. Once again, it was time to start over.

The Saibs had left Baghdad not long after we did and for the same reasons: the political climate had become untenable for most liberal Iraqis. Though long retired by this time, as a senior figure in the civil service Fawzi had seen more than enough of it all. Before the Ba'athists he was a major in the army under the monarchy but, by the time I knew him, he'd been retired for nearly twenty years. Now he was quite rich but his money came from business. He was a well-respected, well-connected man.

After the 1968 revolution, when the Ba'athists seized power and the government were looking for Kurdish candidates to become ministers, Fawzi's name was put on the list. He was an obvious choice given his experience. But when the new president, al-Bakr, saw the names, he said, 'No, I don't want Fawzi,' and that was that. Fawzi never knew why he'd been rejected, but right up until the day he died he always said al-Bakr had saved his life. After Saddam had been put in charge of Iraq's security services, a lot of those men on that list ended up in prison or dispensed with in some other insidious way. Fawzi meanwhile, was left to enjoy his retirement. It was like he'd been pardoned. He never knew if al-Bakr had genuinely *not* wanted him or was just trying to protect him. The two men had a history. When al-Bakr entered the Military Academy in Iraq as a commissioned officer, he and Fawzi were roommates. No one could have predicted he'd go on to become the military dictator of Iraq. Every time Fawzi went back home to Kurdistan, al-Bakr would say, 'Bring me back a bag of tobacco, Fawzi,' and Fawzi would. Perhaps it was this little kindness that saved his life. Even so, Fawzi took the rejection as a slight and the two men never spoke after that. Al-Bakr would often walk past their house, his bodyguard trailing behind at a snail's pace in his car. Fawzi couldn't possibly have missed the man but he refused to invite him in. He was a very stubborn guy.

After retiring from the military in the late 1950s, he moved on to the civil service. In the early 60s, he was made deputy governor of Baghdad and then governor of Nasiriyah. Nasiriyah was about three hours south of Baghdad and a hugely important province. It formed a sort of outpost of the main government. Communication nationally was very limited, and the governor and president would probably speak once a month. The rest of that time he was left to his own devices, so in those days the governor was king and Fawzi had a great deal of power. If you look at photos of their house, you'd think it belonged to the Shah of Iran: huge landscaped gardens and servants on hand for their every whim. But it was all owned by the government. Despite his position, he didn't own his own home. Eventually, he took a job representing Saab's heavy equipment arm in Iraq. It wasn't as glamorous as being governor but it was definitely more lucrative. He was getting on quite well. Too well, in fact. Just as my father had found, the downside of being a success in business in Iraq at that time was that you attracted the attention of the government. And no liberal wanted that.

In 1976, things came to a head for the Saibs. Saddam was beginning to elbow al-Bakr out, and al-Bakr was too old and weak to resist. Both men were dictators but al-Bakr was preferable to Saddam. Fawzi was Kurdish and influential among the senior Kurds in the government. One of his brothers had joined the Kurdish revolution, which put a target on Fawzi's back too. As Saddam grew in power, so too did the number of visits Fawzi received from the domestic secret police – al Amn – to question him about his loyalties. For a time, he managed to convince the police he and his brother were not in touch; that he was just a businessman who disagreed with his brother's anti Ba'athist feelings. But there were those in power who considered Fawzi a threat anyway and decided to do something about it.

It was Fawzi's son, Broosk, who eventually sounded the alarm, but not everyone believed a child of twelve. In those days, there were no seatbelts and Broosk had a habit of kneeling backwards in his seat so he could look out the rear window while they were driving. This is how he saw the white Beetle. It followed their car for a few streets. Where they turned, it turned. When they stopped, it stopped. When Fawzi came to a halt at the lights near the Ministry of Defence, the white car pulled over and a blue

Beetle took its place. 'Baba,' said Broosk, 'there's someone following us.' His father was not amused. 'You've been watching too much *Kojak*,' he told him; but Broosk was undeterred. Every afternoon he took to sitting in the olive tree in the front garden and spying on passers-by, on the lookout for anything suspicious. It wasn't long before he found it. Two men began meeting regularly on the pavement outside, watching the house as they gossiped and puffed on their cigarettes. With their huge, brush-like moustaches and safari shirts, there was no mistaking al Amn. An hour later, they'd leave, driving the butts into the dirt track with their shiny shoes. On his Kodak Instamatic, Broosk took to photographing the men each time they appeared. After two months, he took the pictures and cigarette butts to Fawzi as evidence. Broosk's 'story' was becoming harder to ignore and Fawzi called on a well-connected friend with one simple question: 'Am I being followed?' The answer was a resounding yes. Apparently, Fawzi talked too much and needed 'to go on a little holiday'. Essentially, if he didn't shut up, they'd kill him.

Someone once described the Iraq of my youth as 'one million Iraqis watching the other two' and it was absolutely true: you kept your friends close and your enemies closer. Fawzi was no fool and had always maintained a 'friendship' with Saddam's brother, Barzan – the head of the Mukhabarat. They gossiped and broke bread together over Friday lunches because Fawzi knew that was the best way to keep his family safe. When Barzan heard a twelve-year-old boy had rumbled his intelligence officers, he wanted to meet him. That Friday, Fawzi called Broosk into the dining room. 'So you're the kid who's outwitted my best men?' said Barzan. Best men was a bit of a stretch: Mukhabarat employed the lowest of the low. As long as you were prepared to intimidate or beat a person to death, that was the entrance criteria. 'You'll make a great detective,' Barzan continued, 'show me your spy equipment.' Broosk duly produced the plastic walkie-talkies Fawzi had bought him for his birthday and his Kodak camera. Barzan admired the equipment before sending Broosk off with an avuncular pat on the back and a ruffle of the hair. Everyone in the room laughed at the boy's chutzpah. That afternoon the Mukhabarat sent a driver to confiscate Broosk's walkie-talkies. Anyone with a transistor of any kind was a potential threat to the government, even a little boy. After this it was clear Baghdad was no longer a safe place for Fawzi or his son, and, just like us, he and his family set sail for England's green and pleasant land. The Saibs were our kind of Iraqis. The ones who were wary of the place from which they'd come.

SORRY AMU!

The first time I met them properly was the day they came over for lunch and a swim in the infamous 'Center Parcs' swimming pool for my eighteenth birthday. Technically we already knew them from Baghdad, where Broosk and his sister Lana had gone to the same primary school as me, but there was never more than a passing recognition between the two families. Everyone knew my dad as the son of Nadhim Zahawi and Fawzi as the ex-governor of Nasiriyah, but the acquaintance never amounted to a friendship while we lived in Iraq and I have no memory of their children from school. Even so, the Zahawis and the Saibs were distantly related by marriage and had cousins in common. The roots of most families went back a long way, so this wasn't uncommon in the Kurdish community. I don't know whether it was this or the fact they seemed quite anglicised, but I felt immediately at ease around them all.

By now Broosk was twenty-three and the kind of person you'd describe as an old soul. He never drank or did drugs and, even as

a very young man, his shelves were filled with books on callig-
raphy, art, history and human rights. I was only five years younger
but we couldn't have been more different and you'd have thought
the age gap was far greater. He was probably too sensible and I
was probably too badly behaved, but we were a fit. We liked in
the other what we lacked in ourselves. I don't think Broosk
would ever have got into the trouble I did, but he enjoyed being
part of it from the sidelines, which is probably why he loves my
daughter so much now. Her naughtiness is really quite innocent but if Broosk were to say to her, 'Let's pour a glass of
water over daddy's head' she'd be up for it like a shot. I was
exactly the same. I did it to attract attention, and the day I met
Broosk was about the best example of this he could possibly
hope to get.

The crowd of expats my parents mixed with included many
members from the early days of the Ba'ath Party, before it became
what it did under Saddam. Despite the fact we'd all now left Iraq,
there was still quite a bit of bickering about the past that went on
semi-politely – either face to face or behind someone's back. We
had a common enemy in Saddam, but there was still an element
of friction: 'That bloody Ba'athist. It's his fault; it's his government that's ruined Iraq!' On the day of my birthday, there was
quite a bit of this going on because Dad had invited several senior
figures to celebrate with us. Tahsin Mualla was a Ba'athist who'd
been a prominent doctor with a significant history. In 1959, the
Ba'ath Party were still a minority opposition and tried, unsuc-
cessfully, to assassinate the then prime minister, Qasim. Several
gunmen were sent to do the job and the morning after the coup,
a fellow Ba'athist approached Mualla on his way to work, asking
him to help treat some of the casualties held in a safehouse. One
of those injured was a junior member of the party who'd been
shot in the leg. When Mualla asked where the bullet was, the

gunman said he'd dug it out the night before with a razor blade so it wouldn't fester. Mualla cleaned the wound and gave the man a tetanus shot. The gunman never forgot the kindness shown by Mualla and, later in life, when he'd risen through the ranks of the party, offered him a position as governor of Basra. Mualla, who was then working as a professor at the university, thanked the man but said a polite no thank you; he was happy where he was. It took quite some balls to turn the man down because he was, by now, a very powerful politician. In time, Mualla went on to thwart the man's wishes twice more, refusing to bend to his will when he knew it wasn't morally right, but the young gunman was now very powerful and did not like being disobeyed. Mualla had exhausted the man's patience and knew it was time to leave Iraq. On paper he retired but he always believed – rightly – that his card was marked. In later years, he survived a car bomb in Kuwait and evaded Iraqi agents in Surrey when he'd emigrated to the UK. The young gunman, meanwhile, was by now leading Iraq into the history books – and not in a good way. It was none other than Saddam Hussein. So it's fair to say Tahsin Mualla was used to other people taking him pretty seriously.

At eighteen, I understood all this but at the same time Mualla was just another 'uncle' – or 'amu', as we called all our elders; another expat who liked to eat and drink and gossip about other Iraqis before falling asleep on the sofa. London brought all sorts of dissidents together, but as a child I was always wary of 'Amu Tahsin'. He had a horrible habit of slapping you on the back of your bare neck by way of a greeting or squeezing your hand when he shook it to see how much pain you could bear – a quirk of some Iraqis to try and toughen up young men. A lot of the kids were frightened of Mualla, but I'd perversely let him carry on. I wasn't about to be cowed by this psychopath. So when my dad's friend Nihad told me to 'push Tahsin Mualla into the pool', it was exactly the nod I'd been waiting for. Mualla was by now standing right at the edge of the water in his three-piece cream linen suit, as if poised for the denouement of a sitcom. All I had to do was barge him lightly and that would be that.

For a brief moment after he'd gone under the water fully clothed I thought he might drown, but he finally hoisted himself up on his elbows and hauled himself out with maximum theatrics. I rushed to his side with everyone else. 'I'm so sorry, Amu,' I said, 'I was just walking past. You must have stumbled.' Mrs Mualla was having none of it. She knew very well how mischievous I was and left in a giant huff, taking her dripping-wet husband with her. Even though Dad made me go and apologise to the Muallas later that evening, until the day he died, Tahsin never knew who it was that told me to do it. I might have been naughty, but I was no snitch. The incident of Saddam Hussein's doctor and the East Sheen swimming pool was as good an introduction to me as Broosk was going to get, and it kicked our friendship off with a bang.

BROOSK

By the time we met, Broosk was already totally anglicised and on the lookout for kindred spirits. When he saw this kid who spoke English like a Londoner, it was a breath of fresh air. The Ba'athist in the swimming pool was an added bonus.

Broosk looked like he belonged to a previous generation. Dark, wavy, slicked-back hair, blazer and jeans, expensive white shirt: he was like a cross between Peter Sellers and Ralph Lauren. He was the sort of guy you'd expect to find at Johnny Gold's table at Tramp or eating shrimp cocktail at The Elephant on the River. At twenty-five he was already married and divorced, loved opera and drove a metallic-turquoise Rolls-Royce. Christ knows where he got it. It looked like the sort of thing that belonged to Keith Richards.

Broosk was a gentle, generous and urbane character and, I thought, probably the best-dressed man in England. He was resolutely his own man stylistically and knew exactly what he liked and where to get it. One Thursday morning he called me at six to say he wanted to take me shopping. Fortunately, I'd not yet gone to bed so we began the day with a fry-up at a greasy spoon. We pulled up on a little bridge in the shadow of the Trellick Tower in North West London and strolled down what looked to me like a dive of a street. The Brutalist tower block loomed large over us as we walked down the Golborne Road and headed towards Portobello Market. Even at this ungodly hour there were people here, crowded in little clusters, jostling for position around the traders. These guys were here for the best stuff. Shop owners scratching around for the gold in the dirt to take back to their shops to mark up and sell on. The stalls were very hit and miss. On some you might be lucky and find a hand-cut crystal decanter or an early pressing of the 'White Album' in mint condition, at another it was just discarded Tupperware and souvenir milk jugs from the coastal towns of Great Britain. Broosk knew exactly what he was looking for. He was still living at home then, but when he got his own place a few years later you saw the fruits of his labour unfurl and the pieces he'd accumulated found homes on shelves and in cabinets. Broosk had the kind of style you couldn't replicate overnight and was invested in the art from a young age. It was no surprise to me that he went on to become an interior designer.

I was still doing my A-levels but, even after I went to university, there was no one else like him. Most of the kids I met were eating baked beans out of a can and chipping in for petrol if they were lucky enough to know anyone with a car. Broosk was like someone who'd walked off a film with Lauren Bacall. There was just no competing with him.

Over the next year or so we grew to be friends, but it was when my father lost his money that I found out just how good a friend he really was. As Broosk was always saying, Iraqis are very fickle. And they gossip. When Aubrey C. Briggs and his Air Knife went to the wall, the Saibs were one of the few families from home to stand up for us. It wasn't just that they gave us their flat to live in; they defended our reputation in our community which, I suspect, would prove far more costly. Fawzi was still a very influential man and purposely saw my dad on a daily basis, taking him out and about so their being seen together would act as a seal of approval for my dad. I know Broosk fell out with friends over us and I wouldn't be surprised if his parents did too. Iraqis have a long history of having to switch sides at a moment's notice, and perhaps this was why some were so ready to write us off. But not the Saibs. When things came crashing down, the first thing I did was ring Broosk to ask him to come and pick me up. 'Where's your car?' he asked. I told him the news and half an hour later he pulled up outside to collect me. Until I got myself on my feet financially, Broosk's car became my car. Everything he had, I had, and he never, ever made me feel uncomfortable about it.

Like Max before him, Broosk had a kind of star quality. I've always been attracted to people who surprise me – make me think I need to find out a little bit more – and the really great friends I've had over the course of my life have all had this in common. In the case of Broosk, it was about talent and his innate eye for things. It was something I'd never really seen before. His dressing room was like something from a movie; everything was so covetable and beautiful. I'd been pretty parochial up until then. My whole life revolved around Max and the pub and suddenly, with Broosk, I was seeing the world. Even going to a restaurant rather than hanging out with a bunch of reprobates at the local pub was a culture shock.

When we first met I already had a girlfriend, but it quickly became clear I was going to fall in love with his sister, Lana. It was only a matter of time. Lana had honey blonde hair, big dark brown eyes and a smile that looked like laughter. Theirs was a very tight-knit family and she and Broosk were both still living at home, so my plan to win her over was to try and spend as much time at their house as humanly possible. Any excuse would do. My crush on her no doubt added to my friendship with Broosk because, as much as I liked him, I was round their house at least ten times as much as I would have been had it not been for her. Quite early on I made it clear that I was in love with her, and she made it equally clear she had absolutely no interest in me and in no way took me seriously as a suitor, which I decided to ignore. I knew I could go the distance. She had an air to her that was magnetic and exuded something difficult to put your finger on: a magical combination of innocence, beauty, glamour and a tinge of arrogance that made her untouchable. She became the star at the centre of my universe and I orbited round her, happily waiting for the times she'd shine her light on me.

Occasionally, she'd flirt a tiny bit, which would sustain me for another year or so, and that was pretty much how I operated until we finally got married eighteen years later in 2004. She was just the kind of girl you waited for. I was in love with her then and I'm in love with her now. The fact that she and her family stood by our side when we needed it most was no small part of that equation. When she eventually agreed to be my wife, she brought with her one of the greatest gifts I could have asked for: two wonderful boys – Ahmad and Jaafar – from her previous marriage. In 2012, our daughter Mia became the fifth member of our little team. Over time Lana would become the person to take care of our family and our lives and put herself aside for my career, and the only way I can think to show my true appreciation now is to honour her wish of privacy by not writing more about our home life in this book.

One of the biggest draws for me with Broosk was that he was the only young person I knew who had a job. Everyone else was studying or still at home. I was out raving every chance I got and had no real idea where I was going in life. Broosk had trained as an interior designer at the American College in London and, on graduating, had persuaded Fawzi to invest some cash in a two-bed flat on Princes' Court round the back of Harrods. It was expensive but not quite as absurd as that sounds now. Broosk got in straightaway with the marble bathrooms and polished wood and began the renovation. In short, he was a grown-up and I liked being around that. I took to turning up at the flat after lectures to revise and Broosk pretended to listen as he worked on the renovation. There was no furniture, so I'd sit on the floor and read out loud from my textbooks: 'An increase in the speed of a fluid occurs ...'. Any chemical engineer will tell you that until you get your head around Bernoulli's four-page equation on fluid flow through pipes, you've got no hope of ever building an efficient factory, and that bloody equation haunts me to this day. I imagine Broosk feels the same. Whenever he objected to my revising in this way, I'd remind him it was me that needed to memorise this stuff not him, but doing it like this helped me absorb more. Left to my own devices I just couldn't get my head down. Broosk had taken the place of Auntie Farida, and that was the way I got through my first-year exams. We were a team.

By the time I was in my third year Broosk had started designing for other people and had opened a small office in Knightsbridge in a serviced block in Collier House. It was a tiny room with no window where you paid for everything from secretarial services to photocopying. Filter coffee was still a relatively new thing and we drank it all day long from the communal percolator, which for some reason always smelt slightly revolting. Seeing Broosk expand the business was exciting and I wanted to be a part of things. Eventually, I came up with the bright idea of my running an estate agent in conjunction with his design service, and Broosk Estates was born. I had no training or experience, so it won't surprise you to hear that the partnership was not a success. Suffice it to say there were more experienced agents in Knightsbridge with better connections who weren't also studying for their exams in the back room. Arguably you learn more from failure than success, so it was a good introduction to working life, nonetheless. After that our careers would diverge, but Broosk stayed in the same lane. As time went on, there'd always be a flash of something Great and British in his work: a flag or a nod somewhere to the monarch. Despite the fact he'd left Baghdad when he was thirteen, Broosk, like me, always considered himself to be British. It just took a swimming pool in the back garden of a suburban south London home and an elderly Ba'athist to bring us together.

CHAPTER 10

DISORDERLY CONDUCT

BRASS IN POCKET

In my late teens I learned a valuable lesson: it's not until you've done a job you absolutely loathe that you get a sense of what you'd rather not do for the rest of your life. For me, that job was my first. What I hated was less about the work and more to do with my boss, but more than anything it was an exercise in how to deal with a manager who despised me with the heat of a thousand suns.

After the averted catastrophe that was my O-levels, I managed to secure a place to sit my A-levels at King's College, Wimbledon. I was doing well enough in class for Mum to okay my getting a holiday job at the end of the first year. She came from a family of doctors, dentists and biochemists and was desperate for me to follow the same path. She dreamt of being able to utter the words 'My son, the doctor' but for now was happy to settle for one who worked as an orderly at Kingston Hospital. It was a small step nearer her goal. While I liked the idea of having my own money, the realities of earning it were a total shock to the system. No teenager wants to get up at 4 a.m., least of all to manhandle an industrial floor polisher with a hangover, but that was what I'd now be doing for the next eight weeks.

DISORDERLY CONDUCT

The orderlies at Kingston fell into two groups: the part-timers and interns who were passing through on their way to 'better' things, and the people who took it seriously and committed themselves to doing it properly. I was in the first group and my boss hated me for it. For the sake of discretion I'll call her Sue, but I'll also tell you she was a dreadful harridan. At least I thought so at the time. The other orderlies were largely hard-working women in their forties and fifties, with a handful of guys thrown in. They were the silent motor of the hospital. They made sure the machine purred smoothly in the hours of darkness and slipped away unnoticed before the doctors swept through on their daily rounds.

Let me be the first to say I wasn't going to win any awards for effort at Kingston, but there was something else Sue didn't like about me. Sue considered all interns lower-class citizens and took great pleasure in kicking them into shape. In short she was a bully, and the lesson Dad taught me on holiday five years earlier rang in my ears the minute I met her. 'Don't let yourself be bullied, Nadhim.' I couldn't tackle Sue to the ground, obviously, so I did the next best thing: I smiled and ignored her and refused to rise to her bait. It was a battle of wills and one in which I had the upper hand. Unlike most of her other staff, I was a teenager; my family weren't relying on my income to survive. I didn't *have* to stay at Kingston and Sue knew it, and *this* was what she didn't like about me. What I didn't like about her was the way she treated the people who couldn't afford to walk out. I'm guessing she enjoyed the feeling of power it gave her, which was very sad. She'd have gained much greater satisfaction from sharing her experience with others on the way up. Instead, she chose to intimidate and humiliate people who had no choice but to stay and take it.

The funny thing was, whenever I was with the patients I had a great time. My favourite wards were maternity and gynaecology because they were full of women who all wanted to chat. It was like being at home with my grandmas. The male wards were more monosyllabic, but all you had to say to the ladies was 'I'm going to be a doctor' and it triggered a full-length episode of *This Is Your Life*. I loved it, but it was just one more thing for Sue to dislike about me. There was a clear hierarchy in the hospital and the person at the top of each stratum was the one most likely to defend their territory most fiercely. For Sue, this meant making sure no one was seen slacking or chatting, which amounted to the same thing in her eyes. In fact, there was a lot to be said for providing inpatients with a bit of company, but that was another conversation for another time. At Kingston the chain of command started with the nurses, followed by the senior nurses, then junior doctors – whom the nurses all fancied – and then the consultant, who was king. If they came through the ward with their vast entourage, you hid in a cupboard. You were not to be seen in your grey overalls or, God forbid, with your mop and bucket. To be honest, even if you couldn't see me, you'd have been able to smell me; I was followed by a cloud of Dettol everywhere I went. Like Victorian maids in a stately home, we were expected to behave as if we didn't exist. I actually thought this was a mistake, given that we had our ears to the ground in a way that many higher up did not.

When my dad first started work, he trained at a massive crane construction company. At the time my grandfather, Nadhim, was the governor of the central bank and had gone to visit the company's production line. As he toured the facilities with the director he spotted my father sweeping the floor outside in the apprentice yard with his broom and his overalls. My grandfather excused himself for a moment and went to speak to my dad. 'When you become a manager,' he said, 'now you'll know where people hide the dust and the dirt.' He was absolutely right. Often the best bosses are the ones who've done every job on their way up. They know exactly where the dust has been swept.

Being on the wards taught me it wasn't the work I didn't like; it was that I didn't want to work for someone like Sue or in an environment like the one she'd created. I wanted to matter in the scheme of things. I wanted what I did to make a difference, even if it was a little one. When the time came, I decided I didn't want to be a boss like Sue either.

More than fifteen years later when my friend Stephan and I started YouGov, we put our offices in the middle of the building, made them out of glass and facilitated an open-door policy for one and all. If Sue had taught me anything it was that the person with the most power was not always the one with the best ideas. Moreover, if you had any sense as a boss yourself, you'd harness the capabilities of your whole workforce, not just the people at the top, especially if you wanted them to take pride in their work.

Fundamentally, I don't believe anyone goes to work in the morning wanting to do a crap job, but learning how to get the best out of your team is a skill that comes with time. Abuse of power, on the other hand, is one of the easiest holes to fall down, but it is not the most rewarding or productive way to run a business. If you pick the right people, you should likewise be prepared to listen to their ideas, otherwise why pick them in the first place? In fact I'd go so far as to say, surround yourself with people even more talented than you are if you get the chance. The ability to deputise and empower those around you is one of the most commonly overlooked skills – particularly in a growing business. If you don't get a handle on it, the likely outcomes are failure or killing yourself trying to succeed. Micromanagement is the downfall of many large institutions, and government is no exception.

I imagine most people would assume the minister of any given department has oversight across every single decision made within it. If I tell you that each one is bigger than most FTSE 100 companies, you might change your mind. The Department for Education alone, for example, employs roughly 9,000 people internally as well as nearly half a million teachers. In the coming year, it will spend £86 billion on wages and resources. The idea that the education secretary could successfully run that 'business' without effective deputisation is absurd and, in my mind, only a fool would try. Some politicians are well known for their micromanaging, but for me the key is to have a transparent strategy in place at the top that the whole team works to deliver. Provided you've picked your team based on talent, you should be able to empower them to make decisions safe in the knowledge they have a clear understanding of their destination. This only works, of course, when the message from the top *is* clear. If it becomes hazy, it's easy to run into problems. For me, these principles should apply right the way down to the interns. They're as valuable in their own role as you are in yours, if for no other reason than they'll see things you don't. While it may no longer be your job to get into the corners with your broom, it is still theirs, and a good boss will always want to hear what they've found there. I'm not sure Sue would have agreed.

Juggling my professional and private lives, and making sure one didn't seep messily into the other, was something I never mastered during my time at Kingston. It was no surprise to Sue that if a person came to work direct from an all-night rave, the quality of their work would suffer, and my tendency to do this was one of her few legitimate grievances. My colleague George, on the other hand, had a finely tuned work/life balance. At forty-five, he'd been at Kingston most of his adult life. Lithe and wiry from years of manual labour, he unironically sported an auburn mullet with receding hairline and managed to pull it off. On duty he was the model employee but at home he'd perfected the art of doing nothing. I found this out the morning he invited me back to his flat at the end of our shift. It was clear on entry that this was the home of a man who had neither girlfriend nor spare set of bedding and who only ate food that came from the petrol station. He had the pallor of someone who rarely went outdoors in daylight and would have been perfectly cast to play Riff Raff had the hospital suddenly put on a production of *The Rocky Horror Picture Show*. Despite our nearly thirty-year age gap, George and I bonded immediately over our mutual dislike of Sue. From 4 until 10 a.m. every day he kept his head down at hospital and then, from 10.30 a.m. until the *Six O'Clock News*, he passed the time flipping channels and toking on a large African bong on his sofa at home. He'd pause for snacks and the necessary evacuations, but other than that his day consisted of what's known in the trade as vegging out.

By the summer of 1983 there were four TV stations. Given the paucity of programming, watching television all day was quite a feat of endurance, but George was equal to the task. A typical schedule might mean an episode of *Rainbow* or *The Wombles*, racing of some sort, re-runs of *Heidi*, quite a bit of Ceefax and something with Brian Cant or Derek Griffiths. Expectations of what television brought to our lives pre-satellite were significantly lower than they are now, but the part TV played in shaping our collective consciousness was arguably bigger and more influential. It was also a huge part of my becoming fluent in English after I arrived in London. As well as Dear Deidre, I had *Minder*, *Grange Hill* and *Only Fools and Horses* to demonstrate colloquial diversity. These shows were more helpful than any teacher or textbook because they helped me not just learn the language but how I should speak it if I wanted to fit in. It was George, however, who turned me on to *Countdown*.

ANYONE FOR TENNIS?

By the time I got to King's College my friendship group had shifted. Max and I were still close but I'd met new kids who diluted the increasingly toxic bubble I'd swum in at the local pub. I was still going out almost as much, but I'd finally recognised the need to get my head down at school and was in much more control of my life. Mum, too, had a bit more trust in me because I'd come through the bad patch on my own and she'd loosened up and relaxed the rules a little. The experiences with Max and my near-miss at O-levels had shaken me enough to make me realise that if I wanted a decent standard of living, I'd need to start making plans for it now. I was beginning to think about what I was going to do with the rest of my life.

At eighteen, the biggest drain on my finances was having a girlfriend. Tess was much better looking than I was, but part of my appeal for her was a two-year age gap and my red Ford Escort. I was punching above my weight and the ability to take her into the West End on a Saturday night was my unspoken contribution to the deal.

I was never really a one-night-stand type. I was both too lazy and too romantic. I liked to find a person and stick with them, and Tess and I clocked up two years together. Although it was looks that hooked me, it was personality that kept me there. Tess was a wonderful girl. Kind, funny, smart and beautiful, she came with the added bonus of her mum, who was also pretty awesome. As the single parent of two girls, her mum can't have found life that easy raising her kids alone, but she had a fantastic sense of humour and was relentlessly upbeat. She also had a boyfriend, who unfortunately belonged to someone else. Consequently, he was an elusive character who appeared only erratically but always in a gold Rolls-Royce, a bit like Mr Big. Much to my surprise he did eventually come good and whisked her off to Monaco some years later, though no doubt leaving a trail of fury in his wake. I was quite pleased his attendance was restricted by his other responsibilities; I was much happier in a household of women. It felt like home.

Most kids of my age took their girlfriends to Pizza Hut on date night, but for me and Tess it was dinner on the King's Road in Chelsea, followed by Xenon or The Hippodrome in Leicester Square, where the dress code was 100 per cent *Miami Vice*. In my dark blue, double-breasted silk suit and open-necked shirt, I thought I looked exactly like Don Johnson but, for a variety of reasons, was much more likely to be mistaken for Lionel Ritchie. Our speciality was a choreographed dance routine to 'Trapped' by Colonel Abrams, which I could probably still roll out now in an emergency. Tess loved dancing and so did I. As teenagers, my sister and I would be on every dancefloor at every wedding or family party – like Ross and Monica Geller, but Muslim. From 1979 onwards, however, my party piece was to perform 'Rapper's Delight' to anyone who had six and a half minutes to listen. My blue silk suit came from Matches Fashion in Wimbledon, which was at least ten times as expensive as Burton or C&A where any normal person my age was shopping in the mid-80s. I'm not sure how or why I catapulted over the high street and went straight to boutique shopping, but, once again, I was reminded that with every action there is an equal and opposite reaction, and this applied a thousandfold to money. If you wanted to spend it, you needed to make it. Luckily, I'd met someone at King's College who was going to teach me how.

Darren Ahmet was the son of Big Jak Ahmet, nightclub impresario and owner of Omar Khayyam on Regent Street, the most famous Arab nightspot in London. Jak was a Turkish Cypriot who'd come to the UK with no money and worked his backside off in kitchens, washing dishes, before becoming a chef. From there he opened a kebab shop and then progressed onto his own restaurants and clubs. The 70s was the decade of the Oil Shock – a period in which the West faced substantial petroleum shortages and became increasingly dependent on foreign suppliers for its energy. While this was not great for the UK, it was brilliant for petroleum-rich countries in the Middle East who benefited from increased demand and concurrently higher prices. The Arabs were not only wealthy but they also loved to be entertained. Omar Khayyam catered for Saudi sheiks and princes who came to throw money at belly dancers and listen to their favourite singers shipped in from Cairo. Jak saw a gap in the market and plugged it. His son Darren had the same visionary nature. He took everything he'd learned from his dad and fused it with a new scene he saw unfolding.

The result was some of London's most infamous raves. In the late 80s, acid house and ecstasy sent huge ripples through society and ushered in a new era in London's nightlife. Darren partnered with club promoters Joel Coleman and Graham Ball who did Westworld, and farmed in DJs Danny Rampling, Paul 'Trouble' Anderson and the Boilerhouse Boys for these nights. All those guys were instrumental in setting up the pirate station KISS in the early days of rave, which fundamentally changed the face of dance music. Darren was right in the middle of it all and I hung on to his coat tails, just as I'd done with Max at the football. It was the same type of thrill; the kind of thing you couldn't tell your parents about. Darren and his team were public enemy No. 1; it was mischief in the extreme and I loved it.

Once again, though, I hovered on the nerdier side of the spectrum. I had a lifelong phobia of putting anything up my nose, which meant I was never going to get into cocaine. Ecstasy came in tablet form so didn't pose the same problem, but my love of chemistry told me synthetic drugs were a red flag. In my early days at university as a chemical engineer we conducted experiments every Thursday, and one of the first was to synthesise benzocaine. It immediately became clear that anyone wanting to increase their profit margin could cut their drug with virtually anything that came in the form of white powder. You'd have no idea whether this was self-raising flour or rat poison and, for that reason, I was out. For good. I stuck to my Marlboro reds and trusty Southern Comfort and lemonade, and to this day have never tried a Class A drug.

When the police raided Darren's parents' house on Kingston Hill the night he and his team turned the swimming pool and tennis courts into a Brazilian carnival, I was there. For Darren, getting shut down was kudos he couldn't buy as a promoter, so when the raid appeared as a double-page spread in my old favourite, the *Sun*, it was the perfect advert for his business.

By now I'd swapped my tracksuit for a Lacoste T-shirt and vintage 501s on account of Nick Kamen and his launderette. I loved people-watching at these parties, but the biggest source of intrigue for me was trying to work out where these guys were making their money. At Xenon there'd be hundreds of clubbers, but at a rave you were looking at thousands. I was fascinated where the money was in the scale-up. Outside of tickets and booze, it was obvious some of it came from merchandise – psychedelic T-shirts and glow sticks – and this seemed like an interesting avenue to explore.

Just like Max, Darren was hugely enigmatic and likewise didn't go on to further education. Unlike Max, Darren had a plan and a financially successful father to model. I'd seen first hand what my dad was capable of in business, but Darren was the first person my age I'd met with a true entrepreneurial streak. When I needed cash, I knew there was no one better than him to partner with. The summer we finished our A-levels was the summer we decided to monetise Wimbledon.

For two weeks each June, ticket holders for the tournament queued down Wimbledon Park Road for hours at a time, and Darren and I knew that anyone getting off at Southfields tube would have to pass by the house of our mate from the pub, Usman, who lived with his first-generation-immigrant Pakistani parents halfway down the road. One afternoon in the lead-up to Wimbledon, we approached him with an offer he should definitely have refused: £200 in return for the use of his front garden for the duration of the tournament. Usman was a very sweet guy but evidently an utter moron, given he neither negotiated nor turned us down. Ten days later, Darren and I arrived at 6 a.m. and proceeded to set up shop with two borrowed trestle tables and a couple of money belts. Half a million people attended Wimbledon every year and it was our intention to capitalise on this fact. Darren had all sorts of nefarious contacts from his rave operation, and that first morning two grubby, heavy-set types pulled up in a white Transit and unloaded 600 T-shirts from the back of the van. I'd come to learn that the T-shirt-printing industry that operates outside large gigs and events was run by a bunch of charlatans, which suited us perfectly. Official T-shirts inside the All England Club sold for around £25 each. Ours retailed for £9.99. We undercut the competition by around 60 per cent, made 50 per cent profit on every sale and had a customer base that was the definition of captive. Those who didn't buy on the way in invariably bought on the way out. It was a gold rush. The following day we branched into sweatshirts and caps, and the day after, towels and cold drinks, though this was where we ran into trouble. If the T-shirt business was run by rogues, the ice cream van racket was run by the mafia. The next morning we arrived to find we'd been 'warned', with barrels full of iced Coke and Fanta distributed evenly over Usman's parents' front lawn. The message was clear. Don't mess with Mr Whippy.

At the end of the first day, the white van team returned to run through the accounts, which was really just a Tesco bag of cash and rough numbers. We handed over £3,000 and asked for twice as much stock for the following day. We packed up, changed into our silk suits and went to pick up Tess and Darren's girlfriend, Sarah, in his black Fiat Abarth. In 1985, this was hands down the fastest, most souped-up car you could get, at least in the hatchback range to which he was restricted on account of high insurance premiums for the under-21s. We had fifteen hundred quid each in our pockets. To put that another way, two eighteen-year-old boys went out for the night with the equivalent in today's money of nearly £9,000. You could get a *lot* of Southern Comfort and lemonade for that.

My inaugural foray into the world of sales and commerce had taught me several things. The first was that the people who make real money are usually the ones who can spot an opening. Usman and his parents had been sitting on this opportunity since the day they moved in and had never once capitalised on their location. They never tried to renegotiate or kick us off their plot once they saw how much we were making. All they were worried about was whether they'd still be able to get a parking space in July. So, the moral of the story is, if there's a window and you're not prepared to jump through it, know that someone else will.

The second thing I learned was that you need to be flexible if you don't want to eat into your profits. Darren and I were the salesmen, roadies, marketing men and accountants. The minute you become precious about what you will and won't do in a start-up is the minute your margin starts to dwindle.

The last and most crucial lesson was, no matter how good your business, if you can't sell it, forget it. Sales is the cornerstone of every successful company. Whether the product is T-shirts and Coke or opinion polls and data, the principle is the same: if you can't create a market for it, you're buggered.

The Wimbledon episode was not only a brilliant lesson in business but left me with a fire in my belly. I'd seen my dad do it a thousand times – make a deal, bring home the money – but this was the first time I'd held my own profits in my own hand and decided where and how to spend them. It was my first taste of being an entrepreneur, and I'd unwittingly blundered into what would become my first career.

CHAPTER 11

A GAP IN THE MARKET

HOW TO MAKE MONEY

When Dad lost his money to the infamous Aubrey C. Briggs I was quickly removed from my 'I don't need this job and can afford to walk out anytime you annoy me' state of luxury. In fact, by the time I graduated, I was desperate to work out a way to survive financially but realised this was a fact I should keep to myself rather than articulate. A single day in a school playground will tell you desperation is something people can smell. We're attracted to strength because we equate it with value, while desperation means weakness and a whiff of that undermines your position in any negotiation – including one for a job. So I buried all traces of neediness and went out into the world to make my fortune.

The problem was, I was slightly lost. At twenty-two, I hadn't joined the dots between education and the world at large. Graduation seemed like the end of a long train track. I'd been on the journey for as long as I could remember but with very little thought about what the destination might look like when I eventually got off. There was a bracket of kids who seemed to know exactly what they wanted – who got their degree, signed up for a second to qualify as accountants and then went on to work for one of the Big Four. I wasn't one of them. On the morning my

A-level results arrived I had a shift at the hospital, so Jihan had agreed to open the letter when it came and give me the results over the phone. I snuck out while Sue's back was turned to call from the phone box outside A&E. It was not good news – at least not good enough to take up the place I'd been offered to study Medicine at Trinity College Dublin. To be honest, no one was more relieved about this than me. I never really wanted to be a doctor and now, thank God, I wasn't going to be. But I had to go somewhere and it was Jihan who dug me out of a hole as she'd done many times before. A few years earlier it had fallen to her to convince the headmaster at King's College to give me a place to sit my A-levels despite my applying too late to be considered. My sister was a force to be reckoned with and somehow convinced the man to let me in. I don't know what she said to him, but I do know she never takes no for an answer. This is the reason her son refers to her now as 'The Hustler'. She was just like Dad in that respect. She and I rowed like most siblings, but I always thought twice about taking her on. Equally, I could think of no better person to fight my corner whenever I needed help.

In the mid-80s, university clearing was done exclusively over the phone. It was a heady mix of panic and hold music, and the whole thing was made much more complicated if you weren't by a landline at the time. Jihan and I worked in relay. She called round to find somewhere that would take me with the grades I had and I guarded the phone box to prevent anyone else trying to use it while I waited for her to ring back. When the call finally came, she'd whittled my options down to Civil or Chemical Engineering at UCL. There was no time to mull it over; if you didn't take the place, you'd lose it. I might as well have closed my eyes and stuck a pin in a list for all I knew about either, so I plumped for Chemical on the basis that Civil sounded boring and I'd managed a 'B' in Chemistry. It would not become clear until *after* I'd taken up my place that Chemical Engineering centred round physics, but it was too late to turn back then.

University would go on to provide me with some core skills that would prove very handy later in my career, but at the time, those years seemed more about Pro Plus and the revelation that I could hold much more vodka tonic than Southern Comfort or neat whisky. With university on my doorstep, I never moved away to study and, with few exceptions, kept the same friends I'd had at school. Living at home with my family meant it wasn't the big leap into the unknown it probably was for most people. It would be another few years before I cut the apron strings entirely and moved out.

Four years later I had a BSc in Chem Eng, no money and no better idea of what to do with the rest of my life, but it was time to try and find out. I suppose you could say the journey started with Broosk. Broosk had a friend called Ali, who went to Eton and then Oxford. Ali was friends with a kid called Peter Cowen, whose dad was head of one of the Oxford colleges and lived in a huge university house in town. Once we'd got to know his gang a bit better, we'd drive up and stay the night at Peter's dad's after nights out at student parties. And that's where I met the other Peter: Peter Dubens.

Broosk already knew Pete a little through a connection with his father, but by the time I knew him he was in his twenties. Now living in Edith Grove in Chelsea, he'd often pass by Broosk's showroom on the Fulham Road and drop in for a chat. Some days he'd bring his friend Jonny Sieff. These two were a different kettle of fish to a lot of the other kids we'd met at the Oxford parties. They weren't Etonians or Oxbridge students. In fact, Pete dropped out of university before he'd even started.

After I graduated I'd begun work full-time with Broosk, but it became clear I wasn't going to make a career as an estate agent.

I needed to find something that better suited my strengths. Kingston had taught me I was good with people and my summer at Wimbledon that I could sell, but what to do with this information was another matter. It just so happened Pete and Jonny had the perfect solution.

The thing that defined Pete was his drive to succeed. He was the hungriest guy I'd ever met. Part of the reason, I'm sure, is that he didn't come from money himself – at least not 'family' money – but everyone around him did. Pete always had rich friends. Most of them originated from Gibbs, the exclusive pre-prep he attended in Sloane Square. That's where he met Ed Cadogan, whose family controls ninety acres of prime metropolitan real estate. I can see how having those kinds of friends might light a fire underneath you. When Ed left Gibbs, he went to school with Jonny, which was how he later came to meet Pete.

Pete's grandparents were Jewish immigrants who hailed from Lithuania and, like many immigrants, Pete's mother placed huge emphasis on education. You could say I have her to thank for my success because if Pete hadn't gone to Gibbs he would never have met Ed, and if he hadn't met Ed he wouldn't have met Jonny and none of this would have happened.

Though life started out well for the Dubenses, when Pete was small his mum was diagnosed with cancer and his dad left his job to care for her. When she died two years later, the trauma of losing her was exacerbated by a drastic change in financial circumstances because his dad never recovered from the loss and this affected his career. When the time came, Pete didn't bother with university because he couldn't afford not to work. The damage done to his family was what drove him to succeed. Trauma fuelled rather than curtailed his progress, and in this we were kindred spirits.

By the time Pete was twenty, he was determined to start his own company. It didn't really matter what it was as long as it was something. All he needed now was the right opportunity and the right partner.

In the years to come, Pete would buy and sell companies at mind-boggling figures that make what he does for a living sound like a game of *Monopoly*. He's a serial entrepreneur and a hugely successful private equity manager but, even now, you'll struggle to find more than the same few stories regurgitated about him in the press. Some of this I know is because he'd rather concentrate on business rather than shouting about it in the papers, but I think he learned early on that it never hurts to project an image bigger and more awesome than you really are if you want people to buy into the dream you're selling. Let's face it, there was a reason the Wizard of Oz hid behind that curtain with his megaphone; he didn't want people to see he was just another ordinary human being trying to sell a dream. After graduation, I knew I had to do exactly the same thing: project something bigger and bolder than I really felt, and get someone to buy it.

RIDING THE WAVE

If Pete was hungry, Jonny had a full belly. He came from a very wealthy, well-connected family. The Sieffs weren't just rich, they were as good as royalty in Jewish circles. Jonny's great-grandfather, Israel, had been best friends with Simon Marks, son of Michael Marks – the immigrant barrow boy who parlayed his market stall in Leeds into multi-million pound retail empire, Marks & Spencer. Simon Marks and Israel Sieff had been to grammar school together and became lifelong friends, eventually marrying one another's sisters. Israel began working with Simon at M&S in 1915 and, after Simon died in 1964, took over as chairman and MD. When *he* died in 1972, his ashes were buried next to Simon in Golders Green cemetery. Partners till the very end.

Israel's son, Marcus – Jonny's grandfather – went on to create the M&S food hall, which means I have him to thank for my annual Christmas pudding. So Jonny had some pretty dynamic role models knocking about. I suspect it was a lot to live up to, but he was a great salesman himself. He was also charming and handsome, with a great deal of presence. If Jonny was anything to go by, I could see how and why his family had been so successful. In Jonny's words, his great-grandfather had an aura about him. For me, Jonny was very much the same. He had a confidence in his delivery that made you feel he was going to succeed. It was like a force field around him. When Israel died, his obituary in *The Times* said his relationship with Marks was 'a remarkable combination of two very different minds and personalities which produced the amazing success of Marks & Spencer. The immense practical genius of Lord Marks balanced the percipient, sensitive fascination with any piece of pioneering which was characteristic of Sieff.'* This was a company built on innovation, and now Jonny was taking up the baton. Just like his great-grandfather he was a visionary, and in Pete he found his Simon Marks. Once they got rolling, it was hard to separate them. They spoke as one.

Jonny had already done an internship at an East End manufacturers, as well as a piece of research for the family business on the textile and printing industry. He'd discovered the same thing I had during my stint at Wimbledon: the T-shirt-printing business

---

* 'Lord Sieff – Joint architect of Marks and Spencer empire', *The Times*, 15 February 1972.

was run by chancers, either that or mom and pop ventures operating from sheds and garages at the bottom of gardens. Jonny had identified a gap in the market and Pete was the natural choice of partner to capitalise on it. Jonny was as charming as Pete was determined – it was the perfect match. In 1985, Global Inc was born: a small T-shirt-printing business with a big future.

The two original investors in Global were Jonny's dad and his friend David Wolfson – Margaret Thatcher's ex-chief of staff. The boys took the cash, rolled up their sleeves and started work. In the first instance this was from the bedroom Pete still rented at Ed Cadogan's. When they got enough business they moved into a warehouse on Garrett Lane in Wandsworth.

For a couple of years they went out and sold the T-shirts themselves, driving around in their shared yellow Suzuki Jeep – Pete one week, Jonny the next. But things changed dramatically after a timely tip-off from Jonny's friend Jamie Barshall, and quickly got too busy to handle alone. While browsing a magazine he'd picked up on the train to London, Jamie had seen an advert for Hypercolor – a line of clothing manufactured by a US company called Generra that changed colour with heat – and showed it to the boys. By complete serendipity, a friend of Jonny's father – Walter Schoenfeld – was the chairman of Generra, and the boys swung an introduction. Walter could have taken the lead to anyone higher up in the Sieff family business but knew it needed not just an entrepreneur but one plugged into the right market. Generra's whole product was based around youth, music and clubbing because, as any teenager who'd been to a rave knew, if there's one thing young people like to do, it's crowd into a room, dance and sweat. As young guys themselves, the boys were in just the right space to sell Generra's product. Despite Walter's personal introduction, it still took over a year to get to the point of a conversation with Generra, and even then they had to guarantee $26 million in sales over the next three years to secure the contract: a pretty ballsy commitment for two kids barely out of school.

So when the time came and Pete and Jonny offered me a job in sales and marketing, I didn't need to sleep on it. These were my kind of people.

Hypercolor T-shirts were a fad that lasted little more than a year but, to give you an idea of the scale of that fad, in the US alone the parent company sold $50 million worth of product in the space of four months. It was a hugely successful but simple scientific invention – a dye that changes its molecular structure with body heat – which generated millions in global profits. The worst thing about *that* was that the technology was originally British. The scientist who came up with the idea couldn't get funded in the UK, so the Japanese firm Matsui took it, tweaked it to make sure it didn't hurt your skin or come off in the wash, and sold it to the Americans. Then the Americans sold it back to us. A perfectly flawed circle. I thought about this journey many times when I saw the risk-averse nature of government. It was a cautionary tale about what happens when you don't recognise or protect the valuable things right under your nose.

In Britain, because of our great universities, we're much better at the 'R' than at the 'D' when it comes to the research and development of ideas. If we were as good at taking our discoveries into business as we were identifying them, we'd move GDP substantially because, for every £1 you unlock, you attract at least another £2 from the private sector. The Americans are great at using government as both financier and first client. The CIA and the Department of Defense have their own private equity investment arms that act as first investors in projects championed by the government. Silicon Valley – one of the most profitable industrial locations in the world – was founded on the back of the DoD. Working with Hypercolor was a great example of money that could have been made for the UK with better research and development infrastructure, and the story stuck in my mind. Twenty years later, I got my first opportunity to right this wrong.

In 2010, I ran as an MP for the Conservative safe seat of Stratford-on-Avon, and won. I'd worked as a councillor for three terms so had some idea of what the job would entail but had not realised that every MP functioned just like a small enterprise: a cottage industry, with an office, staff and customers. The product they were buying was your voice in parliament and the currency they paid in was votes. Each MP was a semi-autonomous business under the umbrella of a much bigger parent company in Westminster. The minute you arrive at your new job you're handed a pre-loaded laptop, logged in and secured with your new address, complete with a six-week backlog of emails amassed during purdah from constituents waiting to speak to their new member of parliament. Your office needs to be up and running immediately if you're going to be able to help them. Even in a so-called safe seat, to be an effective politician you need to treat it as a marginal one. Work like you would if you couldn't afford to rest on your laurels. Customer service in parliament or in government should be no different from in business – if the standard falls short, it affects your bottom line, which in this case is whether or not you and your party will be re-elected. A lot of my new colleagues in Westminster told me to hire from within but, from a background in business, I knew the best way to make a company successful was to hire the best person for the job, irrespective of where they came from. Why limit yourself to a predefined pool of candidates? It made no sense to me at all.

Like all MPs, I was given the standard-issue three and a half members of staff to run my office and service my 70,000 constituents and I knew just the person I wanted to start with. I'd met Simon McIntyre three months earlier when he'd turned up to volunteer for my campaign at the Stratford-on-Avon Conservative Association in a beautiful old building next to the church where Shakespeare is buried. He was an extremely sharp, bright guy with a degree in astrophysics but in a pretty bad way when he arrived. Over the weeks I noticed his desk was peppered with hidden red bills; these weren't difficult to spot if you'd ever been in that situation yourself, which I had. I knew better than to ask him outright about his troubles, but as he was a young, newly married man, I could see he needed some financial stability. As soon as I won my seat, I asked him to come and work for me full-time as my chief of staff. Within six months he'd worked out the problem with our existing customer relationship management system – there wasn't one. When a constituent contacted me to say, 'I was in touch with your predecessor two years ago ...', other than dozens of lever-arch files and an outmoded system called CMITS, which ran off Microsoft Access, there was no easily accessible or user-friendly record of their correspondence to build on. To give you an idea, when one person in the team wanted to sync their files on CMITS, it required every other person signed in to sign out and wait for the system to upload. Clearly, we weren't going to get very far, very fast with that approach. Simon was a brilliant tech guy and I knew he'd have no problem building a proper system to replace the status quo, but what he'd never done was build a business. Fortunately by that time I had, and so we made a deal. I agreed to teach him how to create a successful company from scratch, and he agreed to let me use the technology he produced for the rest of my time in parliament free of charge. Over time, Simon built caseworker.mp, which is now used by more than 90 per cent of all British MPs. Five years after he started working for me, it was so successful he had to leave to work on it full-time. This is what we needed to do more of: foster talent and keep it in the country.

Pete and Jonny obviously saw something they liked in me the evening Broosk and I went for a Chinese with them at their favourite restaurant in Pimlico. I always get excited about business and new ideas, whether they're mine or anyone else's, and I love brainstorming and turning things over. I never really care who the beneficiary is; for me, it's about positive outcomes. So, that night, when the boys talked about their start-up, I couldn't help but wade in with my own ideas. I was envious of anyone already in business and desperate to get out into the world. I found their set-up exciting, even though the pleasure was wholly vicarious. Evidently my enthusiasm must have come across loud and clear because by the end of the evening I had a new job: Sales Manager, Global Inc.

When I walked into Garrett Lane on my first day, my overriding feeling was one of relief at having landed on my feet financially, and I was determined to make myself indispensable to Pete and Jonny. On the outside I probably looked pretty confident, but under the surface I was madly paddling away. In all honesty, that never really changes no matter how far down the line you get. If you're good at your job, you should always be learning, and ultimately you never really know if something's going to work out until it's over. I knew I should be able to do the job, but whether I could remained to be seen.

I'd proved I could sell at Wimbledon and had the story in my back pocket if I needed to impress anyone. What I hadn't factored in was that all the sales I'd made to date had been to an end user with a tenner in their pocket looking to buy a souvenir. I'd never yet dealt with a trade customer or for that matter been in any kind of business meeting in my life, which is why the decision to send me to negotiate with the senior buyer at C&A was a novel one. Thankfully, none of this crossed my mind before I set off on the tube with my sales kit in my Adidas sports bag. I'd taken Pete and Jonny's tips and added my own flourishes to the pitch and was eager to take the whole thing out for a drive.

Thirty years on it's easy to dismiss C&A's significance in Britain's retail market. In the early 90s they were still a huge player with cheap, fashionable clothes in prime outlets on every major high street in Britain. Sadly, this combination was also part of their downfall when out-of-town stores started to gather momentum and supermarkets gained ground in the clothing market but, at the time, a meeting with the head buyer of C&A was considered a major coup for such a young company. As a teenager I'd walked past the C&A family mansion in Kingston every time I went to Darren's house, so the meeting was not without its personal significance for me.

On arrival at their HQ in Oxford Street, I was shown into a large office with a big desk, perfect for me to display my wares, which I began unpacking and laying out. The T-shirts came in five colourways: blue went to pink, green to yellow and so on. As I lined them up side by side to begin my demonstration, in walked Mr C&A Buyer, a giant of a man, and, with barely a nod of recognition, sat straight down at his desk and began writing on a notepad. I stood for a moment, waiting for him to open the dialogue, but he didn't even look up. I emptied my bag of its last item – the key ingredient in my tool kit – a 1984 Clairol 850 two-speed hairdryer on long loan from my sister. I wiped my sweaty palms on my trousers discreetly and cleared my throat: 'Would you mind if I used your plug?' Without looking up he motioned to the socket next to his feet. The lead was only just long enough to reach the table and I immediately regretted not buying a newer model with more slack. With my stall set out, I gave another little cough to signal I was ready and was given a wordless, perfunctory wave of the hand from the man still scribbling on his notepad. I took this as a sign to begin and launched into my sales patter. At the pivotal moment in my speech – which I appeared to be delivering to no one – I flipped the switch on the hairdryer to full heat and swept it across the line of T-shirts, leaving a Mexican wave of colour in its wake. I was pretty pleased with myself, having practised this to the point of exhaustion the night before in my bedroom. The trick was to maintain eye contact with the buyer while doing a swoop over the T-shirts low enough to trigger the technology but not so low as to rumple them. I didn't actually say 'Ta-dah', but it was that kind of a moment. It was, however, met with absolutely no response from the audience. He wasn't even watching. I didn't know whether he was being arrogant or trying to intimidate me or was just busy with other things, but there followed a soul-destroying pause. I didn't know whether to speak to fill the silence or just wait for him to acknowledge my presence. We'd still not exchanged a single word and I was beginning to doubt he'd agreed to the meeting in the first place. After what seemed like at least ten years had passed, he finally stopped writing and looked up, shoving five pages of his notepad towards me with an abrupt, 'When can you deliver?' I picked up the pieces of paper which I now saw were order forms rather than his own private musings. Five sheets, one for every colourway, each with an order of 75,000 items. All sound evaporated from my body as I tried to process the magnitude of what was happening. Three hundred and seventy-five thousand T-shirts at £7.50 each. The Wimbledon cash looked like a deer I'd hit in the rearview mirror in comparison with the £2.8 million he'd just signed off. It was paralysing. Finally, I managed a small, strangled 'Let me call the office and get back to you' before he exited to do whatever it is men like him do after spending nearly three million pounds on T-shirts.

News of my coup was conveyed back to the boys at Garrett Lane via a phone box outside Oxford Circus tube station. If there was one, I felt like my probation period must be well and truly over. With my first business meeting under my belt, it was time to try a trade show.

TAKE THAT & PARTY

In 1986, fashion designer Jeff Banks came up with the idea for a TV show that merged catwalk style with high-street budgets and wrapped it up to make it look like an episode of *Max Headroom*. *The Clothes Show* was destination television and there wasn't a person my age who couldn't pick its presenters Jeff, Selina and Caryn out of a line-up. It was a massive hit, with nine million viewers at its peak – which was just about the time the boys decided to take a stand at the spin-off *Clothes Show Live* exhibition at Birmingham's NEC.

Two years previously I'd worked as Broosk's gopher on his stand at the British Interior Design Exhibition at the Chelsea Old Town Hall. The whole place was divided up with MDF walls and each designer got a square on which to build a room from scratch. You had two and a half weeks to put it together before Princess Margaret came to open the whole thing to the public. It was like the Chelsea Flower Show but with sofas and candelabras. The net result was that I was now officially the most qualified person in the office to run our stand at the exhibition and was shipped off to Birmingham with two helpers, a Stanley knife, some packing tape and 500 T-shirts.

We took the basic package at the show, which meant a steel frame, white plastic backdrop, a table and one chair less than we needed. When it came to tarting up the stand it helped that we were in the T-shirt business. I pinned the five colourways to the back wall and stacked up the remaining boxes with Global Inc emblazoned across the front and waited. Two hours later and it was a ghost town; at least around our stand. I called the boys back in the office from the payphone in the lobby to tell them there was absolutely nothing to report. Time dragged on, and Danny, Dave and I did the rounds of other stands and took turns sitting down. Pete and Jonny had arranged for the shirts to be worn by a new band who were performing that day on the main catwalk. They'd met up in London the week before and their burgeoning fan base of sweaty teens seemed the perfect audience for our product. We agreed that if things didn't pick up after their performance, I'd send Danny and Dave back to the office and chalk it up to experience. I looked at my watch. It was 11.05. The band would be on stage now: Mark in pink, Jason in orange, Howard in blue, Gary in green and Robbie Williams in purple. What happened next is the closest thing I've experienced to being suffocated by an avalanche.

Out of nowhere a sea of people swept towards us like a tsunami. The sales patter I'd developed was abandoned as we struggled to manage the sheer volume of customers. The idea of using my Clairol 850 to demo the colour change was now positively laughable. Our carefully planned system – me on sales, Danny on cash, and Dave on wrapping and bagging – dissolved in minutes as we began stuffing money into the empty boxes underneath the display table. The crowds started to spill round the sides of the stand, opening up boxes themselves and impatiently pulling out stock. The two chairs were repurposed as a makeshift barrier, which did little to deter the baying masses. Half an hour later I made the executive decision to release Dave to go and get someone from security to help, which made things even worse for Danny and me at the coalface. Ten minutes later, Dave returned with two Lou Ferrigno types who'd clearly seen this kind of thing before. Within seconds they'd erected a waist-height aluminium barrier and funnelled the crowds back behind it like they do in McDonald's on a Saturday night in Leicester Square. I sent Danny back to the payphone to call the boys with the message: 'Send help and start printing!!'

Six hours later and it was over – at least for the first day. I was like a dry husk and had never been more tired or wired. Paranoid I'd be ambushed on the way back to the hotel, I'd transported the cash in an unmarked duffle bag as nonchalantly as it's possible to carry £15,000 in used notes at dusk in the Midlands. Jonny and Pete drove up that night to celebrate. When they walked into my room I demonstrated just how well things had gone by emptying the duffle bag of notes all over the bed. It wasn't as much as the C&A deal had brought in but it was cash and it was real and it was all there in front of us, tangible evidence of the wave we were clearly about to ride. We were just kids. It was mind blowing. It gave me the same sort of high I'd got from the football and the raves except, this time, I wasn't doing something I could get arrested for and it was okay to tell my mum about it. I rang her from the hotel that evening.

Eighteen months later and the guys knew the colour-change T-shirt fad was coming to an end. We'd sold more than £16 million worth of them; it was time to get out – yet another note to add to my 'lessons in business' dossier. Timing is everything.

After the *Clothes Show Live* I felt I could legitimately add retail to my CV. I'd also had a taste of what it was like to be part of a successful business. Global Inc was a baptism of fire and an entry into the world of commerce like no other, and I felt I had a good handle on how to make money. I couldn't call myself an entrepreneur yet because I wasn't the one who'd taken the risks, put up the cash or spotted the gap in the market, but I realised that's exactly what I wanted: to do it myself. I felt ready. Watching Pete and Jonny jump into the abyss was a great lesson in how to hold onto risk and I was inspired by them to do the same. The one thing I'd not covered with the boys was how to lose money, which, I'd argue, is probably the ultimate lesson in business. I didn't need to worry though; I was about to take a Master's on the topic. And it started with a man named Archer.

CHAPTER 12

BEAN KURD

THE MENTOR

At 83, Jeffrey Archer still has the energy of a man who's roared at himself in the mirror before opening the front door to you. If it's your first encounter, it's quite the experience. Our inaugural meeting was on the back of a cold call. Success in sales often comes down to the best leads and, in April 1991, Pete happened to hear about a really big one. It was to prove life-changing in ways I couldn't have imagined.

When the Gulf War had come to an end earlier that year, my old nemesis, Saddam Hussein, signed a peace agreement with US General Norman Schwarzkopf that prevented him from flying fixed-wing aircraft over Iraq. It said nothing about helicopter gunships, which he promptly dug out and used to threaten the Kurds in the north of the country. They fled to the mountains, where they began to freeze and die in their thousands. Appalling images appeared daily from Iraq. The dead bodies of infants wrapped in blankets by the side of the road; seas of makeshift shelters as far as the eye could see. It's always incredible how quickly these kinds of human disasters throw what were previously 'civilised' people living ordinary lives into conditions that look almost biblical. Girls with pierced ears and boys in Nike T-shirts suddenly barefoot and filthy, waiting in line to share food or scrabble over water. The juxtaposition of these two worlds only serves to highlight just how quickly the trappings of consumerism become irrelevant when we move into survival mode. The public felt both incensed and helpless watching such crimes unfold, crimes that were carried out in the name of a single man and a single party. It was an appalling act of unprovoked aggression by an unfettered sociopath. This was a man whose *modus operandi* I knew first hand, and though I'd long since left Iraq, the people he was displacing were my own. For me, this felt very personal. I knew I wanted to help, but had no idea how.

Jeffrey Archer had been deputy chairman of the Conservative Party and a highly influential figure in John Major's government. The story goes that it was Jeffrey's younger son, James, who questioned him about why the Kurds had been left to fend for themselves; why no one was going to their rescue. Jeffrey was in a position to do something about it and he did. His decisiveness and dedication to a cause were just some of the many things I'd come to like about him.

His plan was the Simple Truth – a benefit gig and campaign in alliance with the Red Cross to give aid to the Kurds via the United Nations. To get something like this off the ground required quite a bit of chutzpah. Most people had never heard of the Kurds. They were a minority group in a region whose cultural, political and religious outlook was seemingly at odds with our own. Why them? Helping would cost money and was one of a long line of demands on an already overstretched budget. Geldof had done it for the Ethiopians but if the government were going to buy into this now, we needed someone to sell it in, just as Bob had done with Thatcher. That man was Jeffrey Archer. He could sell anything to anyone. Though he'd learned to love the finer things in life, at heart he was still your basic wheeler-dealer; an Arthur Daley type who'd duck and dive until he got what he wanted, and he was never afraid to revert to this when needed. His first target was John Major, whom he persuaded to part with £10 million to kick it all off. When George H. W. Bush heard what the UK had pledged, he matched it. All the other targets fell like skittles. Jeffrey's plan to garner support worked very nicely.

When you start to look into your own fragile existence, it doesn't take long to see we're a drop in the ocean of history. This, I'm sure, is why entrepreneurs like Warren Buffett or Bill Gates move sideways from business into philanthropy; they're all asking themselves the same question, 'What am I going to leave behind?' This, I believe, is the situation in which I found Jeffrey the day I arrived at his apartment in April 1991 in the midst of the Simple Truth campaign. When I asked him recently what motivated him to try and pull off such an implausible stunt, he told me it was in part to assuage 'the guilt of success'. He had everything he could possibly want. It was the 'What will I leave behind?' that motivated him now.

When Saddam had attacked the innocent Kuwaitis a year earlier, I resolved to organise some kind of protest. The first stop was a visit to my friend, Hamad, who'd been exiled to the UK after the invasion of his country. Hamad and I had already marched with other Kuwaitis, but he helped me set up a meeting with the organisers of those rallies to understand how you put one together. From Broosk's first-floor flat above a shop in the Fulham Road, I rounded up some mates and worked on the plans for two demos running from Marble Arch to the Iraqi embassy. The idea was to get the Iraqi diaspora out in a show of solidarity to prove not all of them backed Saddam and his illegal invasion. Not long after I'd been to Scotland Yard for the demo licence, I got a covert visit from CID to discuss protection. On the two weekends in question, plain-clothed operatives weaved in and out of the crowds doing their best to keep us safe. I'd done as much as I realistically could, given my circumstances at the time. Now, though, Saddam had gone a step further with his attack on the Kurds and I was determined to put them front and centre of people's minds. It might have been 4,500 miles from what I now called home, but I felt no less connected to the tragedy.

Jeffrey felt likewise determined to help, and the highlight of his campaign would be a benefit concert broadcast across thirty-six countries and staged in four. When Pete turned on the radio one morning on the way to work and heard Jeffrey's announcement about the gig, he was straight on his newly acquired Motorola to Cynthia Crawford to ask for Jeffrey's number. Crawfie, as she was better known, was the shared secretary of Margaret Thatcher and her ex-chief of staff, David Wolfson – founding shareholder of Global Inc – so quite happy to hand the number over. When Pete called to ask if Global could make the merchandise for the concert, Jeffrey invited him over there and then. Within thirty minutes he and Jonny were at Jeffrey's front door ready to make their pitch. Evidently they did something right because Jeffrey offered them the contract on the spot. The deal had been conceived, negotiated and closed in the space of an hour. Just as they were leaving, Jeffrey asked the question that would mark the beginning of my political career: 'I don't suppose you boys know anyone Kurdish?'

As I rooted through a box of mislabelled XXLs back at the office, line one lit up with a breathless call from Pete: 'Can you get down to the Embankment to meet Jeffrey Archer?' I'm pretty sure it was a rhetorical question because, for a certain type of right-leaning thinker, Jeffrey's apartment was the mothership: a microcosm of the world at Westminster. In 1991, I was one such right-leaning thinker, though, at twenty-four, still a long way off any thoughts of a career in politics. That didn't mean I wasn't well versed in the subject. Given where I came from, it was impossible to avoid. The topic followed me everywhere. In Baghdad, my parents were liberals in a socialist state, but in the UK I'd chosen the Conservative Party as the best match for my political ideals, which, for some, might seem an odd choice. My initial decision to vote blue, however, had more to do with chance than choice.

THE SOCIALIST WORKER

The day I arrived for Freshers' Week in September 1985, I was one of UCL's more puny undergraduates. Skinny, small and brown with a mouthful of goofy teeth, at eighteen I looked three years younger than I was. As I walked towards the main entrance of the Union I was greeted by a bloke who looked at least thirty, handing out copies of *Socialist Worker*. I knew I'd be loaded down with leaflets once inside so said a polite 'No, thank you' to his offer of a free magazine. This was apparently *not* what he wanted to hear. Without warning he launched into an aggressive tirade that tied my refusal to take his socialist paper with my being 'a race traitor', and delivered the whole rant two inches from my face. As his spittle flecked my cheeks, I felt the ire rise from my gut.

I had no interest in politics. I'd just come from a place where tyranny was billed as socialism and socialism as equality; where going into politics meant losing your head. I was not about to be pushed by a guy on the street purporting to believe in freedom while dictating that all brown people should adhere to his political bias. It was the holiday bully, the chanting crowds at Sheen Comp and my dad's slap round my face all over again: 'Don't let yourself be bullied, Nadhim.' Not only was I not interested in his politics, I was now utterly furious. Given my size, I thought it unlikely I could take him down, so my comeback would need to be mental rather than physical. Like most siblings, my sister and I had baited each other relentlessly as kids, but, since she was bigger and stronger than me, I'd learned that the best way to get my own back with her was with mind games. I realised now this was no different; the quickest way to get under *this* guy's skin would be to find out what the other side had to offer. I extricated myself from the situation and walked through the Union doors with a revised agenda for the day. I was now there to seek my revenge.

I didn't have to go far. The Conservative Collegiate Forum, as it was then called, had a trestle table right near the door. Even better, it was manned by a really good-looking blonde girl. When she told me she was doing a PhD in Chemical Engineering I thought it must be fate. When she said she was part of the university showjumping team – a hobby close to my heart – I felt like the planets had aligned above me and some sort of rousing classical music was about to start up from a hidden orchestra pit. Actually, she just got me to fill in some forms but it was a pretty exciting start to university life.

So the decision to become a Conservative was initially based on incandescent rage, but it led me to a place where I felt happy with my choice. The party, she told me, believed in freedom. I came from a country where there was none. They believed in opportunity and so, I realised, did I. Even my standing there in front of her now was the result of one – a UK education was one of the best in the world. Today, I'd say opportunity defines me and I've taken advantage of every one I've been given. They haven't all worked out, but at least I've been free to take them. That was what being a Conservative meant to me. The freedom to choose. I never found out the name of the socialist who accosted me all those years ago but, given that I went on to become chairman of the Conservative Party, I have to tell you now my friend, that was the most spectacular own goal.

So did I want to go to Jeffrey Archer's apartment that day? I could hardly get my coat on quickly enough. My appeal to Jeffrey was much more rudimentary: he needed a Kurd with an inside understanding of the problems they faced in Iraq. When he'd learned Pete and Jonny 'had one back at the office', his response was an emphatic 'Get him in!' And so it was I made my way to Peninsula Heights on the Albert Embankment for what would be the first of many visits.

Jeffrey's penthouse is both a political landmark and a living monument to a different era. From outside, the building resembles an office block that was architecturally quite exciting when it was conceived, but now looks like the sort of place you might take a speed-awareness course. Unless you were to stand on the other side of the road on the petrol station forecourt and crane your head back, you'd have no idea the very top floor even existed, let alone housed one of the most influential men in politics. It's the sort of place a misunderstood superhero could lay low if he were on the run – the perfect place to see the police scurrying around below while hidden from sight. And then there's 'The View'. To say it's incredible is a spectacular understatement. I have no doubt Jeffrey's decision to buy the penthouse was as much to do with his love of the vista as the fact it immediately disarms anyone who enters, which is no bad way to start a meeting with someone you're hoping to dominate or win over. As you pad across the marble tiles towards the wraparound glass walls, all London is gradually revealed. It's how I imagine Mount Olympus might feel – the highest possible place from which to survey your kingdom.

The first time I met Jeffrey he was living four floors down in the same building and had yet to purchase the top floor, which then functioned as Bernie Ecclestone's bachelor pad. The 10th floor view, however, was no less staggering than the 14th. I'd been to all the tourist sights in London but to work in a building with that kind of aspect would make you want to get up in the morning. When Jeffrey asked if I'd like to come and help on the campaign, there was no doubt in my mind this was where I wanted to be.

By the time we arrived on the scene he had three weeks left to pull the project together and needed all the extra hands he could get, so I dragged Broosk along to the next meeting. Jeffrey got two Kurds for the price of one, and 'Bean Kurd' and 'Lemon Kurd' became a team. His nicknames for us set a lot of tongues wagging, even though he must be the most colourblind person I've ever met. Fundamentally, he was interested in outcomes; he didn't care where you came from or what your background was, as long as you were the best person for the job. Years later the press put their own, less affectionate, spin on our pairing and dubbed us the 'Gucci Kurds' on account of Broosk's shoes and what they considered to be Jeffrey's selective choice of immigrant.

While Pete and Jonny took care of the merchandise, I was seconded to Jeffrey's flat for the remaining twenty-one days of the campaign. My contacts in the Middle East and understanding of everything from the culture to the landscape made me a valuable asset. The reward was being around Jeffrey and watching him work. If Max was magnetic, Jeffrey was the neodymium.

Broosk and I weren't the only ones on hand to help. Jeffrey gathered people like a kid picks up stones on the beach. He always had an eye out for anything shiny or interesting to put in his bucket. In the three weeks I spent holed up in that apartment, I'd estimate 100 people clocked up around 20,000 man hours between them to pull the show together. To put on an event of that scale, in that time frame, was an absurd undertaking by anyone's measure and exactly the kind of thing Jeffrey was good at. What we achieved was testament not only to the energy of everyone involved but also his powers of persuasion. Like Geldof, Jeffrey wasn't afraid to cut corners or spin a few tall tales to get the job done. If he needed to tell Peter Gabriel that Paul Simon had already committed in order to get him on board, that's what he did. He knew exactly how to stroke an ego to best effect. People did it to him all the time.

Up until then my working day consisted of schmoozing buyers and textile manufacturers and dropping off boxes round the back of C&A. The campaign, I thought, would be just another sales job with a different product. On one level I was right, but it was also a big gear change to find myself taking calls in which people routinely said things like, 'President Bush will talk to Jeffrey at 3 p.m.' I absolutely loved it. It was the old familiar thrill I'd got from the football but now I was able to channel that adrenalin into something productive that I really cared about. I thrived on it. I couldn't sleep at night and I didn't care. Who needed to go to bed?

Jeffrey believed in throwing people in at the deep end, and in this respect was an incredibly generous, selfless boss. He didn't keep the best bits for himself. There was never any suggestion I was too junior to make the call or share an idea. It was like a teaching hospital where everyone scrubbed in because the consultant knows there's no better way to learn than on the job. The fact that anyone could challenge him was one of Jeffrey's great strengths. The responsibilities were shared and so were the rewards.

THE MOMENT OF TRUTH

In time Jeffrey would have a great deal to do with my getting into politics and likes to tell people I wanted to be a minister from day one. Looking back, that's something he identified in me rather than something I knew about myself. Had it not been for him, I'd almost certainly have carried on in business. It's what my dad had done; it was what I knew. My grandfather's legacy was a common topic in our house, but even my own father had not followed him into the same profession because no sane person wanted any part of Iraqi politics during the 1970s. My heritage was political but my role model was an entrepreneur and it was that path I'd been following until now. Even so, whatever it was that had driven my grandfather must have been in there somewhere because Jeffrey could see it. Until we got to the night of the concert itself, however, its existence was news to me.

I was pulling my weight at Global but the campaign was different. There were other people relying on me in a way I'd not experienced before. At work I had a lane and I stuck to it. At Jeffrey's we were all part of a team driving towards a common goal. Although he was the boss, he set out a clear direction and deputised effectively. I knew unequivocally that the buck stopped with me on the tasks I was given and so made it my business to get round any obstacles I encountered along the way. For the first time in my life I was proving I could handle myself without support. When I faced a problem, I answered it with hard work and made myself invaluable to Jeffrey. I garnered a reputation of being the guy that could organise anything. You want ten cars to go to the airport and another three to the American embassy? I was on it. You need the secretary-general of the UN on the phone? I was on that too. You want a thank you telegram from the Kurdish leader, General Barzani, to read out on the night? Give me five minutes ...

Masoud Barzani was in the middle of a war, fighting the Iraqi army in the mountains. As much as he might be glad of our support, it seemed unlikely I was going to get him on the phone. Instead I went to his representative in London, Hoshyar Zebari. My dad knew Zebari a little, which helped, and between us we eventually got word to Barzani and secured the note. It was a hugely important endorsement of our campaign, so I enjoyed basking in the glory of having been the one to get it. At the end of the gig, a traditional Kurdish band would play the finale, and then Jeffrey would get up and read the telegram out live on air to wrap the evening up. It wasn't until two days before the gig at a meeting with Harvey Goldsmith and the suits from the BBC to run through final arrangements that Jeffrey told me the change of plan. Everyone thought it would be much more authentic to have someone Kurdish read out the message, which didn't leave many options. It could only be me or Broosk. During the campaign, it became clear that Broosk didn't have the right kind of drive to become a politician. In Jeffrey's words he was a saint, and you couldn't be a saint *and* have ambition 'unless of course you're Mother Teresa', who was apparently the most ambitious person he'd ever met.

Knowing him as I do now, I think Jeffrey always knew it would be me who'd do the reading but preferred to test my mettle by springing it on me last-minute. Looking out onto 12,000 people was enough to paralyse anyone, but as I stepped out on stage I found myself detached from the magnitude of what was happening. It was like I was a separate person from the kid standing in front of the microphone. When I view the footage today, I look like a revolutionary Jeffrey's just pulled off the street and realise it's been a hell of a journey between now and then. When I came off stage that night, something had shifted in me. It was the culmination of the previous twenty-one days' work; of putting the whole plan together. It was the cherry on the cake and it tasted all the sweeter because I'd helped make it myself.

My father's financial collapse had presented me with two primary issues. The first and most obvious was money – we didn't have any, and I needed to make some. The second was the need to repair my family's reputation, which was a longer-term project. Dad had borrowed money from friends and the fact he'd lost it all put a question mark over whether we were decent people. I wanted to shout from the rooftops that we were. I was! Delivering that speech was a step towards addressing the issue of my family's shattered reputation and I felt a weight start to lift from my shoulders. The ultimate kickback from the Simple Truth was the feeling I got from standing in front of a crowd of people at Wembley Arena – and God knows how many millions watching on TV – and knowing they could see I'd done a good thing. That I *must* be a decent person. More than that, I'd participated in something I felt passionately about that had helped people unable to help themselves. I knew I was a good salesman but now I'd used this skill for something that really mattered. I knew immediately it was something I wanted to do again.

Before I met Jeffrey I'd been buried in short-term goals, with no real vision of where I was going in life. He had much better seats, evidently, because he seemed to have a clearer view of my future than I did. Jeffrey had come far enough on his own journey to go beyond money and into something he considered more important, and he clearly believed I was capable of functioning in the same space. What he wanted for me was the same thing my father had been driving at all this time: they wanted me to make a difference. It just so happened Jeffrey was in a position to give me the chance to do it.

THE ELEPHANT IN THE ROOM

I can't talk about Jeffrey properly without mentioning the elephant in the room. Jeffrey is a guy who's very easy to criticise. His mistakes have been very big and very public. He was always more than just a politician because his persona pushed him into the realms of an entertainer – which are dangerous waters to swim in. Just like Boris Johnson, Jeffrey was the one you'd rely on for a good soundbite if you shouted a question at him as he left Downing Street. But his charisma and forthright nature made it equally easy to tear him down. It's much more difficult to pillory someone unremarkable, and Jeffrey was never afraid to put himself out there and be the target. But when I got to know him, I saw he was also someone with what I considered to be some very moderate, rational core beliefs that are easy to lose sight of in the crossfire of his errors. It's boring but true: Jeffrey Archer was much more measured and sensible than you might want to believe. He hated division and extremes – thought them a complete waste of time – and his desire to find a middle ground made perfect sense to me. In taking chances on guys like me, Jeffrey had demonstrated that what drove him was outcomes. From my years in both business and politics, I can tell you that is much less common than you might want to believe.

He'd worked his way up from the very bottom and knew that the best results came from the best teams and the right people for the right jobs. In this he operated entirely without ego, and it was an inspiring thing to see up close. For all Jeffrey did wrong, the things he did right became the cornerstones of how I'd choose to conduct myself for the rest of my career.

I was too young to be thinking about a legacy but I liked the feeling I'd done something without personal gain. For the first time in my life, I'd begun to think about that bigger question, 'What am I going to leave behind?' If I pick apart my past, delivering my speech that night was the catalyst for a phase of life I hadn't even known I'd wanted to embark on.

Coming down from the high of that evening made it very difficult to go back to my day job. Although I loved Pete and Jonny, the added responsibilities I'd been given while working with Jeffrey had given me a taste for more. There was no doubt in my mind I wanted to be my own boss and I wanted to make my own money. Luckily, I knew just the man who might want to invest ...

CHAPTER 13

DEATH OF A SALESMAN

HOW TO LOSE MONEY

Whenever Pete talks about success now, he likes to refer to the scene in *Fiddler on the Roof* where Topol sings 'If I Were a Rich Man'. 'The most important men in town would come to fawn on me! They would ask me to advise them like a Solomon the Wise ... And it won't make one bit of difference if I answer right or wrong. When you're rich, they think you really know!' Not true at all he'll say; just because someone's wealthy or successful doesn't mean they know what they're talking about. In fact, the true mark of success is to be open to the idea you could be wrong. That you don't, in fact, know it all. The truth is we make mistakes every day, and understanding how fragile things really are is a good thing to keep in the back of your mind when you next make an executive decision. I was about to learn this first hand.

In the film of David Mamet's play, *Glengarry Glen Ross*, there's a scene in which veteran salesman Jack Lemmon does his best to close a deal that's hanging by a thread. If you've not seen it, the film centres on a group of real estate agents threatened with dismissal if they don't make one of the top two slots on the leaderboard the following week. It's famous for its examination of man's innate drive to survive. It's a brilliant film but tense and anarchic enough to make for horribly uncomfortable viewing. The first time I saw it was at the cinema while I was working for Pete and Jonny, and I couldn't stop raving about how great it was. The second time I saw it was a few years later, late one night on TV at home, and I cried like a baby most of the way through. So what had changed in between? The simple answer is, I'd learned what it meant to have skin in the game.

In 1994, Pete and Jonny sold Global to Coates Viyella. I stayed on for a while but knew I didn't want to work for someone else long-term. The business had expanded, and I'd become well versed in finding and purchasing new merchandise licences for them to produce. I got good at spotting a gap in a market within a market. Often the licences had more than one interested party and you'd need to make yourself the most attractive buyer. Sometimes that came down to a really great dinner out with the CFO or a common love of Man U with the head of sales. I'd learned that business was about much more than numbers on a piece of paper, and that making and maintaining connections was key to staying ahead of the game. Fortunately, I loved that part of it: hearing new stories, learning new things.

Most of our products came from Bangladesh but sometimes, if we had a gap in production, we'd use smaller, UK-based factories to fulfil our orders. One of those companies was a manufacturer in the Midlands called Ray Allen. The son of the owner, Kevin Higgs, was a rep I knew well who'd helped us out many times by plugging a stock gap at short notice. We got on well. After Pete and Jonny sold up, I began thinking about next steps. I'd accumulated a lot of experience and been well paid, but I'd just watched two kids my age pocket £4 million each; it was time to start making some proper money for myself. When Kevin suggested he and I go into business together it was the perfect next move. He'd oversee manufacturing from his dad's factory in

Hinckley and I'd head up sales from London. I'd find the licences and he'd make the clothes, and we'd split the profits from the licences down the middle. I had a long list of contacts and Kevin's father had years of experience in manufacturing. What neither of us had was capital, but I knew a man who did.

In the wake of the Simple Truth, Jeffrey and I had become close friends. Close enough for me to be able to approach him about investment and, in July 1995, he agreed to put £400,000 into my new business with Kevin. Allen Hinckley Ltd was registered at Companies House, with Kevin and me as Company Directors. It was the culmination of the previous five years' work. I felt like the king of the world.

The scale of my ambition was best summed up by the fact I persuaded the freeholder of the offices we rented in Battersea to let us put our logo at the top of the whole building despite the fact we only leased one floor. I knew Maurice and Charles Saatchi had done the same in Berkeley Square, which should give you an idea of how I saw myself at the time. It was the Wizard of Oz trick all over again. For years after, I drove past that building with the logo still on it every day on the way to work. It would come to be an effective reminder of my errors.

As head of sales at Global, I knew everyone in the industry and had a good reputation. My speciality was children's licensing because we'd had the contracts for Warner Brothers and Disney. Children's licensing was pretty niche, so everyone knew everyone. Each year you'd meet the same faces at the same trade shows. Everyone was on the lookout for the next big thing and most had a story about the one that got away. Mine happened the day I went for a meeting at a dishevelled, ramshackle office in the cheapest district of New York to meet a man palpably hanging on by the skin of his teeth. We talked at length about how their brand was going to be revitalised but, from the looks of their offices and his obvious desperation, that seemed unlikely to be happening any time soon. I walked away from the meeting feeling pretty sorry for the guy. The company was obviously on its knees. On reflection, this episode was possibly the greatest lesson I could have had on how and why not to judge a book by its cover. That company would eventually morph into the multi-billion-dollar phenomenon that is now Marvel. At the time, I felt like you could have bought the entire franchise for a few million dollars.

Despite this miss, when the BBC went looking for a manufacturer to produce the merchandise for their newest kids' TV show, I was one of the people who got the call from Sarah at their commercial division. The show hadn't yet aired, and I got a courier package of some VHS tapes which I watched that morning over breakfast. By the time I left for the office, I knew there'd be competition for the contract and prepared to schmooze on a large scale. It was go big or go home, and I pulled every string I could. Fortunately, Sarah, like me, was a Formula 1 fan, so I knew exactly where to take her. When we took our seats that weekend at the European Grand Prix in Jerez, Andalucía, I knew the deal was as good as done. The loudness of the engines, however, made it the worst possible place to try and conduct a business meeting. On top of which, coming from Iraq, I found the whole thing pretty unnerving, sounding, as it did, exactly like endless rounds of mortar fire.

If I thought the Hypercolor licence was big, what was on the table now had the potential to blow it out of the water. In 1997, if you asked most under-fives what they wanted for Christmas, it was a Teletubby – the slightly trippy children's TV characters created by Anne Wood, owner of Ragdoll Productions. In March that year, the BBC had broadcast the first episode of this show, which would go on to run for nine series. Demand for merchandise outstripped production at a staggering rate, with many stores resorting to rationing purchases. I liked the show; it was clever and silly and my instinct was it would do well. I didn't know it would end up being the most lucrative show in BBC television's history, coining in over £1 billion in merchandise sales by the end of its run in 2001. Whoever won the licence for clothing merchandise would be set for life. Or so you'd think. Hasbro and Golden Bear had already signed for the toys and, that Monday, I signed up for everything else.

In layman's terms, *Teletubbies* was the biggest hit on earth. Sales were rolling in and I was sending the contracts up to Kevin in Hinckley for production. If we sold a million pyjamas at £9.99, we'd get 20 per cent of that £9,990,000, which we split down the middle with the BBC. It was a winning formula. But I also knew from my experience at Global that a successful business shouldn't rely on one fad if it wants sustained, long-term growth. So, despite the orders mounting up, I put my sales hat back on and started looking for new products to expand our offering. My schmoozing trip to the Grand Prix with Sarah had got me thinking about Bernie Ecclestone – the then CEO of the Formula One Group. F1 as a concept was a conglomeration of brands under one umbrella, but no one had capitalised on that umbrella. Each F1 team involved did their own thing to greater or lesser success, but Bernie had no ownership over the merchandising of his overall concept. It was a gap in a market that I thought we could fill.

As luck would have it, Bernie had not long sold his penthouse on the Embankment to Jeffrey, who'd then moved upstairs to the 14th floor. Jeffrey, as ever, was the perfect person to get me a meeting with Bernie and, as an investor in our company, he had a vested interest in doing so. My plan was to build a retail business around the F1 brand with Bernie and Jeffrey and, in addition, have Allen Hinckley own the licence for production, which we'd sell into other retailers such as BHS or M&S. Kevin and I chatted it over and I prepared to meet Bernie and Jeffrey with his blessing. If we did this right and added it to the *Teletubbies* contract, Allen Hinckley would be huge.

When we presented to Bernie, he liked the idea of a retail concept but said we'd have to convince Ferrari and McLaren too. Knowing we'd need more investment if we pulled this off, we went away and set up a shell company called A to Z, so we'd be ready to move if we got the green light. A to Z would form the retail arm and licence into Allen Hinckley. Sadly, Ferrari and McLaren did not feel the same way as Bernie. Neither company wanted to relinquish ownership of their own brand and the project failed to take off. A to Z, therefore, was now nothing more than a dormant company on the shelf at Companies House. Given how excited I'd been about the project, its failure to launch was a disappointment but not a problem, given the volume of sales we were doing on the *Teletubbies* licence. I put the idea to bed and chalked it up to experience.

EH-OH!

The success of the show had been so hard and fast, most manufacturers struggled to keep up with demand, so when I got the odd call from customers saying they'd had their order late or not had it at all, I thought things would iron themselves out. Kevin always had an answer for the delays and I trusted him. When he called to ask to meet in London, I had no idea there was anything wrong. When he told me we were in trouble, I thought he must be panicking under the pressure given the number of orders I'd brought in. When he told me we were losing money, I was dumbfounded. Surely that was impossible? Not, it turns out, if your cost base is too high. Not if every T-shirt you sell at £5 costs you £5.50. You do that a million times, and it's half a million quid down the drain straightaway. Unbeknown to me, this is exactly what was happening up at Hinckley. Worse still, the bank was about to foreclose on his father's factory and Kevin's suggestion was to ask Jeffrey for an additional £400,000 to save it. Given that he'd already given us close to a million in today's money, I was pretty reluctant to go back and ask for the same again.

The BBC had gone to manufacturers they believed could deliver, and Ray Allen's factories looked pretty decent when you went to visit. What I didn't see was a gaping hole in the basic fabric of the company. As with all competitive markets, retailers always pushed for lower prices and for us this meant trying to compete with imports from Bangladesh, which was nigh on impossible. When Kevin and I went into business it was the licensing end of things we shared. He retained ownership of his father's factories when his dad retired and kept 100 per cent of that income. What Kevin had inherited, however, was a fundamentally flawed model – a business with a margin too narrow to function. Jonny's grandfather, Marcus Sieff, had once come to visit us at Global and I took the advice he gave us at face value. 'If you have the sales, you can pay for everything else.' Kevin and I had no shortage of orders so I'd assumed we were doing well, but I'd made the fatal error of making a judgement on faith rather than evidence, and this was my undoing. Running a business, I realised, was not the same as being the head of sales. If you're not watching the bottom line, you're buggered.

Considering the length of time Kevin's father had been in business, it seems unlikely to me now that he did not realise his company was in trouble before we met. I'd like to think, however, he was in the same situation as my dad had been with Aubrey C. Briggs, hoping to fix things on the never never; that he'd thought he could bring in enough money to right the ship. If not, I must entertain the idea his subterfuge was intentional and that I was purposely used to prop up a failing business – which I'd really prefer not to believe. The fact was, his miscalculations meant *I* was now in the same situation as my dad had been. On top of the immediate practicalities, the situation was overlayed with a sort of PTSD from my teens when we'd lost our home. For all the issues I'd had with my dad losing his money; for all the questions I'd wanted to ask him; for all the ways I'd doubted his capacity at the time, here I was now in the same situation. Just like dad, I'd believed my partner was taking care of his end of the deal. That he was operating to the same moral code as me. Just like him, I'd taken investment from a friend and my reputation was now on the line and my integrity in danger of being called into question. Just like him, I was naive not to check these things for myself. I wanted to do exactly what he'd done and hide under the covers. Sadly, there was no time because things were about to get worse.

When I refused to approach Jeffrey for more money, Kevin's attitude changed pretty quickly and the situation went from stressful to weird. The atmosphere between him and me was now distinctly chilly, and I was in the unenviable position of having to try and repair the company with his help. What I wanted to do was walk away, but it wasn't just my money on the line. On one level we were lucky it didn't belong to the bank, but on another it was worse: it belonged to a friend, and the most intrusive, sickening feeling of guilt weighed me down as I left Kevin that day and called Jeffrey to ask to talk.

I knew there was no point in sugar-coating the pill for him. The fact he was an experienced businessman who'd invested at his own risk did absolutely nothing to lessen the feeling of shame I felt when I walked out of the elevator and into his penthouse the next morning. When I told him what had happened he asked to see Kevin, who arrived the following day with his wife. When they spoke about their financial troubles and asked Jeffrey to invest more to try and salvage things, Jeffrey was sympathetic and handled things very sensitively. But when Kevin accused me of mismanagement and of having been distracted by the F1 venture, things took a different turn. Jeffrey knew what Kevin was accusing me of wasn't true and had my back. When we left the meeting that day, I knew we'd reached the end of the line. I felt I'd tried my best to hold things together but the dissolution of good faith between Kevin and me made things completely untenable. I had to face the fact that my first business venture was a failure. I'd done exactly what I'd seen my dad do all those years ago and put my trust in the wrong person.

That night, as I flicked through the television channels, *Glengarry Glen Ross* appeared on my screen. As Jack Lemmon stood in the pouring rain, doing his best to hang on to the sale that would save his job, I suddenly felt the weight of what was happening wash over me and it knocked me off my feet. Now I understood what Jack felt and what my father must have felt, because here I was going through it myself. The stakes were high and the fallout huge. It didn't matter whose fault it was; I was the one who'd asked Jeffrey to invest and I was the one who didn't check the bottom line or do my due diligence. I was the one who felt sick to my stomach knowing that what was to come was out of my control.

It was clear to me now that we were as good as bankrupt and I suggested we declared voluntary insolvency. The Insolvency Office take a very dim view of things if you don't deal with declaring voluntarily. As far as they're concerned, you make a mess, you clear it up. If they have to put their own people on your case, it's their time and money, and if they think you've behaved irresponsibly, you can be struck off as a director. Apart from the obvious, this was not something I wanted on my record for two very good reasons. A few years before, Jeffrey had encouraged me to stand for local council and I'd won the seat for Wandsworth. In eight months' time I was due to stand for a second term, then run as a candidate in the General Election as MP for Erith and Thamesmead the following year. Being struck off would have seen the end of my political career before it had even started. The stumbling block now was that Kevin wanted his own accountants to provide the documentation, but the atmosphere between us was such that I no longer trusted him or them to do it properly and so refused.

From that moment on we were at loggerheads, and in the end it was fought out – needlessly, and at great expense – by lawyers; in my case, paid for by my dad. The accusations of mismanagement were thrown out but the process was horrendous and extremely traumatic. On top of that, the embarrassment of letting my friend down was something that stayed with me for many, many years. In time, Jeffrey would make a lot of money from another investment I brought to the table, but it took until then for me to feel my debt was paid.

The silver lining of this 'failure' was that it helped me reconcile myself to the way my dad had behaved during his own business troubles. I saw first hand how a person could become so desperate to save something that they'd do anything to try and avoid admitting defeat. It had been more than a decade since Aubrey C. Briggs had come into our lives, and I'd walked into exactly the same situation and exposed myself in exactly the same way. In many ways, Dad and I were quite different characters but what I took from the experience was that we were both victims of our own naivety. Our tendency to want to see the best in others was genetic. When he got himself back on his feet, Dad worked for a range of huge multinationals and saw up close the scale of due diligence carried out in those set-ups. From then on he applied the same stringent checks to his own endeavours. He never made me feel bad or questioned me about my error in judgement because he'd done the same thing himself. He knew what was happening was more than enough of a lesson. He didn't need to rub my nose in it.

I'd entered into Allen Hinckley with the belief I had the necessary skills to run a business. It wasn't until after it failed that I really understood the difference between being the boss and being an employee. If you're the person who goes home at night and worries about other people's wages or whether you can service a loan, it's a very different experience. I felt like I'd been naive, but I suppose now I'd be kinder to myself and say I was inexperienced. As my dad would tell me, you don't learn everything in life all at once, but when the stakes are high, you do learn very quickly.

CHAPTER 14

A SENTIMENTAL JOURNEY

THE ART OF DIPLOMACY

One of the many things Jeffrey knew was that, if you were going to get involved in charity work, you'd better make sure the financial set-up was squeaky clean. Even the mighty Geldof was wrongly pilloried over the supposed misuse of money after Live Aid. Fundraising on a grand scale was not as easy as it looked. So when Jeffrey embarked on the Simple Truth campaign in 1991, rather than set up a standalone charity he made sure all funds went directly to the Red Cross and UN, thus circumventing any other bank account. How could he be accused of any wrongdoing if he didn't touch the money? Well, I'll tell you …

The problems really began when Jeffrey stood in front of the world's press with a giant novelty cheque for £57 million to show off the total raised in the name of the campaign. It would later transpire this figure had been somewhat massaged, though not, as some might secretly have hoped, by Jeffrey. However, when he was convicted ten years later for perjury and perverting the course of justice during his libel case against the *Daily Star*, over allegations that he slept with a prostitute called Monica Coghlan, it understandably rekindled press interest in the topic of Jeffrey, his money and his morals, and a formal investigation was launched. The net result was an additional two weeks for him in a Category A prison while they looked into the complaint.

After two years, during which time Jeffrey's name was dragged through the mud, the head of International Aid at the Red Cross, Patrick Healey, admitted it was the charity's own 'junior and inexperienced' staff who had unintentionally pulled together an inflated total for the appeal.* The much-talked-about £57 million was, in fact, a conflated number drawn from a variety of sources and filed collectively under 'The Kurds'. When dissected, only about a quarter of that figure came from Jeffrey's campaign. When asked whether there'd been a cover-up by the charity, Healey said, 'It was a cock-up followed by a cover-up. But it wasn't seen as a cover-up. It was seen as the Red Cross not wanting to jeopardise on-going fundraising.'† In other words, it was good PR for the cause and so they rolled with it. Finally, in 2012, an audit by KPMG on behalf of the British Red Cross found 'no evidence of misappropriation' and Jeffrey was cleared of any wrong-doing.‡ Sadly, none of this matters now: ask anyone about the work he did for the Kurds and it rarely comes without this unpalatable footnote.

Did Jeffrey take that inflated figure and run with it? Almost certainly. It was £9 million more than Geldof raised and Jeffrey loved winning. He was also in the business of selling a cause. Of that £57 million, only around £3 million came from the concert itself. I say 'only', but that's still a staggering amount to have generated in the space of an evening. Would the American and British governments have put up their additional

---

* https://www.telegraph.co.uk/news/uknews/1335019/Charity-cover-up-over-Archers-missing-57m.html.

† Ibid.

‡ https://www.standard.co.uk/hp/front/archer-cleared-after-charity-probe-6335523.html.

£10 million each anyway? Probably, but that's easy to say in retrospect. The fact was, without Jeffrey, there *was* no campaign. When he set up the Simple Truth he knew it would be no different from any other venture; if he couldn't sell the product, the company wouldn't stand up – however worthy the cause. So if Jeffrey put a bit of a spin on things to get it off the ground, I'm okay with that. In my experience there are far more people willing to sit commenting on the sidelines than ones prepared to get up and act, and Jeffrey put his life and soul into the project.

A year after the concert Broosk, Jeffrey and I were off to Kurdistan to see how the money from the fundraiser was being used. Armed only with M&S thermals and thick socks, we embarked on the journey with huge buoyancy and goodwill but wholly unprepared to tackle the press backlash. The money Jeffrey raised had been added to what the Red Cross and UN were *already* doing in Kurdistan, and we should have been clear that this was a trip to see how *they* were spending it. Not us. There was no standalone pot of cash sitting in somebody's safe that we could hand over to the Kurdish leaders struggling to feed their troops. If Jeffrey made a mistake, it was that he didn't disabuse anyone of that fact. He had no access to or control over any money, so when we arrived empty-handed, it felt like the cavalry had turned up without their horses. Relief work happens slowly and systematically, but with no representative from either the UN or the Red Cross in our party, Jeffrey was the face of the campaign and the only one there to try and answer questions. He did a great thing for the Kurds, but his naivety around the expectations and complexities of such a large-scale appeal bit him on the behind. Hard. As ever, Jeffrey's ethos was 'let them talk'. As long he was helping the Kurds, he let the noise wash over him. It was simply not in his nature to be held back by negativity. I see myself as a very positive person, but in this scenario I was the Piglet to his Tigger; his ability to shrug things off and bounce back was awe-inspiring.

TWO TRIBES

It was the ruling Kurdish political parties in Iraq who eventually invited us to come out and see things on the ground. The West was looking to help 'the Kurds', but there were two very different factions under that umbrella. Jointly they were now in control of their homeland in the northern part of Iraq, which was itself divided in two. The Barzani tribe, led by Masoud Barzani, ran the Kurdistan Democratic Party (KDP), which bordered Turkey to the north and Syria to the west. The Talabani family, led by Jalal Talabani, controlled the Patriotic Union of Kurdistan (PUK), which sat to the east, bordering Iran.

Political differences between these two families had meant many divisions and rivalries over the years. In broad terms, the KDP were right-leaning and the PUK, left. Just as with British politics, it was rare for the two sides to agree, and not long after we left a full-scale civil war broke out between them. So although we were there to support the Kurds in their fight against Saddam, the atmosphere between the two parties was not without its own tensions. We walked into an extremely sensitive and potentially volatile situation, and the floor creaked audibly with every delicate step we took.

I thought I understood what had happened to the Kurds but nothing could have prepared me for what we'd encounter on the trip, and I'm sure Jeffrey and Broosk felt the same. It was mentally and physically stressful in a way I'd never previously experienced. If the three of us were friends before we left, we were family by the time we returned home. Visiting the territory in the aftermath of war was nothing like living through it, but, up close, you couldn't escape the devastation. There was no looking away. It was like second-hand trauma and has never really left me. I imagine it's what aid workers must be faced with on a daily basis, and I take my hat off to them.

OUR PARTY

Our trip would take a week, with two and a half days as the guests of each party. In all, we were a group of about twenty-five, including journalists from all the major papers, the BBC and ITN. From London we'd also brought Hoshyar Zebari – the KDP representative who'd secured my telegram the year before – and in Turkey we picked up one more Kurd – Shahzad Saib. As well as being Broosk's uncle, Shahzad was the PUK representative from what was effectively the Kurdish consulate in Ankara. Our travelling companion from the *Guardian* was John Vidal. I liked John, but his dispatches home always seemed to delight in the negative rather than the positives of the trip. Jeffrey, he wrote, had a 'self-selected investigative team' to help search for the money and it was clear John was unimpressed with what he believed to be Jeffrey's choices.* Broosk and I were painted as two public school boys 'rapidly going native carrying Kalashnikovs',† while Jeffrey was the self-important, wealthy buffoon desperately trying and failing to fall in with the indigenous troops. There was also a doctor whose daughter and son-in-law had been murdered the year before, on a mission to try and find their killers, and 'a distinguished Georgian archaeologist who wanted to study ancient funerary transcriptions',‡ whom

* https://www.theguardian.com/uk/2001/jul/26/iraq.archer.

† Ibid.

‡ Ibid.

Broosk repeatedly assured me was an MI6 spy.* Vidal's spin on the group made us sound less like a party of well-intentioned volunteers than the self-absorbed, elite cast of an Agatha Christie novel just waiting to be tripped up by their own foibles. Like Jeffrey, Vidal had his own story to sell.

In fact, other than Broosk and me, Jeffrey had not chosen anyone in our entourage. Each was someone already in contact with the Kurds, tagging along with their own agenda. Kurdistan was hardly tourist territory at this point, so if its leaders were going to transport three visitors 4,000 feet up a mountain in treacherous weather, they might as well take twenty-five and get them all out of the way in one go.

Vidal's snide suggestion that everyone in Jeffrey's entourage was 'unsure what was going on' was correct. No one – including the rest of the journalists, the Kurds or John Vidal himself – had a firm grasp of things. How could they? The situation in the region was incredibly volatile, with in-fighting and backbiting just as common as attacks from Saddam's forces. Our journey was punctuated by constant stops to reassess and renegotiate with the Kurdish soldiers along our route. Every step of our journey had to be checked and re-checked lest we inadvertently set off any hidden politically explosive element – of which there were many. The atmosphere was so charged with tension you felt like every corner of mountain road might bring another surprise. We were all doing our best to feel our way in the dark, John included.

THE JOURNEY

We'd flown from London to Ankara and from there to Diyarbakir – the closest airport to the Kurdish region of Iraq. A fleet of taxis

* Ibid.

took us towards Zakho to meet our Kurdish hosts at the border. The drive from Diyarbakir in Turkey to Zakho in Iraq was the single-most hair-raising experience of my life, and I include in that a trip I'd take some years later to the frontline on the outskirts of Mosul with my friend Rory Stewart and the Peshmerga – Kurdistan's military force in Iraq.

It was a three-hour journey that should have taken five, given the distance and appalling weather. Jeffrey, Broosk and I were in one car and the rest of our party split between additional taxis bringing up the rear. I have no idea how they found their journeys but I had multiple concerns about ours – the biggest of which was a road liberally strewn with fuel oil. There was a huge amount of black-market activity between Turkey and Iraq at the time. Smugglers would come in with containers packed with cigarettes and return with tankers full of cheap fuel. The Kurds took a cut as the tankers crossed the border and did their best to make a living that way in the absence of a normal income. The trouble was, it's one thing to carry thousands of packets of cigarettes in a makeshift container welded to the bottom of an articulated lorry, and quite another to try and transport flammable liquid in the same way. With every trip, these DIY extensions leaked gradually but persistently onto the roads below. Driving on them in a taxi at high speed was like being on an ice rink, but one that could engulf you in flames if you were unlucky enough to hit anything. It didn't quieten my nerves to learn that these were some of the most dangerous stretches of road in Turkey. In fact, this was exactly how and where Broosk's PUK Uncle Shahzad would die a decade later.

To add to the tension, our driver spoke no Arabic, Kurdish or English – which exhausted my repertoire – and drove at around 90 mph irrespective of conditions, traffic or road width. Jeffrey had a front-row seat and I wondered whether he was actually going to have a heart attack but was too frightened myself to worry. It was every man for himself. Not ordinarily known for the habit, I nevertheless spent the entire journey praying, while Jeffrey repeatedly slammed his fists onto the dashboard and called out from the depths of his soul for the driver to slow down. His shouts were met with a jaunty 'Okay, okay,' and no slowing of pace. The driver's only job was to get us to the border and bugger off as quickly as possible, which is exactly what I'd have wanted to do in his shoes. The roads were still hotly disputed and I imagine fear was a regular part of his day-to-day job. He wasn't in the business of allaying anyone else's.

THE WRONG KIND OF SNOW

When we reached the border we transferred into the hands of the Peshmerga. They drove us to the north bank of a shallow river where a fleet of white Toyota Land Cruisers surrounded the car of Masoud Barzani on the opposite side. As if choreographed and timed with our arrival, the convey pulled off in unison and drove dramatically through the waters towards us, coming to a halt in a perfect line. One by one the Peshmerga got out until finally their leader stood at the centre. Physically very small and quietly spoken, Masoud had an understated authority about him. In fact he was quite Zen-like. He dressed, like most Peshmerga, in combat uniform – just like Ukraine's Volodymyr Zelenskyy – khaki-coloured Kurdish sharwall and shirt with the signature Barzani red-and-white turban. It was easy to tell the two families apart because the Talibani head gear was white and black. The war may have been officially over but, as far as anyone living there was concerned, it was still all to play for. Masoud was a high-value target for the Iraqis and his presence at our meeting put him at significant risk. I was in no doubt how privileged we were to be standing in front of him. I'd lived in the UK for about fourteen years now, but an overwhelming sense of pride flooded through me. I knew I was Kurdish, but coming face to face with their leader and his army for the first time, I suddenly felt it.

It was too dangerous for Masoud to travel with us so he assigned his twenty-five-year-old nephew, Nechervan, to take care of us instead. Nechervan was confident, charming and charismatic – someone you instinctively felt would go far. Jeffrey nicknamed him 'The Movie Star' on account of his looks. I was not surprised when he was eventually elected both prime minister and then president of the Kurdistan regional government some years later. His father and grandfather had dedicated their lives to fighting for Kurdish freedom and he was doing the same. For now, though, he'd be our chaperone. With him was another of Masoud's nephews – and Broosk's childhood friend from Baghdad – Sirwan Barzani. All in all, I felt like we were in much safer hands than the ones we'd just left.

Now we were in Iraq, however, in many ways it was out of the frying pan and into the fire. As we made our way to the mountains, the signs of a territory still in dispute were clearly visible. There were constant threats and skirmishes – particularly along supply routes on which the Kurds still depended for food and aid. We swapped our kamikaze taxi driver for a convoy equipped with truck-mounted Soviet machine guns manned by Peshmergas. Each time we stopped, the guards at the back of the convoy would switch to stop their hands freezing onto the handles of the guns. Bombed-out bridges were navigated with the help of two sets of Peshmerga – one on either side. Burnt-out tanks peppered the roadside, no doubt with their dead still inside, and mounted machine guns sat at intervals along the track in constant readiness for an attack. As we passed more guards and more armoury, you realised you weren't just driving down Kurdish roads; you were driving along the frontline.

It quickly became apparent that this was a no-frills kind of trip, but trying to help Broosk balance over a ditch in his tailored Turnbull & Asser jacket behind a piece of corrugated iron while he did his best to go to the toilet summed things up nicely. In Zakho, we camped at an ex-military base in sleeping bags next to gaping holes in the walls where the heating units had been ripped out by the Iraqi army. In Dihok, we were lucky enough to stay at the home of the leader of the Doski tribe, who graciously re-located his wife and children upstairs so our entourage could sleep on the floors downstairs. We could have washed at the sinks in some places but it was far too cold to undress. The best bet was to sleep fully clothed under your coat and hope you weren't frozen to death in the morning.

Just outside Dihok, it was clear that Jeffrey was coming down with a serious bout of the flu. Despite the freezing conditions he spent most of the time sweating furiously with a temperature that hovered worryingly around 40 degrees. Jeffrey is renowned for his positivity; if something is negative or wrong, he simply refuses to discuss it. This included his being unwell, and Broosk and I were forbidden to tell anyone he was ill, journalists in particular. This was the Kurdish frontline and the Kurds don't do weak. He didn't want to be perceived as falling behind or for anyone to accuse him of being a slacker. For my part, I was acutely aware this was a war zone, which meant no easily accessible hospitals or medical assist-ance in an emergency. I didn't care if Jeffrey looked weak; I just didn't want to find myself 4,000 feet up a mountain with a corpse. I was thirty years younger than he was and even I was finding the trip backbreaking. When we finally arrived at a tiny converted guest house in Saladin for a press conference, I felt like we'd arrived at The Dorchester and breathed a massive sigh of relief.

There was a bed and running water and I temporarily stopped worrying Jeffrey was going to die in the night.

Everywhere we went, our biggest obstacle was the snow. I'd been on holiday to the mountains many times as a child, and in the spring they were beautiful. In the snow, however, they were perilous, and 1992 was the coldest winter in over twenty years. There were peaks and valleys and twists and turns that meant it would come out of nowhere and surprise you. Sometimes we'd be lucky, and the Peshmerga would be able to reach us from the opposite direction and dig us out, and sometimes they couldn't and we'd have to turn back. All this was exacerbated each time we came face to face with an articulated lorry coming down in the other direction on its way back to the border with its contraband. The snow was definitely the 'wrong' kind of snow and slowed our every move to a snail's pace.

Just outside Zakho, on a mountain pass en route to Erbil, we were brought to a resounding halt by a seven foot wall of it. I'd never seen anything like it. This wasn't holiday snow or like being stuck in the Alps where you'd have equipment and assistance readily to hand. This was a 200-foot drop and black ice. But, as far as the Peshmerga were concerned, this was normal. It's what they did every day. The Kurds, they say, have no friends but the mountains, and it was obvious this was just another day at the office for the Pesh. They were brilliant. Jeffrey did his best to rally the troops, and everyone, including the journalists, was expected to join in and dig. If the press didn't like him before, they liked him even less after that. Their dispatches implied he was resented by the Peshmerga but quite the opposite was true. No one wanted to shovel snow and I'm sure there were grumbles, but that would have been the case with or without Jeffrey. I think they were intrigued by this little Englishman in his blue puffer jacket doing his best to boost morale. He was an eccentric curiosity, but I never had the sense they didn't want him there.

QUSHTAPA

We were treated with great respect and the utmost courtesy every-where we went, but there was no getting round what had happened to the Kurds. It was an apocalyptic landscape. Before the war, the region had been dotted with small, self-sufficient farms and holdings; people living incredibly rural, archaic, basic lives. Hamlets with their own ecosystems and infrastructure – some with as few as twenty or thirty houses – almost untouched by the modern world. As we drove from place to place now, all we saw were burnt or bombed-out villages, sometimes with a cluster of tents pitched on top of the rubble, where people had returned to their homes after the ceasefire to try and rebuild their lives.

Saddam's strategy was that if you burn the villages, people will have to move into towns and cities where you can more easily control or, better still, kill them. Many Kurds were moved south to Basra and, in turn, some Arabs were moved north in an attempt to dilute the ethnic concentration. In total more than 3,000 Kurdish villages were torched and 180,000 Kurds killed in Saddam's 'Arabisation' programme. But they were used to being attacked. The mountains were riddled with caves and hideouts because the Kurds had always been a people who refused to be occupied or integrate, and they knew how to defend themselves. As soon as they took back control of their territory, many of those displaced returned, but the villages they came back to were now refugee camps with no proper heat, light or sanitation, with some housing thousands of people. The only thing they did have was fresh water because of the rivers and streams in the moun-tains. It was a silver lining in an otherwise bleak landscape.

The house on the corner.

A delegation from the Central Bank of Iraq to meet the UK chancellor, Rab Butler, *c.*1954, led by the governor of the bank, Dr Abdullillah Hafidh (far left with cigar), accompanied by my grandfather (two seats down), who would later take over the role.

My grandfather Nadhim Zahawi Sr (centre), head of the Iraqi delegation to the meeting in Baghdad for the creation of OPEC.

Mum and Dad on their wedding
day, 21 March 1963.

Dad, Jihan and me (in traditional
Kurdish head cap), Kurdistan.

Me and Auntie Farida,
Kurdistan.

School photo. I'm back left
in the stripy top.

Broosk and Lana, Cairo.

Joe Cool?

The girl I fell in love with.

The Zahawis and the Saibs
before they became one.

On stage at Wembley Arena, reading out KDP leader Masoud Barzani's telegram at the Simple Truth benefit gig, 1991.

At a press conference with Jeffrey Archer, Masoud Barzani and Hoshyar Zebari.

With Sirwan Barzani at the Qushtapa camp, 1992.

With Lady Thatcher and Broosk at Jeffrey and Mary
Archer's silver wedding celebrations, 1991.

Conservative Party candidate for
Erith and Thamesmead, 1996.

At Westminster with Lady Thatcher
when I was selected for Stratford-
on-Avon, 2010.

With Jeffrey and Denis Thatcher at one of
Jeffrey's garden parties in the early 90s.

My 'Institutional Memory' education secretary dinner, 2021.

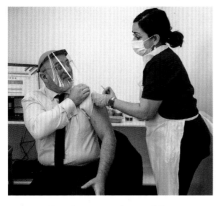

Getting vaccinated by
Nikki Kanani, March 2021.

Holding a press conference as
vaccines minister, 2021.

Leaving Downing Street after
becoming chancellor, July 2022.

Boris is late again for an official
cabinet photo, July 2022.

In the prime minister's office, discussing
the Queen's illness, September 2022.

The Queen's funeral,
19 September 2022.

With Lana and the boys.

Lana, the star at the
centre of my universe.

My little team.

Despite the widespread destruction, Jeffrey drew crowds of people everywhere we went. Rain, snow, freezing winds: it didn't matter. He was the guy who'd put their name on the map. They cheered and chanted and held up banners to welcome 'Sir Jeffrey' and Barzani. It was difficult to judge numbers because the rallies were mainly outside, often with people as far as the eye could see. At times, I'd guess there must have been up to 60,000 people.

When we got to Qushtapa about half an hour south of Erbil, there was something different about the people that came to meet us. Virtually every single one of them was female. In this village, all the men were either dead or missing, presumed dead.

As far as Saddam was concerned, the Barzanis were the leaders of the Kurdish revolution and, as such, a major pain in his behind. He'd already destroyed many villages and pushed the displaced Kurds into camps, but in 1983 he went a step further. Ba'athist soldiers marched into areas that housed displaced Barzani families near Erbil and even Baghdad, and abducted between 5,000 to 8,000 men. Unless you were too small to walk, you were taken. A generation of men and boys gone and never seen again. Everyone in Iraq knew this story, but if you were Kurdish it was even more resonant, a testament to how barbaric and clinical a tyrant Saddam could be. It was ethnic cleansing, pure and simple.

As soon as we arrived at Qushtapa, the legacy of what he'd done was brought into sharp relief by the thousands of women who crowded to meet us. Each one held aloft a photo of a missing loved one. Many thrust pieces of paper into our hands with their names scrawled in ink. This wasn't an exercise in nostalgia; they were still holding out hope these men might be found and found alive, but not one ever was. Years later, mass graves were discovered and tales would be told of how others were melted down in baths of acid, but at the time these women still held out hope that the future would include their men. Our KDP companion, Sirwan Barzani, was still a young child when I'd left Iraq. He'd brought us to Qushtapa now to tell us the story of what had happened to him as a boy. Sirwan had the bittersweet honour of being one of the only male survivors of the Barzani cull.

When Saddam's troops arrived at his Baghdad home in 1983, he was eight years old. His father was a very senior member of the Barzani tribe and guards told him he was being taken for questioning. Other men, in other locations, were told they were being taken to work labouring for the day and would return home that evening. Sirwan hung on to his father's jacket and begged to go too, and, after tears were produced, his father relented. Along with many other male members of the tribe in many other villages, his father got into a waiting vehicle and was driven away. The guard next to Sirwan in the back of their car stared at him persistently. Eventually, without warning, he reached across, opened the door of the moving car and pushed Sirwan out into the road. As he lay in the dust, his father's shouts echoed in the silence as they continued on without him. Covered in blood and several miles from home, Sirwan managed to make his way back to the house. His arrival was a clear signal something dreadful was amiss, but all the family could do was wait. Just as with the other villages Saddam had attacked, none of the men came home that evening, nor the next day, nor the one after that. On the third day, more troops arrived and took all the women – as well as Sirwan – to a place called Qushtapa, where they stayed, confined by a barbed-wire fence, for the next twelve years. A building in the middle of the village housed the Iraqi army, who'd throw sacks of tea, sugar and flour into the compound. Qushtapa was not a refugee camp; it was a concentration camp. The women left behind built schools and everything needed to raise any children left. No one ever explained what had happened to their men.

Even after the Kurds were liberated, most of the women stayed on in Qushtapa. They had nowhere else to go. As we stood that day on the site of these events, I asked Sirwan why he thought the man had let him go that day. 'I don't know,' he said, 'maybe my eyes reminded him of his own son, or he thought I was too young to be melted down.' As Jeffrey, Broosk and I stood in this same village, I turned to look behind me at the young girls standing guard on the roof: some with guns, one with a rocket launcher. It was impossible to rationalise what had happened to Sirwan and his fellow Barzanis, but the really frightening thing was how events like this had been absorbed into the fabric of the region, normalised even. My family had left the country only four years before Qushtapa and I'd adjusted to the freedoms of the West, but nothing had changed for the people we'd left behind. At the end of the week I'd get to go home, but for them this was real life. I realised that for my generation of Kurds, there was no such thing as a childhood if you'd stayed in Iraq.

ANYONE FOR SECONDS?

For the next stage of our journey, the KDP would take us to see their office before handing us over to the PUK at theirs. From there, Jalal Talabani would be waiting at their mountain head-quarters for our arrival at the appointed time with a lunch to welcome us. Without telling anyone, the KDP had mischievously laid on their own welcome party – a lunch and rally at *their* own HQ. Etiquette dictated we couldn't ignore the KDP supporters or the party's hospitality. Added to that, we were all starving and it didn't take much to persuade everyone to tuck in. Jeffrey took a seat with the journalists, and Broosk and I sat a little further down the table. No sooner had I put a fork to my lips than a figure clad in black appeared at my side like an omen. He didn't need to speak for me to gather whatever he was going to say was not going to be good. 'Mam Jalal,' he said, was expecting us 'now', which I interpreted as a polite way of saying we needed to round everyone up and get in the cars immediately. I put down my food, sidled up to Jeffrey as discreetly as possible and gave him the news. Predictably, he had no intention of being rude to our current hosts and said we'd finish our meal first, so I sloped off back to my seat.

Half an hour later and the representative was back. Now he was cross. The PUK commander, Kosrat Rasul – or the Strongman of Erbil, as he was otherwise known – was waiting to receive us in his office to take us on to Jalal and was now officially very hacked off. I sensed we were on the brink of a diplomatic incident and did my best to convey this in the tone of my voice when I returned to Jeffrey. Kosrat is a lovely guy under more relaxed circumstances, but I also knew he was a soldier with multiple military victories under his belt and a reputation for being hard as nails. I certainly didn't want to be the one to tell him we were just starting on dessert and could he give us another hour or so. Jeffrey assured me we were nearly done and I returned, once again, to my seat.

After ten more minutes, the Milk Tray Man reappeared by my side with the news that, since we were now an hour late for our meeting, Rasul was cancelling the entire second leg of our trip. This was clearly a code red and we were back in the cars within ten minutes. When we finally got to Kosrat's office he had steam coming out of his ears and a gun on the table. I reasoned with myself that this was normal in a war zone, but it did little to lower the temperature. Just when it looked like things were about to fall apart, our secret weapon kicked in: Jeffrey turned on the charm, apologised profusely for our inadvertent rudeness and managed to calm the waters. Nevertheless, there was still another hour's drive into the mountains to meet Jalal and, by the time we arrived, the sun was setting and the scheduled lunch had morphed into a dinner. But Kurds are wonderful hosts and, as we sat facing one another at the long table over our meal, the almost-incident seemed entirely forgotten. Good food and wine, I realised, went a long way in matters of diplomacy.

Jalal Talabani was a famously urbane and articulate international politician. While Masoud operated with a translator and my limited Kurdish, with Jalal we spoke English. He was extremely polished. Several years later he came to the UK and asked Jeffrey to arrange a meeting with the now retired Margaret Thatcher. Although John Major was by then PM, Jalal still wanted to meet the great lady, and Jeffrey and I went along with him to her home in Belgravia. Jeffrey and I sat to one side on a little sofa while these two powerhouses sat opposite one another, Frost–Nixon style. I'd met Margaret the year before at Jeffrey and Mary's anniversary party, but this was my first time in her presence as a leader, albeit a retired one. She was phenomenal. She delivered a lecture on Middle Eastern and Iraqi politics that would rival T. E. Lawrence. When it came to the Kurds and their tribal nuances, not a beat was missed. I don't know whether she was just well briefed or had a genuine understanding of the topic, but she spoke for an hour and a half with passion and confidence. And Talabani's no wall-flower. He's known in Iraq as a larger-than-life personality, but even he was put in the shade by her. They called her the greatest prime minister of her century and I'd just seen why first hand. There were many fantastic things I witnessed as Jeffrey's bag carrier, but this was up there with the best of them.

Our time with the PUK was even more covert than it had been with the KDP and most of our meetings were in secret or at night.

At the end of our two and a half days, we were transferred back into the hands of the KDP in Sulaymaniyah and the lovely Nechervan was once again assigned to accompany us to the border. Dusk was the safest time to travel and we left as the sun dipped behind the mountains. Not long after we set off, Nechervan got word the Iraqi army were coming the other way on the same road and planning an attack on our convoy. Without fuss, he dropped off the road and down onto a dirt track that ran along the river bank.

It was by now pitch black and we were on an unlit stretch of land, with God knows what up ahead. We all knew the war was still fluid but this was a definite shift in the tone of our journey. Before now, the only time Broosk or I had held a gun was to have our photo taken with one in a pathetic attempt to look macho. There'd never been any suggestion we'd ever have to use one. Tonight was different. The Peshmerga switched from hosts to soldiers in a matter of seconds and routinely offered the three of us a Kalashnikov each. Jeffrey point-blank refused to take one. 'Absolutely not. I've never handled a gun and don't intend to now,' but Broosk and I both took the weapon and awaited further instruction. Those instructions were pretty succinct. 'If someone shoots at you, shoot back.' Introduction to Firearms was a shorter class than I'd have liked but there was no time for anything more. Up until then, what we'd clearly been watching was the Peshmerga on alert, and now they were kicking into action. Even second-hand the adrenalin rush was instant, and I suddenly understood those stories where a woman lifts a car off her injured child or a man outruns a tiger in the jungle. I'll never know how I would have reacted had we come face to face with Saddam's army because the Pesh knew the terrain inside out and we managed to avoid an engagement, but it gave me a brief sense of what it must be like to live on your nerves. In terms of stress, that journey along that river bank ran a close second to the one from the airport, but of course we still had that to look forward to again on the way back ...

In 1992, I was twenty-five years old: two years earlier I'd been selling T-shirts at the *Clothes Show Live*. Now, somehow, I found myself in the middle of a war-torn landscape in the hands of the oldest tribes in the Middle East at the side of one of the most recognised politicians in the UK under the microscope of the global press. The trip was a masterclass in the art of diplomacy. You put a foot wrong, you lost your head. From a political point of view Kurdistan was not yet a functioning democracy, but what we witnessed were the embryonic days of its formation and it was fascinating to see close-up. A new nation was emerging and we were there at its inception. The tribes that turned out military leaders passionate enough about their homeland to fight for it bare-handed, morphed into political parties with enough skill and stamina to create an imperfect, but nevertheless functioning, government. Seeing the force of personalities at play and the depth of feeling in their beliefs was enough to make me want to achieve something with my life that went beyond the everyday humdrum of making money. It was such a visceral and levelling experience that it was hard to see life in the same terms as before. Now I found myself thinking about what I wanted to leave behind. From the teenage girls we met in Erbil who formed their own female regiment to the leadership skills of Masoud and Talabani, none of these people were what you'd call 'normal'. In one way or another, they were all people whose stories would find their way into the history books.

There are many pieces in the press that will tell you how badly Jeffrey managed his interactions with the Kurds or how insensitive he was around the intricacies of tribal customs and rivalries, but there are not many politicians who'd make a trip like that and handle it with as much chutzpah. I also doubt there are many Westerners so well versed in the nuances of Middle Eastern tribal history that they themselves wouldn't have put a foot wrong in the same circumstances. It was a very good lesson in how even the purest of efforts can be misconstrued if the media want to spin it that way. From where I was standing right next to him, I thought Jeffrey did a great job. I think I'm right in saying he was the only politician – or Westerner for that matter – with any real clout to visit Kurdistan in the aftermath of Saddam's attacks, and I certainly didn't see anyone else offering to do it.

The trip was a mind-blowing gear change for a kid who could easily have ended up spending his days kicking the can down the street with the other dropouts at the pub. When I look at photographs of myself on that trip, I can see the lack of experience in my face. I look like a boy. But I also see a strand of fearlessness. I'd been given an opportunity and I took it. I had no idea what it might entail, but I knew I liked the feeling of risk. Perhaps I was more like my dad than I'd wanted to admit? I don't know whether it was naivety or just the blind confidence of youth that carried me through Kurdistan that winter; I imagine a bit of both. I was out of my depth but oddly invigorated by it all. I liked the feeling of sitting next to Jeffrey and Masoud at a press conference and knowing that I was part of the equation. That people were relying on me to make a difference. I had no idea how I'd weave this sensation into my everyday life, but I was now in no doubt that's what I wanted to do.

PART THREE
TO WESTMINSTER

CHAPTER 15
A TOE IN THE WATER

COUNCILLOR ZAHAWI

After Kurdistan I returned to my day job almost as if nothing had happened, although of course it had. I'd caught the bug. A year or so later I began the slow descent into politics, and by 1994 was a paid-up member of the Conservative Party and beginning my first term as a councillor for Wandsworth. Jeffrey had pulled some strings with his old friend Eddie Lister to help me on my way. Eddie had been a member of Wandsworth Council since 1976 and was now leader of Thatcher's flagship borough – the one that had delivered zero council tax to its residents alongside outstanding service. 'I've got this exceptional young man,' Jeffrey told him. 'I'm sending him round to learn the trade from you.' Eddie would be the first to admit that he's not a Churchillian speaker, but he was the definition of understated delivery and a no-nonsense pragmatist. Not only did he help me get my seat on the council, working under him was a fantastic way to learn the ropes.

There are various routes to Westminster but, for me, this one was easily the best. Local council is a microcosm of parliament and, as such, a great bootcamp if you want to become an MP. If you do succeed, you'll need to be prepared to move, often at short notice, from department to department, so it's no bad thing to have had a taste of things across the board. The other great advantage to being a councillor was that it didn't necessitate giving up your day job. Council work took around twenty hours a week and most meetings were held in the evening, so it was possible to do both. The world inside Whitehall can be very small, and to my mind it didn't do to cut yourself off from the rest of life too early. The skills you learned outside would prove very useful once you got to the backbenches.

Local government was also a good place to learn from your mistakes. A great example of this happened during my time in Wandsworth when we were looking to contract out refuse collection. Stupidly, we went for the lowest bid, got exactly what we paid for and were quickly forced back to the drawing board. The Left would probably say this was because the private sector couldn't deliver and that we should have stuck with a government-delivered service. With my business hat on, I felt it was a question of sourcing the right supplier, no matter what the origin. I realised the one we'd chosen wasn't right but equally, the reason we'd moved away from council-delivered services was because it wasn't what we were good at: it wasn't what civil servants did best. Once we'd revisited the problem to understand why we'd got it wrong, we fixed it. I was confident we'd find the right people for the job, but it wasn't always possible to get things right first time.

Local and national government might seem like other-worldly institutions operating in splendid isolation, but they're no different from any other business. The people that run them sometimes make mistakes. Even the good ones. If you fired everyone who made a wrong decision or slipped up, you'd never give a person space to learn and develop or for the company to grow and expand. There is an expectation that government officials should perform outside the boundaries of reality, and the truth is they don't. Everyone working there wants a great boss, inspiring leaders, good pay and long holidays. People still take sneaky days off sick and perform badly the morning after a night out. Government is probably no different from wherever you work now: it's full of human beings. We have to be cognisant of the fact there'll always be people who set up business in five minutes with a view to making a quick buck from government contracts, but I don't believe that should stop society from thinking about better ways of delivering services, and my time in local government was a good grounding in this principle.

One of the greatest lessons I learned during my tenure was that there's very little that can't be resolved by talking, provided you're also prepared to listen. It was what my mum had been telling Jihan and me since we were kids. Each time our arguments got loud enough to be heard in the street, she'd intervene with a predictable, 'Now you two, let's sit down and talk about it. I'm sure we can work something out.' And now here I was, mirroring her behaviour in my work. Looking at it now, the influence of my mum is laughably clear in my political demeanour. When the situation requires a calming voice or a reasoned approach, I instinctively revert to her words, 'Let's sit down and talk about it.' In everything from neighbourly disputes to high-level diplomacy, understanding that your words or actions can be felt differently by the person on the receiving end is critical. It would become the cornerstone of so many situations in my career. I have a very powerful belief that human beings are much more capable of compromise than we give them credit for. The ability to see the other side is in our DNA and one of our strengths as a nation, but it's a strength we must work hard not to lose. If council work taught me anything, it was that if you could just manage to bring people together, face to face, most would find a solution somewhere, somehow.

THE PATH TO WESTMINSTER

I think Jeffrey always had a bigger plan for me, and after a few years we began to talk about next steps: the path away from local government and onto Westminster.

As long as they're a member of the Conservative Party, almost anyone can stand as a Tory MP, but there are a few hoops to jump through first. The fact I'd already been a councillor worked in my favour but it was by no means a done deal, so I knew to expect some pushback. The process starts with a few forms and an initial bit of questioning about why you want to be an MP, followed by a proper assessment if you get over that first hurdle. This takes the form of a weekend away to a country house hotel where you're put through your paces on everything from teamwork to debating skills. If you pass that, you're put onto an approved list of candidates by Conservative Central Office, who pass it out to local associations for consideration. From there, names are short-listed and twenty go forward for a lengthy interview by party members. It's then reduced again to six or seven candidates who are grilled comprehensively on everything from national policy to issues of local importance in the constituency. I made it through the away day and came back pretty buoyed up by my performance. I thought I could probably improve on my oratory skills but felt I'd done well on team tasks and was quietly confident about my prospects. I was therefore quite surprised to get a letter in the post saying, 'We do not think you're suited to becoming a Member of Parliament for the Conservatives,' but perhaps I could consider doing something else to support the party such as fund-raising or volunteering. Jeffrey was livid and convinced the real reason I'd been rejected was the colour of my skin.

Of the twenty-two members of the cabinet as I write, five are of an ethnic minority – including the prime minister. Within

190

Blair's first ministry *and* the outgoing Conservative cabinet, there were none. I genuinely don't know if Jeffrey's theory was right, but whatever the reason, I was seriously disappointed about the rejection. Not to be defeated, Jeffrey told me to go and see a lady called Trish Morris with his endorsement. Trish was party vice chairman with responsibility for candidates. Having bagged myself an appointment, I handed her the letter I'd received from Central Office. After reading it through carefully, she wordlessly tore it in half and dropped it in the wastebasket next to her desk. 'I'm really sorry, Nadhim,' she said, 'you can go for an interview next week.' Trish is now Baroness Morris of Bolton, known for the changes she instigated in the selection procedure to improve both the quality and diversity of candidates. Anyone who knows her now will tell you that not only is she kind and decent, but she is also passionate about social mobility. I don't know if this was what I was seeing in action that day in her office, but I was grateful for the second chance.

And so it was, I found myself put forward as the prospective member for Erith and Thamesmead. The *Independent on Sunday* drew up its traditional list of 'Rising Stars' based on those candidates others in the corridors of political power think most likely to succeed. The 2020 Conservative cabinet of the future, they predicted, would include Chris Pincher, Chris Grayling, Robert Buckland, John Bercow, Boris and me. In the accompanying article I talked about my admiration for Thatcher, who'd built the kind of economic climate that attracted investors, and I described the UK as 'Great Britain plc'.* There could be no clearer indication of where I stood on matters of growth. Twenty-seven years later, my attitude has not fundamentally changed. In fact, if

---

* https://www.independent.co.uk/arts-entertainment/the-cabinet-of
-tomorrow-1277684.html.

anything, I feel more strongly about it now than I did then. I was in wholehearted agreement with Margaret about the fact that, when you strip everything else away, we're in politics to improve the lot of the country; otherwise, why bother? And, like her, I believe that if you have a strong economy, you can do anything. Yes, the well-off might be even more well-off but critically, you can pay for the services needed to support the people who can't afford to support themselves. If you look at the history of the civilised world, the countries who've focused on economic strength have tended to be the ones who've prevailed. It was just like Jonny's grandfather, Marcus Sieff, had told us that day at Global Hypercolor in my early days as a salesman: if you can generate the cash you can do anything, but without it, your business will collapse.

Despite the *Independent*'s hype, when the day came I was thrashed by a Labour majority of 17,424 and did not enter parliament that year. The 1997 election saw Tony Blair sweep to victory, bringing the Labour Party back to power after nearly twenty years out in the cold. Erith and Thamesmead was a safe Labour seat and I hadn't had a hope in hell of winning it, but running had been a great way to cut my teeth in national politics. Securing a seat was destined to be a much longer and more arduous task, and would need both persistence and luck. I knew I had one, and the other I'd have to leave to the gods, but, for now, it was back to the day job.

CHAPTER 16

THE MAN WHO WOULD BE KING

THE CAMPAIGN

After I'd lost Jeffrey nearly half a million pounds in the Allen Hinckley debacle, to his credit he and I remained friends. He'd chalked it up to experience and I managed to come out the other side with a new job working for one of the suppliers who'd helped me out of my fix. Smith & Brooks designed and distributed licensed character clothing, with everyone from Marvel to Thomas the Tank Engine as clients. If you bought kids' pyjamas with a cartoon character on the front any time in the late 1990s, the chances are we made it. At thirty, I was one of the highest-paid marketing managers in London, with a £120,000 salary, company BMW and the remnants of my own hair; the planets had aligned momentarily and all was right with the world. In some respects it was a backward step from owning my own company, but likewise a welcome break from the soul-destroying experience of losing one. I'm not sure whether it was nature or nurture, but I'd learned not to sit around moping. Mum was a relentlessly opti-mistic person, Dad fantastically determined and Jeffrey the human Weeble, so my immediate role models were overwhelmingly posi-tive; there was no room for self-pity in my world. I got back up and wasted no time embracing the perks of my new job. I was young and cash-rich, and segued seamlessly into the excesses of

90s fashions. This meant high collars, deep cuffs, gold watches and quite a bit of attitude. I was happy. Happy with life, happy with my career and the slow trickle of politics running in the background. Not bad for a boy from Baghdad ...

And then came the call that would take me on a temporary detour. Once again, the person responsible for the diversion was Jeffrey. 'I'm gonna run for mayor.' In 1986, the Greater London Council had been abolished, leaving London without a directly elected government for the first time in nearly a century. When New Labour swept in under Blair in 1997, their manifesto included a commitment to re-establish a dedicated tier of government for Londoners and the election of a new mayor. As far as I was concerned, Jeffrey was hands down the best man for the job. He was the guy that got things done.

Even among those who liked him, however, there were many who had concerns about Jeffrey's suitability for the role. The first time we met I was still fairly green but could see nonetheless that he was the kind of man whose cupboards might contain a few skeletons. Even so, when the person in question is charismatic, bright and dynamic, it often delays a reckoning. I imagine most people who knew and liked him would be hard pressed to untangle the good from the bad. He was a chancer and an entertainer, and those types always attract a crowd, even if the audience knows the show is probably three parts smoke and two parts mirror. I'm not ashamed to admit I bought a ticket, sat in the front row and thoroughly enjoyed the performance. Five stars. I'd go again now. But it was more than just his showmanship I appreciated. Part of the reason I liked him was his interest in me. When you come face to face with someone who sees you for something you've not yet seen in yourself – let alone articulated – it's both disarming and motivating. When someone recognises you for your mind and effectively tells everyone else about it with their endorsement, it's hard not to feel flattered. So when he asked if I wanted to volunteer for his campaign, I asked him where to sign. And I wasn't the only one. Over the years, Jeffrey had collected people he liked or admired and who liked and admired him. It was these people who came together now to support him in his bid to run London – his most ambitious plan to date.

THE TEAM

Jeffrey was always brilliant at spotting talent. His ability to find and nurture it within his party was what gave him such longevity in his career. He'd have made a wonderful scout in any profession; it just so happened his passion was politics. Ironically, for someone many consider to be quite egocentric, Jeffrey was always a team player. He liked leading and his personality certainly dominated events, but he was incredibly selfless when it came to opportunities and I was happy to take them. Later in life, I would come to see that one of the biggest differences between someone like Jeffrey and someone like Boris Johnson was that Boris 'ruled' as an individual whereas Jeffrey believed in the power of the team. If the team did well, so did the captain. I think it's fair to say that one of Boris's weaknesses is not knowing how to build teams. When he ran for London mayor he had the brilliant Simon Milton to do that for him. When Simon prematurely passed away, Eddie Lister stepped in and delivered for him in City Hall and continued to do the same in No. 10 when Boris became PM. When Eddie decided it was time to hang up his boots, it felt to me like a big moment and a turning point in Boris's premiership. Ultimately, he was not able to rebuild the team himself, which created a vacuum and he began to stumble. In life, I've always worked on the premise that if you can get three out of five things right every day, you're winning. If that ratio flips and you start making mistakes, that's when it kills you. I think for Boris the ratio changed with Eddie's departure and he never quite recovered.

For Jeffrey, politics was a team sport. Even when he worked for Thatcher and Major, he was essentially a bag carrier and, when it came to identifying and pushing forward those with potential, he seemed uniquely able to put any ego aside. The net result was that eight of the ten volunteers in his inner team on the campaign ended up as ministers: Sajid Javid, Priti Patel, Shailesh Vara, Kwasi Kwarteng, Tobias Ellwood, Charles Hendry, Robert Halfon and me. Five of us made it to cabinet. If you were a betting man you could do worse than take advice from Jeffrey.

Saj's parents had emigrated from Pakistan, Priti and Shailesh's from India, Kwasi's and Adam Afriyie's from Ghana, and mine from Iraq. Over half of us were first- or second-generation immigrants with brown faces, and we were united in our passion to do something for our adoptive country. Today this doesn't sound particularly remarkable, but I imagine it was the first time blond-haired, blue-eyed Tobias Ellwood had found himself working somewhere in which he was the minority. It would be 2005 before Adam become the party's first mixed-race MP. At a time when race and gender were still a determiner, Jeffrey was completely blind to both. He didn't care where you came from or what you looked like; if he thought you were right for the job, you were in. If you proved yourself unable to carry out your duties, however, you were out just as fast.

In 1998, Jeffrey was about the age I am now, but a huge number of his volunteers were significantly younger. He loved the energy we brought to the table. 'You can knock them on the nose and they just come flying back,' he'd say. Everyone had to pull their own weight and fight their own corner. If he berated you or said you were useless or pathetic, what he was waiting for you to say was, 'Well, give me a bloody chance!' He was looking for people who'd get back up when they'd been knocked down. If we were thinking of going into politics, he knew this was what we'd need to do many times in the course of our careers because it was exactly what he'd had to do himself. So if you whimpered off into the corner, he had no problem in kicking you up the back-side. His approach was simple: if you showed a weakness, you didn't make it onto the team. Only the fittest survived and the group grew stronger as a result. It was Darwinian. We were all volunteers but the 'payment' was far more valuable than any wage: not only were we part of something meaningful, we were being given the chance to learn from the best. When Jeffrey told a friend that he and I 'were both a couple of barrow boys', I took it as one of the greatest compliments I'd ever received.

Jeffrey would say we were all the same as him; that we all, ultimately, wanted to be prime minister and that's exactly what he looked for in people – the drive to rule the world. At the time, none of us were even MPs but we all wanted to be, and Jeffrey took it upon himself to train us up. He was like a tennis pro, constantly testing and pushing us to improve our backhand. His favourite trick, however, was the spot test. If you were part of the team, you knew that at some point you were likely to be thrust into the spotlight without notice. In the early days you kept your heart permanently in your mouth when you went to one of his events. 'Prime Minister: Nadhim Zahawi will walk you to your car,' was the way I found out I was in charge of accompanying Mrs Thatcher to her Jaguar the first time I met her at Jeffrey's annual summer party. And, 'It's very good of you to have come, Prime Minister. Mr Nadhim Zahawi will now do the vote of thanks' was likewise how I learned I'd be toasting Mr Major at the end of one of Jeffrey's dinners. If you didn't swim when he threw you into the deep end like this, you knew not to bring your trunks next time because he wouldn't be inviting you back to his pool the following summer.

Jeffrey always loved giving people grand titles and it was decided I'd be Director of Field Operations on the campaign on account of my organisational skills. At this point, it was still a battle between Conservative candidates – Jeffrey and Steven Norris – which meant Jeffrey couldn't draw on the party centrally to run his campaign. Instead, we would need to create our own team of volunteers and activists, and develop a database of Conservative members in London we hoped might vote for us on the day and it was my job to build both. The only salaried member of the gang was a guy called Stephan Shakespeare. Stephan would reluctantly call himself chief of staff but in private always referred to himself as a policy wonk. Where I was there to organise people, his role was to organise content and come up with policy ideas. Like everyone else on the team, Stephan knew exactly who and what Jeffrey was. It was impossible not to. He was a huge celebrity at the time, and not just in politics. Stephan was aware of the criticisms levelled at Jeffrey but reasoned that, since nothing he'd been accused of had led to anyone getting hurt, he'd make his own judgements about the guy.

Stephan and I hit it off immediately. It was clear from the outset he had a brilliant mind capable of truly original thought. I was now thirty-one, with a reasonable amount of business experience behind me, but Stephan had an eye for detail I'd never seen before. In the years since, I'd like to think I've grown more like him but, at the time, Jeffrey would tell you I was still more of a showman than a businessman. Had Jeffrey ever become PM, Stephan would have been the guy he'd have chosen as his chancellor if he could have. Like me, Stephan had run in the 1997 election but lost to the Lib Dem candidate for Colchester by roughly 1,500 votes – a small margin for a safe seat. So the question was, what next? When he tuned in to hear Jeffrey announce his plans to run for mayor on the radio, that seemed like a good place to start. In his previous life, Stephan had been head of special needs at a Lambeth comprehensive and writing articles on educational policy in the press. He had a much more considered, intellectual demeanour than me but could clearly turn on the salesmanship when he wanted. When he rocked up at Jeffrey's to pitch for the job of campaign manager, not only did Jeffrey say yes on the spot but he handed him a cheque for £10,000 as his first instalment. Not bad going for a policy wonk.

MONICA

In July 1992, on the back of his work with the Kurds, Jeffrey had been made a life peer by John Major. It was his second run-up at it, having been turned down by the political honours scrutiny committee at least once before. In 1985, when Thatcher appointed him deputy chairman of the party, Lord Whitelaw had warned her Jeffrey was 'an accident waiting to happen', and he had any number of reasons to think that. Arguably the biggest black mark in Jeffrey's copy book was Monica Coghlan – a prostitute to whom he'd given £2,000 in 1987 via an intermediary on Platform 3 of Victoria Station. At the time, the *Daily Star* claimed Jeffrey had not just paid her but slept with her – a point that he vigorously denied. The net result was that Jeffrey stepped down from his post as deputy chair because of 'his lack of judgment in offering to pay Miss Coghlan money for a trip abroad – and for that alone'.* He then sued the paper for defamation and walked off with £500,000 in damages.

---

* https://www.theguardian.com/uk/1986/oct/27/archer.politics.

All this pre-dated the campaign by more than a decade, but Stephan and I knew from the start that if we were going to run into problems it would be because Jeffrey had a certain kind of reputation. Stephan even addressed the issue directly with Jeffrey before taking on the job and was assured there was nothing we need worry about. We decided to take a belt-and-braces approach, nonetheless. His long-term PA, Alison, agreed that if there were any unusual night-time movements at the flat, she'd tell us immediately so we could get out in front of any scandal. We settled on a coded message to use in any such emergency and went about our jobs with our fingers quietly crossed behind our backs.

It was eight in the morning and I was about to make a presentation to my bosses at Smith & Brooks when I finally saw that coded message in a text from Stephan: 'The Axe is falling.' Adrenalin immediately flooded my system and I excused myself from the meeting to call Stephan for an update. Alison hadn't been sure of the details but the top line was, the editor of the *News of the World* was on his way over to speak to Jeffrey about a story he was planning to run in the paper. Whatever that detail was, it couldn't have been good: Phil Hall did not get out of his fiefdom and head to you at that hour of the morning unless he was about to nuke you. I left work immediately and headed to the Embankment.

Jeffrey and I have been friends for over thirty years, but to this day I don't know whether or not he actually slept with Monica. Anyone who knows him will tell you that if he finds something unpleasant or difficult, he just doesn't talk about it. He filters everything but the positive out of his life, and for that reason we've never discussed it. In truth, it was none of my business. In the end, it was Max Clifford who brought the news of his deception to the *News of the World*. Max's brother had gone to school with Ted Francis, whom Jeffrey had used as his alibi the night he was supposed to have slept with Coghlan. The story goes that some years later, Jeffrey had humiliated Ted at one of his showbiz parties over an unpaid loan while Ted was in the middle of trying to impress the actress Susan George. Some say it was this slight that prompted Ted to come forward, while others suggest that he just wanted to stop Jeffrey from getting his hands on London. Whatever the cause, it had the maximum impact. Jeffrey had just beaten his opponent Steven Norris 71 to 29 – unheard of in a two-horse race. Ted's revelations couldn't have come at a better time for Jeffrey's enemies.

Our campaign HQ was directly opposite Jeffrey's flat, between a pub and the Texaco garage. I arrived to find everyone anxiously waiting to hear more news. At nine o'clock, Alison called to say Jeffrey wanted to see us. Five minutes later, Stephan and I entered the penthouse to be greeted with the immortal line, 'Sit down, chaps. There's a small matter I need to share with you. I don't think it's a resigning matter but ...' The words hung in the air like a speech bubble as he proceeded to fill us in on that morning's goings-on. An apparently disgruntled Ted had approached the paper with the truth about his alibi. Phil Hall told Ted that if he could get Jeffrey to admit he'd asked him to lie on the phone, they'd pay Ted £14,000 for the story – just enough to replace his clapped-out car. Ted succeeded in doing so, and when Phil arrived that morning at the penthouse, he helpfully brought the tran-script of that conversation with him. If Jeffrey was happy to give them a quote, said Phil, they promised not to put the story on the front page. Stephan and I took it all in before asking to see the transcript ourselves. 'I gave it back,' Jeffrey said. 'I didn't want Hall to think I was worried.' This wasn't ideal. Alison quickly got on the phone and asked for the document to be sent over while Stephan and I hovered anxiously over the fax machine. A few whirring and clicking noises signalled news incoming, the standard cover sheet unhelpfully prolonging the agony. As the first page came through, the verdict was crystal clear. 'We're fucked,' I said to Stephan, stating the bleeding obvious.

After a brief confab, Jeffrey called his lawyer, the formidable Lord Mishcon, and all three of us got in the car and drove to his office. Mishcon was by now about ninety but still had, in Jeffrey's words, a brain 'like a bloody Rolls-Royce'.* He treated Jeffrey like an errant schoolboy who'd been called to the headmaster's office one too many times, and he didn't mince his words. 'This is very serious, Jeffrey,' he said. It was all there on paper. Jeffrey had lied and now Mishcon was going to do his best to limit the damage. To assist further, Jeffrey called on Tim Bell to complete the team. Bell was Thatcher's PR guru, a larger-than-life, chain-smoking ad exec who'd buddied up with the Saatchi brothers when they launched their own agency in 1970. Nine years later, when they won the Tory account for the forthcoming election, Bell was the one who liaised with Margaret. From there they became lifelong friends. All that aside, I'm pretty sure it was Bell who – deliberately or otherwise – flagged up the present situation to the then leader of the party, William Hague.

Jeffrey was due to speak at a school in Kingston upon Thames that afternoon and it was agreed he'd keep the appointment, then Stephan and I would drive him to the family home in Cambridgeshire to see his wife Mary and break the news face to face. I'm sure Mary knew the kind of man she was married to, but I could tell by her reaction that morning that she didn't know about *this*. Clearly Jeffrey understood the magnitude of what he'd done too, because it was the only time in all the years I've known him that I've ever seen him cry. On top of the distress she must have felt personally, Mary also had the worry of how to

---

* http://news.bbc.co.uk/1/hi/uk/1436200.stm.

protect her family. This wasn't the first time they'd been in the press spotlight but it looked like it might be the most serious. Mary herself had testified, unwittingly, on her husband's behalf more than twelve years earlier, and now that had been shown to be in error. Of all the people around Jeffrey, Mary was far and away the most honourable and high minded. She outstripped him intellectually and he'd often joke he couldn't understand her. 'My darling, what does that mean in English?' She was a rare breed and it was horrible to see her readying herself for another onslaught.

By the time Stephan and I got back to Jeffrey's flat in London, it was surrounded. The press had evidently been tipped off that something was about to break and were waiting for Jeffrey to appear. The only sliver of good news was that we'd already got him away to the country and didn't have to work out a way to get him out past the cameras. We drafted a statement and I went downstairs to deliver it to the press. It was the first time I'd experienced the full force of the fourth estate, but it would not be the last.

On Sunday 21 November, the *News of the World* ran with the story and Jeffrey stepped down the next day. Stephan was called to go on *Newsnight* the following evening and told them honestly how small Jeffrey felt in the wake of what he'd done. There was little sympathy for Jeffrey around the table except from his old friend, the novelist Fay Weldon. When the journalist Michael Crick said a proven liar could not be put in charge of London, she replied, 'Well, I don't know where you're going to find a politician who's not a proven liar,' which was a very loyal riposte but did little to suggest Jeffrey was anything but guilty. Max Hastings, editor of the *Evening Standard*, summed up the general mood of the collected guests with his description of Jeffrey as being 'no more capable of not lying than a fox is staying away from the chickens'. Two things were very clear from the programme that evening: Jeffrey was probably guilty, but also maddeningly popular and influential in government. When Hastings had apparently voiced his concerns about him in a private lunch some months earlier to William Hague, the prime minister had told him, 'Let the public decide.' It seemed Jeffrey was both the party's greatest but most volatile secret weapon and one that many, many people had been happy to use when it suited their cause.

In June 1998, Hague set up an ethics and integrity committee to make sure that the party's name would never again 'be blackened by one candidate being guilty of some gross misconduct',* and Jeffrey had finally fallen foul of it. On 4 February 2000, Jeffrey was expelled from the party for five years. Stephan and I knew it was over the minute we'd read the first page of that fax, but now there was the issue of protecting Jeffrey's family and friends. The Monday after the story broke, we began the business of dismantling the team and returning campaign cheques. Everything was packed away into boxes and phone calls were made to explain the situation to everyone involved. It felt like clearing up at the end of a wedding where the groom had run off mid-dance with the bridesmaid. The balloons were all popped and the vol-au-vents unceremoniously scraped into the bin. The party was over.

We gave Jeffrey some time alone with Mary and the boys to gather his thoughts before revisiting the situation. When I did eventually see him, what struck me immediately was the renewed bounce in his step. Here was Tigger again, back up from what I'd assumed was a total knockout. As time marched on and the case eventually went to court, I realised Jeffrey was in a complete state

* David Frost interview, 7 June 1998.

of denial. I don't think he thought of it as lying, more that he had his own version of reality in which he was going to be cleared of all wrongdoing. Until he was actually convicted of perjury I don't think he let himself believe he would be. Jeffrey doesn't confront difficult truths. Clearly there was a body of evidence against him, but even during the trial he seemed not to have contemplated an alternative ending to the story. On reflection, it wasn't the first time I'd seen someone create their own reality when they found themselves backed into a corner; it was exactly what my dad had done with Aubrey C. Briggs.

So what was the moral of the story? For me, there were several. The first was that human beings – however well known, important, influential, well paid, seemingly experienced, wise or responsible – make mistakes. In fact everyone does, but most don't have to do it in public. Most are not in such a visible position that they don't get the chance to sit down with their families in private and say, I'm really sorry, I've messed up. I learned that however obvious a resolution it might seem to an outsider, confronting the truth is often the most difficult part of the equation. But it's probably what matters most. It was also the bit that neither Jeffrey nor my dad – in his own spiralling crisis – had been able to do. Both men waited until the truth smashed into them before they chose to acknowledge it, and the mess was far worse as a result. Not just for them, but for those around them. When I sat across from my friend now, watching him lost in his own reality, I felt desperately sad for him but also hoped I'd never find myself in the same situation; that I would keep a firmer grasp on my own reality than he had on his. The friend in me looked at him with great warmth and pity; Jeffrey was a force for good, but no one is perfect.

We never visited him in Belmarsh. His son Jamie did and advised us not to. Instead, we waited until he'd been moved to a

Category C prison. Even so, the first time we walked in we were searched and sniffer dogs circled our feet. Broosk went as white as a sheet and Jamie had to reprimand him: 'Please wipe that look off your face. We have to leave him here at the end of the visit!' But in all the time he was inside, Jeffrey never once alluded to being uncomfortable. He made it look like he was busy and kept us smiling. I read in the press that at one point he'd contemplated suicide but that 'the thought of failure [was] just too awful to contemplate'. That didn't sound like Jeffrey to me. He never dwelt on anything. Even after he was released, we never talked about the experience. If we wanted to know the details, he said, we could read about it in the diaries he wrote about his time inside.

It's a testament to Jeffrey's charm and loyalty that not one of the people on his campaign turned against him when he was convicted. They sat out his sentence and when he came home, they were there, waiting to greet him and carry on as normal. That was the kind of faithfulness he inspired if you'd worked up close to him. Though I know he was desperately sad to have ballsed up his chances of becoming mayor, he'd have been sadder still to lose the friendship of anyone working on his campaign. Even twenty-five odd years later he still instinctively refers to us as 'his team'.

I'm sure he'd tell you himself that the blame for the fact he never was party chairman or mayor sits squarely at his own feet. He's a chancer but he's also a realist. His fall from grace was spectacular but, in a funny way, I'd argue he has something much more valuable now: the ability to speak freely. Whether it's the upcoming novice or the seasoned pro tottering on the edge of a bad decision, Jeffrey is able to counsel them all from the comfort of his armchair. No longer a leading man himself, he directs the players on the stage without being confined by the sins of his past or the party line. He's free to guide and support his team exactly as he wishes, and this, I believe, gives him a great deal of pleasure. As a person who's picked up the phone to him more than once over the years, I can attest to how much I've appreciated the trusted voice of someone who doesn't sugar-coat the pill on the other end of the phone in a moment of crisis. If life knocks you down, you get back up. It's as simple as that.

As of 2022, Jeffrey Archer has raised over £50 million as a charity auctioneer and accrued more than 275 million book sales. Not bad for a barrow boy.

CHAPTER 17

GREASY SPOON

THE BIRTH OF YOUGOV

And that was it. Overnight, I went back to Smith & Brooks, the volunteers filtered back to their normal lives and Stephan, as the only paid member of the team, was officially out of a job. Jeffrey was eventually tried and sentenced eighteen months later, and in between, life carried on almost as normal. As a stopgap, Stephan and Jeffrey had set up Shakespeare Fine Art, a gallery specialising in pop art, in a disused industrial space on the Essex Road. A month after Jeffrey's resignation, Steph and I met for lunch at a nearby greasy spoon to discuss the future.

For the past two years, we'd spoken daily during the campaign and both felt we'd like to work together again; but on what? I'd never left my job at Smith & Brooks so there was no immediate need to do anything, but Stephan was drifting. He knew he didn't want to go back to teaching and had expanded his skillset enormously during his time on the campaign. Having him work in a gallery was like getting Steve Jobs to do a shift at the Carphone Warehouse: a total waste of his talents. Finding a suitable alternative required a good brainstorm and some form of sustenance. I was still young enough not to worry about having a heart attack, and we sat down to discuss our ideas over a full English and a strong cup of tea.

In 1999, the internet loomed large in day-to-day life, and had he been tasked with running London, one of Jeffrey's biggest challenges would have been successfully harnessing its power for the good of the city. As a result, e-government was something Stephan had spent a huge amount of time thinking about during the campaign. Everything from parking fines, bin collection and taxes would inevitably move online, and this was something we had to be on top of. There were two interlinked subsections of e-government that seemed worthy of consideration. The first was e-consultation – the process of listening to people's concerns online in order to give them a voice – and the second was e-polling, which differed from consultation in that it was anonymous and more likely to give a non-biased indication of how the public might lean in a vote. As part of the campaign, we'd bought opinion polls and were struck by how costly and slow the process was, and how little there was in the way of granular data. Leading pollsters like MORI and Gallup still carried out their polling face to face or on the telephone, and both methods had their limitations. You only ever got that five or ten-minute window with a candidate and the sample of respondents was easily skewed. If you knocked on the door and someone was out, did that mean they were more socially active or affluent than the person next door, and, if so, how might that influence the data? An online survey would be accessible 24/7 and the account holder could be contacted again and again, meaning we'd be able to build up layers of information from the same person. It was cheaper and more nuanced, and the data could be modelled much more effectively. But at that time, the internet was not without its own issues. In 1999, a relatively small proportion of the adult population was online and that percentage were all early adopters, which, in itself, said something about the nature of the candidate. They were predominantly younger and more affluent, which affected the data. While this was a consideration, it was one that would diminish in significance over time as the technology became more mainstream. When that happened, we'd be left with an audience unfettered by the problems that plagued face-to-face and telephone models. We just needed to bide our time.

Jeffrey's campaign might now be defunct, but that didn't stop Stephan thinking about how and where the concepts he'd developed could be used instead. He was a brilliant, original thinker, but back then he was not an experienced businessman. His background was teaching and campaign management, and neither gave him the skillset to set up and run a company. That's where I came in. In simple terms, I needed Stephan's mind and he needed my expertise, and we stepped back into the same roles we'd had during the campaign. He came up with the ideas and I got them done. It was the perfect marriage of minds. As we sat in the cafe that morning, we batted things back and forth until we had the outline of a viable company. Somewhere in a cupboard there's a biro triangle on an egg-stained napkin that captures the fruits of our labours that morning. The three pillars of YouGov's original construction right there in black and white: e-government, e-consultation and e-polling. We were ready for take-off. Sort of.

Our intention was to create a platform on which local government and its constituents could talk. We were back to my mum's old lesson: 'Let's sit down over here … I'm sure we can work something out.' It was a business model centred on communication. We knew the equilibrium between the people and the executive – whoever that might be – was shifting in favour of the people and that the internet would give them much greater say over how their lives would be governed, and we wanted our new company to be part of that equation. That all sounds pretty rudimentary now but, twenty-five years ago, the way you communicated your views on life to the powers that be was in a letter to your MP, newspaper or *Points of View*, and even they'd stopped accepting correspondence by 1998. But things were about to change. Not only had we identified a gap in the market but it seemed like we might be in a position to plug it.

There was one problem, though. Our initial idea was a romantic one – something we both felt passionate about but not necessarily something we saw as a big money spinner. In itself, this was no bad way to start. If you set up a company because you want to get rich, the chances are you'll fail. There's no correlation between your desire for money and success. Jobs and Zuckerberg didn't set out to become rich, they went into business in the belief they could make the best computers or social networks. They were obsessive about their inventions; the by-product was financial success. We had total faith in our idea; we just had to keep our fingers crossed that investing in consumer democracy would eventually pay dividends.

When it came to a name, we wanted something that represented this new world order. The Blair government had just launched their own e-government portal called me.gov and Stephan's initial idea was a play on that. 'LondonGov' would give the electorate the chance to have a say in how their city was run. If it worked, we could move on to other cities and replicate the model: BerlinGov and so on. With my business hat on, I knew that a commercially successful company would need to think bigger. Why restrict our ambitions to London? This was a national, if not global, concern, and our name should reflect that scope. YouGov was an amalgam of two words: you and govern. It was consumer – or citizens' – democracy. In truth, we always thought we'd find something better but the name stuck and we grew to love it. It summed up exactly what we intended to do. Sometimes the simplest ideas are the best.

By the time our plates were cleared, we had our napkin and our name but, once again, no money. Stephan wasn't earning a vast amount at the gallery and was in no position to put in any cash. I, on the other hand, was earning a great deal at Smith & Brooks but was spending it just as fast on clothes, cars and showing off, so didn't have any savings to invest either. And there was another stumbling block for me. Having already lost a business and got back on my feet, I was also very, very nervous about giving up my salaried job. I knew it was a big risk, and this time I actually understood first hand what taking a chance like that could do to a person if it backfired. I was torn between wanting the security a salary brought and the adrenalin rush that came with the thought of going out on my own and succeeding. I felt like I had Mum on one shoulder and Dad on the other. My dad and sister had always had a much greater appetite for risk than me and Mum, but there was still a strand of it running through me. I reasoned that as long as I could justify them with good, solid evidence, there were some risks worth taking, and if I was going to make the jump again I'd be hard pressed to find anyone any smarter, more capable or trustworthy than Stephan to do it with.

None of this answered the question about where to get the money we needed. Although Stephan and I were both close to Jeffrey, I still felt hugely indebted to him and very uncomfortable about going to him again now. Whether he articulated it or not, my instinct was there was a grain of resentment that I'd lost him a lot of money – and justly so. Instead, we came up with the idea of approaching Neil Bruce-Copp – an old school friend of Jeffrey's who'd been a donor to the campaign. Stephan had built up a great relationship with Neil during his time as chief of staff and Neil admired Stephan enormously. Neil was another great entrepreneur, whose gap in the market was laptop cases. In the early 80s he'd come up with the idea after reading a discarded trade magazine on a train from Leicester to London and realising that anyone buying a newfangled portable computer had no way of transporting it safely. After securing orders from IBM and ICL, he went on to found Targus Group. By the time he sold up in 1996, it had won multiple awards and was turning over millions. We wrote a one-page outline of our new company and Stephan took it to Neil, who became our first investor.

The next target was my dad, who had his own pros and cons. By now it was nearly fifteen years since the collapse of the Air Knife and, thanks to his vision and tenacity, he was currently enjoying the most spectacular turnaround in fortunes. In the wake of the breakup of the Soviet Union, he'd read that a lot of the Baltic states looked quite exciting commercially. Having never stepped foot in Eastern Europe, in 1993 he got on a plane to Lithuania and started his business life again. When the Soviets exited the country they left behind a huge facility called the Mazeikiai Refinery – the only oil refinery in the Baltic states. As a relatively poor country, the Lithuanians were looking to raise money by privatising the facility and Dad decided he'd be the guy to get someone to buy it. He gradually made connections and eventually found himself representing a Canadian company who were keen on the idea, and for the next two years he represented their interest in setting up the deal. A wage was coming in and our family were getting back on their feet. If the deal came off, however, he'd be a *very* wealthy man. And that was the moment the board pulled out of the deal. Another two years of his working life were about to be flushed down the drain. Whether it was because of what had happened with Aubrey or just his innate personality, Dad was not about to be outdone again. He scoped-out an alternative buyer, got on a plane to the US and persuaded Williams International to pick up the pieces of the deal. Not long after, they became the brand new owners of a second-hand refinery.

So the one thing I knew about my dad was that he was very happy handling risk. He'd also come a long way in understanding the mechanics of huge international companies and how we might apply some of those rules to our start-up. I knew the pitfalls we'd encountered with Allen Hinckley and felt confident Dad's experience would help me avoid the same thing happening again. Given the success of YouGov today, it's difficult to frame its inception in the same way I did twenty-five years ago. I didn't feel like we were a two-man band – I was beyond that – and we had ambitions to be global, but at the same time I had no way of knowing whether we'd sink or soar. What I did know was that I had to be prepared for either eventuality. In fact, my mum was so appalled by the idea of my leaving a sensible, well-paid, full-time job, she burst into tears when I told her I was giving it up. So, with the benefit of hindsight, while it looks like YouGov was a sure thing, at the time it was just another start-up and I, just another guy taking a punt, but I felt much better doing it with the backing of my dad.

While I was confident about the operational side of things, my track record was less than perfect when it came to the 360° management of a business. I knew Dad's expertise would prove invaluable going forward, but he was nothing if not business savvy and wasn't about to give it to me for nothing. I was in no position to pay him as a consultant, so the only way I could afford him was to offer him equity, to give him shares in exchange for his time and expertise. Given the company was then worth nothing, I just had to hope he'd be prepared to take it in lieu of his services.

The other consideration for me personally was that I owed my dad, big time. When Allen Hinckley collapsed and I'd needed legal representation, it was Dad who'd paid the fees and bailed me out. He never quibbled or questioned or made me feel bad; he just stepped up. When I found myself in financial difficulties he subsidised my mortgage and helped pay my bills. Had it not been for Mum and Dad, I'd have very quickly lost my flat. In all, the legal fees were around £25,000 – closer to £60,000 in today's money. At thirty, I had absolutely no hope of finding that kind of money elsewhere and was fortunate I came from a family whose first instinct was to protect and support one another and that my dad had made enough money back to provide me with that sort of cash. So, when it came to him taking equity in the new company, not only did I not mind, I felt I owed it to him. Stephan and I split our holdings down the middle with a wage and shares. I gave my shares to dad and hung on to the salary. In return I got a £17,000 investment and, more significantly for me, an injection of expertise and moral support. It was the buffer I needed to feel secure moving forward. When Stephan and I met in the greasy spoon that day, I knew he didn't want to embark on this venture alone. Despite his strengths, he wasn't confident he could handle the business end of things, which was why he needed me. I felt exactly the same way about Dad. I did have more experience in this arena than Stephan, but I was still the guy whose most recent venture had failed. I knew there was a gap in my knowledge and Dad was the one person I knew I could ask to fill it. For him it was a punt, and he added YouGov to the list of horses he was currently betting on. It was win win; or it certainly seemed so at the time.

For a variety of reasons that would not present themselves until much later, I could not have been more wrong. Within five years the company had floated and my shares would have been worth more than £7 million had I had them. Unbelievably, that was not the most costly consequence of the decision to give my dad shares, but that is a discussion for a little later …

And so it was, our small team set off on its new venture, wholly unaware just how big it would eventually become.

It quickly became obvious that the part of the equation which really worked was the polling and, as the hull tilted towards it, we leant in. The first thing we had to do was build a big enough database of users to create an accurate representative sample of the general public, ideally somewhere in the region of 200,000. We could then pull off a sample of 5,000, whom we'd invite to complete a survey. Each time they did, we'd pay them a nominal amount. That amount couldn't be life-changing because it could impact how they'd respond. For each survey they did, they'd get a little more and, when they reached £50, they'd get a cheque in the post. Of the 5,000 panellists we figured around 50 per cent would respond, and that would leave us with a sample of 2,500. It was failsafe. All we had to do now was solve the problem of how to get 200,000 people on board. In 2000, we launched 'Interactive News' in an effort to provide us with a solution.

The engine behind this was a gang of graduate journalists we employed to cull the news in shifts, working 24 hours a day, seven days a week. Each article they wrote would include half a dozen questions at the end based on the central theme of the story. You could read the news anywhere, but the idea behind our version of it was customer engagement; getting an audience used to giving an opinion online. In other words, consumer democracy. The next step was finding an outlet to host the articles, and Freeserve seemed like the obvious choice. Freeserve was an internet service provider that would eventually morph into Orange and then EE, and was owned by Stanley Kalms, founder of Dixons and PC World. Stanley was an old-school sort who'd worked his way up from his father's photographic studio and now sat at the top of the country's biggest electrical retailer. He was well known for his acerbic remarks and no-nonsense attitude. When Stephan and I walked into his office on Farm Street in Mayfair, he made his feelings about us perfectly clear. 'You've got five minutes; don't waste my time.' There wasn't much of a bedside manner about Stanley. Forty-five minutes later, however, he called in Ajaz Ahmed – the man who'd come up with the idea of Freeserve – and an hour later we were still going; things were looking good. Freeserve could provide us with eyeballs and in turn we'd provide them with content, but Stanley wasn't about to give us any money for our input. At this stage of the game we'd have to be satisfied with giving our content away for free and keeping our fingers crossed it would prove to be a loss leader rather than a straight-up loss. As a start-up, we were in no position to argue.

The first time we knew we were really onto something was the night I got a text from Ajaz to say, 'What the hell's going on with your service?! The servers are frozen.' A quick call to our IT guy told me a deluge of responses to an article on fuel costs had swamped the server. Three months later, lorry drivers blocked UK motorways in protest about rising fuel prices, and Steph and I realised that what had happened that night had been a precursor to these events. If we could replicate that again, we had a valuable predictive tool on our hands. If we wanted to make any money out of it, however, we'd have to prove it. We needed a way to demonstrate the accuracy of our product and decided the best place to do that was in politics. It was an arena in which we were both comfortable and one where people couldn't get enough of predictions.

During every general election a large group of academics are funded to study how the electorate vote and, in 2001, this was outsourced to leading pollsters, NOP, Gallup and MORI. By now we had a handful of employees, including a guy called Joe Twyman who'd come on board as a research director. Joe ended up staying for eighteen years but was then a young political graduate with ties in academia. Through him we were approached by Essex University, who asked whether we'd like to give them our raw data for analysis to include in the mix. It was a fantastic chance to showcase our service. Unfortunately for us, all their funding was already allocated to the other pollsters, meaning, once again, we'd have to hand over our content for free. Given we were the insurgents, we decided the opportunity was far more valuable than any fee and signed on the dotted line.

When Labour won (again), YouGov turned out to be the most accurate out of all the pollsters. The new kids on the block were the smartest. It was a huge leg-up for us and, on the back of it, we started getting interest from the papers. Given our overheads, no one was going to get rich from one £4,000 survey a fortnight, but it was worth more to us than that in exposure. Every time the papers ran one of our surveys, I insisted on branding our work. Having our logo appear regularly in the *Telegraph* was advertising we could never have afforded ourselves, and it was another foot up the ladder.

The political polling worked well as a shop window but the money would end up coming from brands. There's nothing more valuable in business than knowing what your customer is going to want next and why, and how to sell them your next-generation product. This was where we really started to gain traction. When we got our first big deal, I photocopied the cheque for £15,000, framed it and put it on the wall in my office. We were finally making headway.

We knew from the Freeserve episode that the public were keen to comment on things that piqued their interest, but if the only respondents were 'Disgusted of Tunbridge Wells' it wasn't a balanced sample. You only had to pick up a newspaper to see how hugely people differed in opinion, and we needed to hear from all of them. Alongside our 24/7 journalist graduates, we hit on the idea of commissioning 'celebrity' journalists, well known for having a particular audience, to pen think pieces specifically targeted at their readers. Each would write one article a month complete with half a dozen questions at the end in return for a fee of £400.

Our list of writers was an eclectic one. Fay Weldon was the ballsy novelist best known for *The Lives and Loves of a She Devil*; John Humphrys represented the middle- and upper-class newshounds at the *Today* programme on Radio 4; Ian Hargreaves, one-time editor of the *Independent*, veered left, as did Peter Kellner, former political analyst at *Newsnight* and journalist at the *Evening Standard*. Our final columnist was one Boris Johnson, then overseeing things at the *Spectator* rather than Downing Street. When it came to payday, Humphrys swapped his fee for two years for 2 per cent equity. Peter Kellner eventually left the *Evening Standard* and came on full-time, taking a combination of salary and shares. Boris, typically, went straight for the cash. 'I need the money,' he said. 'I've got overheads.' It was my first introduction to this tornado of a human being and I quickly learned that, while his work was always beautifully written and brilliantly crafted, it was also always, always late. He was the only writer we ever had to chase. 'Really sorry, Nadhim, really sorry,' would come in his trademark gruff voice over the telephone, but the apologies never arrived with an excuse. But that was just the package you got with Boris, and I kind of didn't care. Even then he had stardust. Stephan and Boris already knew one another. Boris had edited the articles Stephan had written for the *Telegraph* and Stephan made the approach to him now. Boris had the same magnetic charm as Jeffrey and Max. If you wanted to be around it, you just accepted the trouble that came with it. The one thing you did feel – and I think he felt too – was that he was 100 per cent authentic. At least in the moment. When the company floated in 2005, Humphrys got even richer, Kellner became a multi-millionaire overnight and Boris complained on a regular basis that I should have persuaded him to take the shares. Finances, I would later learn, were never Boris's strong suit but he had other qualities that made him a valuable asset.

YouGov was an amalgamation of all that Stephan and I had learned over the previous decade. For my part, all the mistakes I'd made and treasures I'd collected over the years were sitting ready in my bag for the right time and place to use them. There was definitely a degree of luck in its formation but quite a bit of foresight too. With the birth of the internet, the world was changing and it was clear only the fittest would survive. Luckily for Stephan and me, when the fish developed legs, we were the first ones on the riverbank selling shoes.

CHAPTER 18

GAME OF THRONES

A RETURN TO BAGHDAD

It was around two o'clock one afternoon in April 2003 when I got a call that would mean another trip east. I picked up the telephone to hear a broken, crackly line but a voice that was easily recognisable as my dad's. 'You'll never guess where I am,' he said. I had no idea. The last I knew he was in Kuwait, where he'd been contracted by the US construction and engineering firm Kellogg, Brown & Root (KBR), after selling up in Lithuania. Three weeks before the call, the US had launched a military campaign in Iraq and driven Saddam out of office. Baghdad lay in tatters and, with their leader now in hiding, the Iraqis rioted and looted and took whatever they could in the absence of any recognised authority. KBR were there to provide life support to the US army while they got on with rebuilding the city, and my dad was the man in charge.

Unbeknown to most people, KBR had been operating from villas at the Hilton Fahaheel Hotel in Kuwait months before the war even began. In the dead of night, they made tracks into Iraq, spraying the roads with liquid asphalt to prepare them for the heavy tanks and trucks that would be sent in when word was given to attack. After months of preparation, General Jay Garner and his team would drive from Kuwait to Baghdad to set up the

Office of Reconstruction and Humanitarian Aid – or ORHA – and oversee the rebuilding of Iraq's infrastructure and the establishment of an interim Iraqi government. Garner would eventually be replaced by the US ambassador Paul Bremer but, as current director of ORHA and temporary replacement for Saddam, at this point he was the most powerful military official in the country.

After ten years of UN sanctions and a further three weeks of US bombing, Iraq was in a pretty dire state. The most pressing issues were reconnecting civilians with water and electricity where possible. In the wake of the invasion, civil servants and politicians had fled and the country was wholly without government or properly functioning services. Everything, absolutely everything, had to be thought of and implemented. It was a colossal task and a monumental responsibility, but you don't say no to being part of something like that; at least you don't if you're someone like my dad.

Early on the morning of 19 April, the first convoy of four-wheel drives left Kuwait. Garner drove in an armoured GMC and Dad followed behind in an armoured Toyota Land Cruiser. At around 1 p.m. that afternoon they arrived at the now deserted Republican Palace, from where dad was now calling me on a Thuraya satellite phone. 'I'm in Saddam's office,' he told me. For a kid who'd been driven from his home by this man twenty-five years earlier, there was no other response to that statement than 'I'm on my way.'

When I landed in Kuwait a week later, Dad had organised for me to go to the Hilton and for KBR to take me into Baghdad in the next available convoy. But before the driver had a chance to collect me, I got a call from my friend Sam Chalabi, who was standing – somewhat unbelievably – outside in the car park. 'I'm going to Baghdad to see my uncle,' he said. 'Why don't you come with us instead?' Sam had a convoy of Land Cruisers to transport him and three journalists to the city, and that sounded much more fun than going in with my dad's friends. Sam's uncle Ahmed was another brilliant but flawed human being and a hugely influential but controversial figure in the history of Iraq – but that's a story for another book. At this point he was odds-on favourite to take over from Saddam with the backing of at least part of the American invading body and had set up camp at a place called the Mansour Club to meet with anyone wanting to kiss the ring.

When I got into the passenger seat the next day, the first thing Sam asked me was whether I knew the way to Baghdad. Sam was born in Iraq but educated in the US and UK and had not been back for more than twenty-five years – but neither had I, so God knows why I told him that I did. From the Hilton it was a seven-hour journey across the border into a war-torn landscape dotted with tanks and burnt-out cars. Saddam had actually built some pretty good motorways that helped us get through Iraq itself, but half an hour outside Baghdad it became clear I had absolutely no idea where I was going. In UK terms, I'd effectively got us as far as the M25 but now had to get to the Hippodrome in Leicester Square without a map. It quickly became clear that I could not, but no one seemed too worried though. We were a pretty convivial gang. When one of the cruisers overheated, no one made a fuss.

The convoy parked up and we all got out. One of the journalists was a lovely Jewish guy who'd brought some traditional Jewish cake in honour of Yom HaShoah – the day on which Jews commemorate the Holocaust. As the sun went down, he passed it round and we shared it by the roadside as we waited for the engine to cool down. It was an oddly beautiful evening given the circumstances. Back on the road, we behaved like any other gang of tourists and pulled over to ask anyone who'd stop for directions. Given the previous three weeks, most passers-by were understandably jumpy about anyone who didn't look like them and, with my shaved head, wraparound sunglasses and O'Neill T-shirt, I wasn't passing for a local. On top of that, my Arabic was pretty rusty and my accent even worse, so when I wound down the window and started accosting people I had the added disadvantage of sounding like a seven-year-old boy. Eventually, we reached the Mansour Club, where I transferred into the much safer hands of KBR, who actually did know where they were going. Half an hour later, I arrived at the Republican Palace and hit the ground running. There was no time for pleasantries.

KBR had an open-ended contract with the US Department of Defense to supply life-support services to the US military wherever they wanted to go in the world. Food, medicine, technology, tradesmen: anything and everything you could think of to get a place back up and running would be handled by KBR and its contractors. For the past three months, Dad and his men had been assembling teams to do everything needed to rebuild the city. Sanitation and refuse management had to be thought through in detail, glazers were needed to replace blown-out windows, plumbers to fit toilets and change boilers, thousands of cleaners to make buildings habitable and drivers to distribute fuel to petrol stations all over the city. US missiles were incredibly accurate and had taken out the necessary infrastructure to bring the government down, and now that infrastructure had to be put back. It was a colossal task on a huge scale and Dad and his team worked flat out to get the job done. Seeing the operation in action was totally awe-inspiring.

Most surreal of all were the helicopters that landed regularly on the palace lawns. Soldiers formed orderly queues to take off pallet after pallet of millions and millions of neatly stacked dollars. In all, the reconstruction of Iraq would cost the US around a trillion dollars and most of it came to the palace to be stored in Saddam's own safes. You would have thought this would be the most money I'd ever see in my life, but nearly twenty years later I got to see something even more mind-blowing. In July 2022, I was (briefly) made chancellor of the exchequer and invited to lunch with the governor of the Bank of England, Andrew Bailey. As part of my visit, Andrew took me down to the vaults that store the UK's reserves and I got to see what 437,000 gold bars look like when you lay them out on pallets and stack them up six feet high. Oddly enough, the vast doors at the Bank of England were the same design as those that guarded Iraq's reserves in their own central bank. In years gone by, the Bank of England had printed the Iraqi dinar and Chubb had manufactured the same doors for the vaults of both banks. When Saddam fell, the building was attacked by looters who attempted to get to the gold with the blast of a rocket-propelled grenade launcher. To Chubb's credit, the RPG round failed to get through the doors but did damage the hinges and neighbouring sewage pipes. A secret mission of Chubb engineers was sent from London to Baghdad to wade through the debris and repair the historical doors. It was just another story that sprung from the complicated ties of our past with Iraq.

The sheer physicality of so much cash in Saddam's back garden made one thing clear: there were millions to be made from the reconstruction of Iraq, and for anyone wanting to exploit the situation it was a dream come true. For this reason, Dad was determined no money should find its way into the wrong hands. He gave clear orders that not a penny should be spent on bribery and that anyone found to be doing so would be fired on the spot.

What I saw from watching my dad in action was not so different from the lesson I'd learned all those years ago at Kingston Hospital: if you wanted to inspire the troops, the best way to do it was to lead from the front. Dad was hands-on and up for every challenge. On entering the city, the first thing Garner had asked him to do was to find 4,000 workers. Dad hadn't been back to Iraq since the day he left on that Swiss Air flight in 1978 so was not much better placed than Garner to source them, but he made it happen. This was the first time I'd worked alongside Dad in this way, and I realised I'd inherited the same instinct. When you were asked to get something done, you did it. You didn't bother your superiors with your concerns, you made it your business to make it happen. It's exactly what Jeffrey had said he'd liked about me during the Simple Truth project and why he'd asked me to run the mayoral campaign with Stephan eight years later. I had to admit, Dad and I were more similar than I'd thought. Working alongside him at the Republican Palace was like seeing my own reflection in the mirror for the first time.

I'd never been to the palace before; it was not somewhere you went unless you were 'invited'. It was exactly as you'd expect, but jaw-dropping nonetheless. Saddam had gone big on gold taps, swag curtains and self-portraits, many of which still hung on the walls despite the surrounding disarray. His ego was best demonstrated by the enormous gold and red velvet throne that stood in one of the state rooms. I can imagine why he had it but the irony was, when you sat in it, you looked and felt absolutely tiny. It was the greatest metaphor for his complete lack of self-awareness. Like most dictators, in an effort to look bigger than he really was he'd managed to make himself look just as small as he was at heart. It was Putin's long table all over again. The self-indulgence of the man contrasted horribly with the rows of dirty, ugly, corrugated-iron shacks at the back of the palace. This was where Saddam housed his soldiers; the people who protected him. Their squalid living quarters stood in marked contrast to the absurd opulence of his own. Clearly this was not a guy who led from the front.

When Dad had arrived, it was obvious life at the palace had been abandoned at a moment's notice. Had it been a crime scene, the body would still have been warm. A huge side of beef hung over a pool of bloody water in the kitchens, defrosted when the electricity had been cut off. Rooms that had housed Ba'ath Party surveillance were abandoned in the same way, exposing the amateur nature of their operations. The secret police systems were incredibly crude. Where the West had imagined there might be sophisticated technology, they found microphones in the frames of windows and thousands of pages of banal, handwritten notes documenting hour upon hour of trivial conversation. These rooms were a clear demonstration that the 'wizard' behind this curtain was just a small, trumped-up, paranoid little man, doing his best to look important. I took a sheet of paper from a huge stack on one of the desks. On it was scrawled a coded conversation between an aunt and her niece overseas about how 'nice the grapes had been that season'. Just like everyone else in Iraq, these poor people coded even the simplest of conversations in an effort to evade the unwanted attention of their dictator. I folded the note in two and put it in my pocket as a reminder of the world my family and I had escaped.

Every night around 250 soldiers and officials slept on camp beds on the palace floors; rows and rows of men and women huddled up in their sleeping bags like sardines in a tin. As the operation scaled up, their numbers grew. In the evenings, there was nothing much to do except smoke cigars and drink whisky. We shared stories and rations and talked into the night. This was where I met the American officer who'd been put in charge of the Ministry of Municipalities and was consequently now responsible for all local government. As well as hailing from Iraq, by now I also had nine years under my belt in local government so had a fairly good idea of the task he was faced with. When

Saddam fled, so did the vast majority of the city's officials, leaving the ministry without oversight and the buildings exposed to looters. Their country had been invaded and their leader, however awful, had been deposed. Most of them were now wondering what the hell was going to happen to them and were incredibly frightened. The US officer – who, for security's sake, I'll call Joe – had managed to round up all the senior civil servants – or director generals – the week before and convince them to come back to work. He'd promised them their jobs were safe, their salaries would be paid and the ministry would be protected. He was due to meet with them for a progress report the following morning and, given my background, asked whether I'd go with him.

The next day, twelve director generals arrived at the palace. The safest way to travel was together. Introductions were made, flak jackets put on, and we set off in a convoy to the ministry to meet the junior civil servants who'd been working to clean things up. On arrival we were met by around 200 very angry men and women. While the army had posted a tank at the front of the building, they'd failed to protect the back, leaving it wide open to looters. Everything these people had done over the past week was wasted. Thieves had taken anything they could sell but worse still, destroyed things of even greater value. Technical maps of the sewage systems in Basra and blueprints for all the major cities had been burnt. Hugely important documents for the proper workings of the city, gone in an instant. Water pipes were smashed and floors flooded; furniture and equipment scorched and blackened. Looters had attacked many buildings in the same way. The National Museum of Iraq, which housed thousands of years of cultural history, was stripped of many irreplaceable artefacts and the Baghdad National Library was burned to the ground, taking with it thousands of manuscripts dating back as far as 7,000 years. It was a devastating aftershock to the horrors of the bombing and completely needless. The collateral damage of war was devastating and long-lasting.

The interpreter did his best to convey their collective fury but too slowly and inaccurately to be helpful, so Joe asked me to step in. I explained to them that this was an accident and they in turn told me they felt let down; that they'd cooperated and put their trust in the Americans and had been left completely exposed – which would never have happened under Saddam. They were conscientious about their work but were also scared. The straw that broke the camel's back for them was that the Ministry of Oil building, which sat diagonally opposite, was completely untouched. It didn't take much to interpret this as a bid by the Americans to control their country's natural resources rather than just a stupid mistake made by the military police who'd put a tank at the back of *that* building but not theirs. Joe was understandably livid. He'd put a lot of time and energy into convincing these guys to get on board with the programme. This error made him look like an idiot, and he was crystal clear about that when he gave the head of the military police a dressing-down in front of the entire staff of the ministry.

When we left, the mood in the car was pretty sombre. The situation was an unmitigated disaster and Joe knew it. As we drove back to the palace we passed building after building covered in the graffiti of whichever organisation had now claimed it as their own. Hundreds had been broken into and taken over by political parties flooding back into Iraq from Syria, Iran and even Kurdistan. Each one was now daubed with the name of its new 'owner': the Dawa Party, Building No. 560; the Iraqi Communist Party, Building No. 167. It was chaos. To the silent majority looking on, what they were seeing was their country falling apart. A country without a visible leader to enforce the rules. And suddenly it clicked. Iraq was a socialist state and every single building was government-owned. All the Americans need do was find a way to remind everyone of that fact.

When we got back to the palace, Joe asked me what I thought about the events of that morning and I was hesitant about whether to tell him the truth. That surely they must have planned this out ahead of time, right? That if you're going to take over a country that's been ruled by a dictator, you'd better make it absolutely crystal clear who's in charge when you kick him out. I asked how much he knew about the background of the situation. To his credit, he'd clearly read up on the subject, but the theory is quite different from the reality. Sometimes you needed someone on the ground with a first-hand understanding of the climate to be able to convert that theory into practice. It's exactly the reason Sir Percy Cox called on people like Gertrude Bell and T. E. Lawrence after the First World War to help translate the problems faced by the Allies into a language they could understand. I realised that in this instance, it was Dad and I who'd have to translate. Out of everyone there, we were the ones with that local experience. We were the ones who'd lived under the same dictator they'd just toppled and understood that, although his removal was both desired and necessary, a vacuum of power in a country used to an iron fist was a potentially dangerous thing.

For the past forty-five years, the country had been ruled by a succession of bloodthirsty dictators and its citizens were not used to the same freedoms we lived with. During the pandemic, there were many who questioned whether Western countries could successfully implement lockdown in the way the single-party states of the East could. Whether Western citizens would accept the constraints on their freedom in the same way. The cultural divide between those living in democracies and those in dictatorships was the subject of much discussion. Here in Iraq we were faced with a population used to someone being in charge and, while most were happy it was no longer Saddam, that void could not be left open for too long without creating even more serious problems. I decided it would be better to be honest and asked Joe if he'd noticed the graffitied buildings on the drive back. 'Yes,' he said, 'What was that?' 'Those,' I told him, 'are all the political parties you've just unleashed.' I explained these were state-owned properties, and that the US needed to make it clear their occupation was illegal. That he needed to call in the representatives of all the political parties and tell them that, from tomorrow, those buildings must be vacated. If they wanted office space, they'd have to rent it like everyone else. That public property was not up for grabs, and looting and illegal activity would not be tolerated. That they needed to make their authority clear – not just to the silent majority but also to the Iranians, who would not hesitate to take advantage of the chaos given half a chance to infiltrate the capital and use it to take over Iraq. That freedom for those who've lived under a dictatorship would be an evolutionary process. That you could not reasonably expect a people who'd been spoon fed for the last forty-five years to know how to feed themselves overnight.

What he'd not understood from the books he'd read was that Saddam, just like Hitler before him, was a brilliant marketing man. He projected his strength by visible demonstrations of his authority and that was exactly the language the Iraqis left behind understood. If the Americans didn't say, 'That doesn't belong to you,' someone else would come and claim it. That's how Iraq worked then. The initial step was an incredibly simple one and I was amazed it hadn't crossed their minds before now. With Joe's approval, I went to the market and knocked up a prototype sign that read 'ORHA: Property of the State of Iraq: Trespassers will be prosecuted', and told him to make enough copies to put prominently on any and all public buildings. It was a very basic, but

necessary, first step. Sadly, it was too little too late. By the end of
the week, Garner was out and ambassador Paul Bremer was in;
my friend Joe was gone and the whole idea got shelved. Elements
of the Iraqi opposition – including Sam's uncle – persuaded
Bremer to leave the creation of a new political structure to the
country's own parties and to disband the predominantly Sunni
army. In practice, this meant sending home hundreds of thousands of trained men with not only a gun but also a complete loss
of purpose, and hoping for the best. A month ago these people
had been officers in the nation's most powerful organisation.
They had salaries and could support their own families. Now
they were nobodies. In the end, the Shias largely joined the new
political parties while the Sunnis formed ISIS. It was a mess that
felt like it could have been avoided with more forethought. War
viewed from afar is easy to ignore. Seeing the city up close after
the fall of Saddam provided an indelible lesson in the far-reaching
collateral damage of any conflict. The destruction rarely stops
when a ceasefire is called, it's just that it's quieter and less like
headline news.

It was almost twenty-five years since the night Dad left his
own father's house on Al-Tabari Street and neither he nor I had
been back since, but it was where we both gravitated now. By
this point, Mum's brother was living there with his wife and
grown children. A few days before I arrived, three armoured
vehicles had driven my dad back to the Waziriyah district and
he'd slept in his old home. The night I arrived, I went back too.
Everything seemed much smaller than I remembered, which I'm
sure had more to do with what the house represented than its
physical footprint. My bedroom was almost unchanged and the
furniture not so different, but it was a bittersweet feeling to be
back. I went out onto the porch where I'd played cards with my
grandma. I was too big to climb my tree again but it was still

there. The legacy of my grandfather was built into the walls of our home, and what he'd done for the country was carried proudly by Dad and passed on to me, but the Iraq he had known and loved was gone. Destroyed not just by the war itself but by a generation of mental torture that had sucked the spirit out of the city. The heat, though, was just as I'd remembered. I walked back into the kitchen to get myself a glass of water and found myself standing in front of the wall where Dad had written twenty-five years earlier: 'My name is Hareth Zahawi. This is my home where one day I hope to return.' And here we both were now. He'd been as good as his word, but when I looked around me the only thing that remained of our home was the house itself. The rest of our lives had been swept away, lost amid the rubble and confusion of war. The size of the challenge to rebuild a country fit for free citizens was overwhelming. As a boy I'd promised my dad that if they got him, I'd get them too, and I suppose now we had. Somehow, though, it felt like a hollow victory.

CHAPTER 19

RISING STAR?

THE PALACE OF WESTMINSTER

By 2010 I'd spent a decade as part of what was now a very successful business. I'd done what I'd set out to do – find a gap in the market and plug it. I'd also been very lucky in that I'd made quite a bit of cash on the back of it. YouGov had floated in 2005 and, as a public company, required significantly more of my time and attention than before. It also pronounced on politics; the data relied on independence. That meant I couldn't progress seriously in government without undermining the integrity of my business. Something had to give. Sadly, that thing was my political work and, in 2006, I reluctantly stepped down as councillor for West Putney in Wandsworth Council.

Time moved on, and that might have been the end of the story but, much as I loved my job day-to-day, when I looked at my career as a body of work there were still gaps I wanted to fill. There had to be a bigger, overarching meaning to life, surely? I knew a political career would mean giving up my business as well as a significant drop in salary, but when I thought about what I wanted to leave behind for my kids, I didn't want the answer to be 'money'.

In 2008, the country had entered a recession. Thatcher always said that without a strong economy you were nothing, and I knew my experience in business gave me something valuable to bring to the political table. Part of the reason I became a Conservative was because you can't do the things you need to do for the most vulnerable in society if the economy is not working. If there were ever a time to try and contribute to our country's financial reconstruction, it was now. I was nearly forty-three years old and, after a decade in one place, it felt like the right moment for a change.

I resolved to talk to Stephan but knew it would be a bitter-sweet conversation. Our idea had done better than either of us could have imagined, but we were no longer the same two people who'd met at the greasy spoon. Stephan's experience had caught up with the size of his mind; he didn't need a partner anymore. He was also very happy with where he was in life. His 1997 run-in with politics had not left him wanting more, but he knew I'd never really put the idea to bed and his response that morning was a simple, 'Go for it.'

Having been through the selection process in 1997, my name was already on the list of approved candidates so my application just needed reactivating. I re-did my CV and started applying for seats. One crucial thing to bear in mind when you're trying to secure a candidacy is that it's a numbers game. The best chance you have of winning is by applying in multiple locations. If you get knocked out in one constituency, you move on to the next and hope that at least one of them will come good. During the selection process for Devizes, I got down to the last few candidates but lost out to a brilliant lady called Claire Perry. The beautiful Art Deco amphitheatre at Marlborough College was the backdrop to my first proper political defeat. Next up was Suffolk Coastal, where the seat was won by the feistiest candidate of us all, Thérèse Coffey. Nowadays, Thérèse is known as a no-nonsense operator, and she was exactly the same in 2010. The local Conservative Association in Suffolk had become increasingly Eurosceptic so I knew I needed to tread carefully around the topic of what would become known as 'Brexit'. When the subject of the EU came up during the Q&A, I put on my businessman's hat and explained how and why I thought Europe should be reformed from within; how I believed we could create a new kind of EU, modified for the times, to better suit our UK citizens. When it came to Thérèse's turn to talk on the same subject, she responded by putting her Union Jack handbag firmly on the table with an accompanying 'Over my dead body' and waiting for the applause to subside. It was positively Thatcheresque and she unsurprisingly thrashed me.

Unlike Devizes, Suffolk Coastal allowed candidates to bring their families along for the vote so that if and when they won, there'd be someone there to clap. If you didn't win, however, it was a different matter. As soon as the Association had chosen their candidate, the losers and their families were swept un-ceremoniously out of the room to allow the winning party to celebrate unfettered by sour faces. It was a brutal reminder that in politics, unless you're someone, you might as well be no one. After I was bundled off stage and out through the back, I made my way to the car park where I found my wife, Lana, and my sons, Ahmad and Jaafar, huddled by the car. The clouds and grey skies we'd seen on arrival had now turned to premature darkness and a light drizzle. It was back down to earth with an uncomfort-able bump. We embarked on the three-hour drive back to London like a pack of tired, wet dogs. Somewhere just outside Dagenham, the mood was unexpectedly lifted by a call from my old friend Sajid Javid, who'd just heard I'd been shortlisted for the final in Stratford-on-Avon. It was a glimmer of light on an otherwise overcast day.

RISING STAR?

Jeffrey always said politics was a mixture of hard work and luck, and if I'd ever doubted that last part, events in Stratford-on-Avon were about to reconfirm my faith in gambling. Of the 650 parliamentary seats, there's normally a tiny handful of candidates who decide not to rerun at the last minute. After thirteen years in the same seat, John Maples, MP for Stratford-on-Avon, was one of them. With only three months to go before the election, John decided to stand down and I was the lucky beneficiary of that decision. Sixteen years after my first foray into politics, on a freezing February evening in another draughty school hall, I successfully beat my five opponents and bagged myself a plum seat. Now all I had to do was win it.

ELECTION NIGHT

The final four weeks in the lead-up to any election are relentless. Seven days a week, you and your team are out campaigning, knocking on doors, delivering your message. In 2010, I was not yet living in Stratford-upon-Avon, so I'd rented a flat by the canal, and Lana and the boys would come up at weekends to visit. It's a very rural seat: sixty-six villages spread around the constituency with local volunteers in each. My core team consisted of my agent, James Holloway – a lovely man who organised our daily schedule – Simon McIntyre, who'd later go on to work for me full-time, and Gary Jeffrey, who was tasked with driving us all round in a knackered old Shogun to knock on doors. Lunchtimes were sandwiches in a local pub somewhere en route and evenings were an Indian at Hussain's on Chapel Street. After that it was back to bed to rest my feet before beginning the process all over again at eight the next morning. I wore through two pairs of shoes in a month.

On the day of the election itself, the schedule was a little different. As soon as the polling stations opened, we visited them all to thank the volunteers. Tellers outside each one crossed the names of those constituents who'd told us on the doorstep they'd be voting for us off the list and fed that information back to the office. In the evening, it was back to knocking on doors and making calls to get the last votes out. At the end of that evening, when the booths closed at 10 p m , I went back to the flat to watch the exit polls on TV. It looked like Cameron might just about do it. I tried to sleep a little bit but the adrenalin made it impossible. Just after midnight, I gave in and got up and dressed again to go back to watch the count at the local leisure centre – the only place large enough to hold it. The ballot boxes came in and a big team sifted through the papers. At 3 a.m. the returning officer called all the candidates up onto the podium to announce the winner. By now I was as frazzled as a crisp but equally about as wired as it's possible for a human being to get without bursting into flames. No matter how many people had told me Stratford-on-Avon was a safe seat and that I was going to win, until I heard my name called that night I didn't really believe it was going to happen. My phone lit up with a barrage of texts. One from an old university friend congratulated me on my 'meteoric rise', which made me laugh out loud: this win had been twenty-five years in the making. Even so, I still felt like Cantona when he chipped it in to the top corner of the goal at Old Trafford against Sunderland in '96. It was the greatest feeling in the world.

Things are a bit more sophisticated now, but in 2010 the induction pack given to all new MPs was still wonderfully amateur, and I was handed a brown A4 envelope containing three or four sheets of paper telling me I was now representing Stratford-on-Avon and that I should report to Portcullis House in Westminster on Monday morning. There were no further instructions on how to become a member of parliament.

After a few interviews and photographs with local media and a slew of well-wishing messages and calls, I was absolutely desperate to get to bed, but when I did finally get under the covers the adrenalin, once again, kept me awake for all but an hour. I got back up once again, this time texting Mum and Dad to ask to meet for an early breakfast at the hotel where they were staying in town. As we discussed my news over a full English, it was the second and last time I saw my dad cry, and I reacted like any normal teenager would, beckoning the waitress for more drinks to distract from the overwhelming awkwardness of the moment.

The following day I got a text asking anyone who might be in London that Sunday to come for a meeting at David Cameron's office a few minutes' walk from Downing Street, on the north side of the Embankment. On a Sunday morning I knew London would be empty, so I drove into town and parked on Little College Street on the far side of Parliament Square. As I walked under the clock tower of the Palace of Westminster it dawned on me that this would be my office now; this was where I worked. It was a pretty sensational feeling. If I'd been in a 1940s musical, I'd have swung round a lamppost and kicked my heels, but I made do with walking down Whitehall like a really excited ten-year-old boy on a class trip to No. 10.

When I got to Dave's office, I imagined every other member of parliament would be there, but there were only about thirty of us. The Conservatives had bagged 306 of the 326 seats necessary to secure a majority so, for the first time in thirty-six years, Britain had a hung parliament. If we were going to lead the country, we'd need the support of another party to do it. That Friday, Dave had spoken to the leader of the Liberal Democrats, Nick Clegg, to offer his party a coalition. Sitting behind his desk now, shirt sleeves rolled up, ready for business, he said he believed

Nick was going to accept and that we would be moving in to No. 10. It had been three days since my election as an MP, but this was the first moment it had properly dawned on me we were going to form a government and that I was going to be a part of it. This was what I was going to leave behind. This would be my legacy.

The realities of forming that government became clearer the following day when I reported for work at Portcullis House on the Embankment. In a hung parliament it is the incumbent party's right to try and form a coalition government and, believing he could still do that, the Labour leader, Gordon Brown, had refused to visit the Queen and offer his resignation. He'd also refused to leave No. 10, meaning no one else could move in either. So, while I now had a team, a laptop, 800 unread emails and a gigantic bag of backdated post, I had no parliamentary office in which to put them. For the next three weeks, my team and I sat in the canteen on the ground floor of Portcullis House, knocking back Diet Cokes and coffee in paper cups, working from our laptops while we waited for someone to vacate a suitable space.

Eventually, I was given a good-sized office in Norman Shaw North on the Embankment, and my team and I finally set up shop. My 'induction meeting' consisted of Alistair Burt MP from the Whips' Office telling a group of excited novices not to spend too much time in the bar or do anything they'd be embarrassed to read about in *Private Eye*. Alistair was very softly spoken but serious enough for any new boy to know not to mess with him. He told us Whitehall was a place full to the brim with history and wisdom – both good and bad – and that if we had any sense, we'd take the opportunity to learn from the best of them.

When you finally got into the House of Commons itself, the seating arrangements were a mixed bag. While the frontbenches were absorbed by members of the cabinet, the backbenches were a bit of a free-for-all. If you wanted to get a prime position, you needed to think like a German and get there early with your towel – or in this case the 'prayer card' used to mark your chosen seat – to bag the best sun-lounger. This suited me perfectly. I'd always been an early riser and would get to the chamber at eight each morning because the seat I wanted was the one next to the father of the house, Sir Peter Tapsell – at that time the longest-serving member of parliament. When it came to the wisdom Alistair Burt had talked about, Peter had it in spades. He'd been an MP since 1959 and during that time had been Anthony Eden's bag carrier – or principal private secretary, as the job is formally known. Peter was a principled, outspoken and sometimes contro-versial member of the house. He'd come into Thatcher's government via the City, but he and Margaret never got on and she overlooked him for many years despite his skillset. Eventually she offered him a junior ministerial role, which he promptly turned down. She never offered him another job and he stayed on the backbenches for the remainder of his career. I knew that by sitting next to him I'd learn an enormous amount. In time, he and I became great friends, and he affectionately dubbed me 'The Pasha'. In business I'd always set huge store in the value of insti-tutional memory and there was no greater example of this in parliament than Peter. That seat was well worth getting up early for.

Many years later I would go on to become secretary of state for education and remembered what Alistair had said about learning from the best, so I set up a dinner for as many of the previous incumbents of the post as I could get together. For the first time ever, Ed Balls, Ruth Kelly, Charles Clarke, Ken Baker, David Blunkett, Michael Gove, Justine Greening and Damian Hinds sat round the same table and talked. There was more cumulative experience that evening than you could shake a stick at. These people represented the cross-party institutional memory of the past thirty-five years, going as far back as Thatcher's administration; it was impossible to put a price on its value. There was both friction and agreement where you'd least expect, and we stayed until midnight swapping stories and advice. It was the greatest focus group of all time. When the green benches were removed and the cameras taken away, the most interesting thing was how many of us agreed and got on. I, more than most, understand why a single-party country is undesirable, but I've often wished we could focus less on competing and more on outcomes.

THE INSTITUTION

When I arrived in England, you could still walk along Downing Street. A single policeman would sit or stand on guard outside No. 10 and probably even say hello as you strolled past. But there was no real reason to go there unless you were in government. All the surrounding streets were part of the political village of Westminster. There were no other offices or shops or dwellings. You only went there because you worked there. Once upon a time that policeman would sit in the Listening Chair – a comfy, button-backed, green leather seat with a canopy that covered the occupant's head and curved around their sides. A chair designed to amplify any sounds of feet on cobbles or intruders at windows. A tin-lined drawer underneath the seat enabled hot coals to be put inside to warm the guard on a chilly night's watch. Nowadays, it sits inside the foyer of No. 10 as a reminder of a time long gone.

The level of pomp and circumstance outside the doors of No. 10 reflects the fact that some of the most important decisions in global history have been made behind them. Inside, though, there's more of a day-to-day, corporate nature to the atmosphere. There are visual reminders everywhere of the building's history,

242

but there's also a cafe in the basement that could pass for a Costa and one loo that never flushes properly.* Just like every other office, people gossip about 'Julie' from Accounts and question the fact why anyone in their right mind would start a meeting at 4 p.m. on a Friday afternoon. The guarded gates and polished brass make it seem like everyone inside is set apart from the real world, but really, there are no superhumans in government. Just ordinary employees. There's no magic about it.

The greatest example of this for me was the afternoon I saw Mrs Thatcher at one of Jeffrey Archer's infamous summer parties in the gardens of his home in Grantchester. I'd stayed there a few times with her and Denis as guests of Jeffrey and Mary, and was used to seeing her on fighting form. Unlike John Major, who loved to put his feet up with a plate of fish and chips on Jeffrey's sofa and unwind, there was never any downtime with Margaret – at least not that I saw. Even at the weekend she brought her handbag down to breakfast. On this particular afternoon, Stephan and I were enjoying the show as she delved into memories of her past dealings with Europe alongside another of Jeffrey's guests, Peter Lilley. Peter was a Thatcher loyalist who'd served under her for most of her tenure, so when she began to lecture him on how *her* cabinet had done things it took a moment for those of us present to realise what was happening. I knew that Margaret had had dementia for some time, but when you saw her holding forth on subjects dear to her heart, you'd be hard pressed to believe it. It was staggering to see someone so verbally and cognitively adept forget something so fundamental. It just didn't seem possible. But dementia can be very deceptive. Margaret was able to relay reams of information with a level of detail few others could match and it was only her not

---

* The private one next to the chancellor's office.

remembering that Peter had worked under her that made it clear something was amiss; like watching a synapse fail to fire in real time. I hoped she'd realise her mistake and correct herself, but when she continued on, it fell to Peter to tell her kindly, 'But Margaret, I was in your government.' There was a moment's silence before she moved on without explanation, as if it had never happened. It was totally heart-breaking. This was the woman my mum had repeatedly pushed in my face as an example of what the freedoms of this country meant, and now here she was, no different from any other frail old lady who couldn't remember her phone number or where she'd put her house keys. None of our group discussed it afterwards, as if there were a collective reluctance to acknowledge her mortality. It was the perfect demonstration of the fact that however much we want our leaders to be supersonic, flawless versions of ourselves, Westminster is full of normal people, doing their jobs, just like in every other office on earth.

The parliament of my youth was quite different from the one I walked into in 2010. Under Thatcher, cabinet would be attended by the secretaries of state, the cabinet secretary and one more notetaker. There was a clearly defined line between the front-benches and the backbenches, and most people waited a considerable time to move from one to the other. When Tony Blair came to power, however, he brought with him a more relaxed, modern approach to politics that had its upsides but equally its downsides too. In many respects I'm a big fan of Blair – he's one of the greatest communicators of a vision we've ever had in both politics and government. People understood the journey he wanted to take us on and – like all the best leaders – he was not only able to envisage something but sell it too. But I disagreed with his erosion of hundreds of years of formality. Blair was like the cool teacher who gets the class to call him

Tony, and I got that: but for me, Whitehall was a different matter altogether. I hadn't thought so at first, but was quickly seduced by the history inside the chamber walls and began to understand why time inside them had moved more slowly. A respect for the institution was part of the job. My relationship with Boris was a very good example of this. By the time he became PM in 2019, I'd known him for nearly twenty years. He'd worked for me at YouGov and I'd had to chase him for his homework many times. Once he was elected, however, I never addressed him as anything other than 'Prime Minister' or 'Boss', even outside of work. It was a boundary that allowed me to do my job with the necessary objectivity. Some years later, it was that same boundary that would allow me to compartmentalise my emotions from my ethical duty and write him a letter advising him to stand down.

To an outsider, I'm sure 650 people addressing one another as the Honourable or Right Honourable such and such seems absurdly antiquated, but it didn't take much time for me to understand that these traditions had been developed for a reason. Things in the chamber can get very emotional. By definition it's a place where at least two groups of people elected expressly *because of* their opposing beliefs come together to argue their point, and it's easy to get upset from time to time while doing this. So you train your brain not to let things get personal; to know that this is your job and that, in the heat of the moment, having to pause for a second to remember to say the Honourable Lady or Gentleman might prevent that moment from getting the better of you.

The first time I heard the division bell as an MP, I watched open-mouthed as hundreds of us crammed through the underground tunnel that connects Portcullis House and the Houses of Parliament to enter the division lobby to vote. Sometimes this happened several times a day, and the response was Pavlovian.

We'd all drop what we were doing – however important – and funnel as one back through that tunnel and into the chamber. Surely this was an insane waste of human resources? Something that could take thirty seconds was taking at least fifteen minutes and breaking our focus from whatever the task was at hand. Why on earth were we not doing this online? After a time, I began to see more layers in the mechanism at work. I realised that if you were a backbencher wanting to get hold of a minister, there was no better time to do that than during the vote. If your constituents were being hurt by a particular piece of policy, the chamber was the best place to buttonhole the minister and lobby them in person; to refuse to take no or the standard letter of response for an answer. I realised, on reflection, that there was a reason traditions like these had existed for hundreds of years. It was a climate-specific piece of evolution.

So while I understood why Blair felt like the modern world called for a more modern government, I think the slackening of rules around cabinet meetings was a mistake. During his meetings, the room would be filled with not just secretaries of state but also ministers eligible to attend, as well as twenty or so advisors on the outer circle beyond the main cabinet table. The net result was that much of what happened inside those walls leaked straight out – a situation that continues to this day. Once that started happening, it meant the driver was no longer in control of his horses. In fact the cart was now driving the horse. It was impossible to expect such a large, amorphous group to contain the conversation – especially when you added twenty-four-hour news to the equation. That monster needed constant feeding to sustain its output, so the press were always on the hunt for something to say. When social media came into play, it created an even greater, insatiable, appetite for news. There were many more examples of hair-trigger decisions being made in response to media noise, which, to my mind, undermined the very existence of cabinet. Why bother with a group of elected senior politicians debating and turning over evidence as part of a 360° view of government if ultimately decisions were going to be made to manage a headline? That level of short-termism, in my view, is deeply damaging to good governance. In the end, I'm sure Blair must have realised this too because he eventually created a kitchen cabinet where all the really important stuff was hashed out. Effectively, he did away with the old system and recreated it upstairs in the flat. Despite the desire to be informal, there was a reason why the tighter cabinet worked. A respect for the institution was vital to the proper running of government and to maintain control of your own agenda.

I grew up with a cast-iron respect for the institutions and traditions of this country. The British represented a form of dignified control in Iraq that was washed away after the fall of the monarchy and replaced with a bloodbath that lasted almost fifty years. The Iraqi monarchy was uptight and old-fashioned and sometimes unnecessarily formal, but what replaced it was barbarism and totalitarianism. Sitting here now, it occurs to me that perhaps part of the reason I am less inclined to shun the old formalities is because, in my mind, they are inextricably linked to a sense of safety and morality that I preferred to what followed in Iraq. When you're used to your freedom, it's easy to attack the institutions around you simply because you can. Having come from a place where the pillars of society were routinely dismantled, my underlying fear is always that we'll take these freedoms for granted and become apathetic about politics. It's easily done when you've not lived with the alternative.

TO WESTMINSTER

THE SUBS' BENCH

After thirteen years, Labour had been relegated and my team were finally back in the Premier League. When the names of the winning MPs were revealed, I appeared again in the *Telegraph*'s list of 'Rising Stars', which suggested   at least to me   that I was about to be catapulted directly to cabinet on the back of a comet. I wasn't, but practically everyone else I knew was. Sajid Javid, Priti Patel, Matt Hancock and Liz Truss were all speedily promoted under the Cameron–Osborne regime while I sat on the subs' bench for the following eight years, hardly ever getting to play in a match. Occasionally I'd be called on at the last minute for a bit of much-needed energy if others were flagging, but it never amounted to any tangible recognition.

So why wasn't I getting any further? Looking back, I think part of it was that I just wasn't shouting loud enough. It wasn't in my nature. I knew lots of people who believed in 'growth mindsets' and 'managing up', but I came from a background where, if your work was good, that was all you need worry about. Do your job, do it well and someone will recognise you for what you are. In fairness, before I'd come into politics I'd either been an integral support to the founding team or a founder myself, so there'd been no time to sit around strategising about power structures. You got on with the job at hand because if you didn't, no one got paid. I had no idea how to 'manage up' because I'd never had to. I just wanted to work. I did feel I was well liked in parliament, but evidently that wasn't enough. If you wanted to make your way to the frontbenches, you had to be pushy too. As much as Whitehall was supposedly concerned with outcomes, it was also about perceptions, and on that front I evidently wasn't putting enough spin on things.

For a time, I felt like those eight years on the backbenches had been wasted; that while others were making headlines, I was plodding through the mud in waterlogged boots. Actually, they were anything but wasted. I'd amassed a huge amount of additional experience to add to my existing skillset. When I did finally reach the frontbench in 2021, when Boris made me secretary of state for education, I realised my perception of my political career to date had been completely skewed. In business, the leaders I'd valued were the ones who'd worked their way up. They were the ones with a 360° understanding of the company, who could turn their hands to most things if they had to. There was really no reason to think government should be any different.

But there was undeniably a paranoia about how slowly or quickly your star rose in Westminster, and that was partly down to the way our political system worked. The term for a government could not exceed five years. In practice this was often four years or less. As a result, the window in which to get noticed was pretty short. The whips would do their best to keep everyone focused and motivated, and part of the way they'd do that was by making space for new people. Before long, there'd be another election and another intake, and your rising star would be old news. So it's no surprise that many MPs felt that if they hadn't reached the frontbench in one cycle, they'd failed. Interns who end up running a FTSE 100 company within five years are few and far between, so the fact you didn't do this in government should not be regarded as a black mark. Backbench MPs were doing exactly what they were elected and paid to do: represent the interests of their constituents. Having now experienced political life from the 'bottom' to very close to the 'top', I can honestly say that, by a country mile, the best and most fulfilling part of the job has been just that: getting in a room with the people I represented and seeing whether I could work out a way to help them.

Nevertheless, the Holy Grail of getting to cabinet is something that drives pretty much every politician I've ever met; after all, the ultimate historical footnote is that your society decides to elect you as one of the handful of people that leads them. If you happen to come to parliament when your party's in opposition, however, that could mean your entire career is spent without the chance of becoming a minister. There are many brilliant Labour MPs who've never had the opportunity to put their talent behind a department, who've spent the bulk of their career patiently waiting their turn. I've been incredibly fortunate that my entire time in parliament to date has been as part of the party in power. Sometimes, it's just about luck.

Today, the pathways to power are more direct and clearly thought out, but most twentieth-century leaders had an entire career before entering government. The decision to go into politics tended to be something a person made *after* they'd experienced life in the wild. By the time I got to cabinet, I saw there were various members who excelled in one specific field but far fewer with the skills to run the complex systems of a whole department. It became clear that if you hadn't gained that kind of experience before you got to parliament, you'd potentially struggle once you got to the top. On the night of my selection in Stratford-on-Avon, one of my opponents was a lady called Georgina Butler – a retired British ambassador to Costa Rica and Nicaragua – who, at sixty-five, was by far the oldest of the candidates. 'Wouldn't it be nice,' wrote our moderator that night, Matthew Parris, 'if our House of Commons began more to represent, not just the gender, sexuality, class and ethnic backgrounds of the nation as a whole, but its generational cohorts too? ... men and women who have pursued – and completed – distinguished careers outside.' It was a remark that would only resonate when I got to cabinet and saw the true complexities and responsibilities involved in running an entire department.

Historically, you wouldn't expect to make it to cabinet for at least a decade. Thatcher took eight years to reach the shadow cabinet, eleven to take a seat at the main table and twenty to become PM. It took Churchill thirty-six years to get the top job, Attlee twenty-three, Macmillan thirty-three, Callaghan thirty-one, Major eleven, Blair fourteen and Johnson eighteen. So really, I'm not sure what I was worrying about. A slow journey was nothing to be ashamed of.

FROM BUSINESS TO POLITICS

While I'd consider myself to be a fairly bright guy, I was not the same as Dave or George or any of the team that had come up around them. There was a confidence to Dave's inner circle that I can only think came from a certain kind of background. Was my nose put out of joint by this? Probably a little bit. After all, Cameron's premiership dominated my early years in parliament. I had been privately educated for the latter part of my schooling, but as a teenager my copy book was heavily blotted and I wasn't the kind of clever that would have taken me to Oxford or Cambridge. I wasn't serious enough about life and I hadn't been schooled in the right way to get me there. I'd gathered experience over time, but I didn't come from a background where everyone I knew was going to end up 'being' someone. At times it did feel like I wasn't good enough for the Cameron team and, if I'm honest, I found some of them a little arrogant. But the question I had to ask myself was whether I really would have been ready for government – let alone cabinet – had I *not* gathered that experience outside of Westminster. Would I have been ready before the collapse of Allen Hinckley? Before I'd lost money and experienced failure? I honestly don't think so. I'm very fond of telling anyone who'll listen that all the greatest entrepreneurs have lost money before they've made it and it's only in doing so that you understand its true value. It's also a good test of whether you'll find a way to get back on your feet when faced with a problem or come to a grinding halt. For me, losing that money was one of the greatest lessons of my career.

In recent years, there's been a far greater number of MPs whose only experience of the working world has been within the narrow confines of Westminster. They may have a full Rolodex and a pin-sharp take on parliament, but what they've potentially bypassed on the way is life and situational experience. Senior ministers are moved from department to department, often at short notice, and are expected to perform to the highest standards and adapt to their surroundings on the spot. Between September 2021 and October 2022 I went from education secretary to chancellor, to chancellor of the Duchy of Lancaster and then to chairman of the Conservative Party. These were senior jobs in education, finance, operations and marketing. I was expected to do each of them equally well and sometimes with only a day's notice and no material handover. In the public eye, there's no time to get things wrong or learn the ropes, and politics is the only 'business' I know in which something that absurd would happen. One of the biggest issues in our society now is that we sometimes expect people in power to be perfect. This is not only unrealistic but incredibly unhelpful, and even more reason I'd argue that significant real-world experience in a senior politician is not only desirable but necessary. The trouble is, the salary of a senior minister is relatively low compared with that of a senior executive at a FTSE 100 company, especially when you consider the amount of experience realistically needed to do the job properly. Encouraging people with enough of it into govern-ment, therefore, is another matter altogether and will be one of the greatest challenges to face liberal democracies going forward.

All that said, had I stayed in business, I know I'd have been much more limited in my outlook. The upside of those eight years in exile was that I got a taste of a huge range of issues while I was trying to keep myself busy. I indulged my love of global politics on the Foreign Affairs Select Committee and my love of commerce on the Business Committee. When I was appointed education secretary, creating 'learners for life' was the long-term aim of the game: turning kids into adults with a healthy appetite for absorbing new things by developing new facets to their personalities and equipping them with the skills to do that. While I'd scraped through school by the skin of my teeth, those eight years on the backbenches, hopping from topic to topic, felt like another crack at the whip. A second chance at my education. Quite apart from kicking my heels, my years in the wilderness were the greatest apprenticeship I could have had and the best possible training for cabinet.

GETTING STUFF DONE

In 2015, five years after I'd first been elected as an MP, to the outside world I was no further up the political ladder than when I'd started, but that didn't mean I hadn't progressed. I'd gained a huge amount of new knowledge and the select committees were where I'd amassed a good deal of it. For me, the select commit-tees were the part of our parliamentary system that worked best. While the Punch and Judy stuff went on in the chamber on a Wednesday afternoon, behind the scenes the committees were weighing up the evidence and coming to a measured – and crucially cross-party – conclusion. I loved this part of my 'training' and would recommend it to anyone entering politics. The irony of it was, if you rose very quickly through the ranks, the biggest thing you missed out on was the opportunity to sit on one because you could only do so as a backbencher.

Like many other new MPs I was desperate to get my teeth into something meaningful; something that might make a material difference to people on the street. The job of these committees was to scrutinise the executive – be that regulators, unions, government, academics or big corporations – and it made sense that any MP sitting on one should have prior experience relevant to its remit. Given my background, the obvious place for me to start was the Business, Innovation and Skills Select Committee and, in July 2010, when the whips opened the nominations, I put my name forward for my colleagues to vote on. Within a week I learned I'd been successful and took my place on the committee under the chairmanship of Labour MP Adrian Bailey. During the next five years we looked at everything from what went wrong with Kraft's takeover of Cadbury's to Lord Browne's work on the reform of how we fund higher education, and much else in between. It was a wide and varied portfolio of inquiries.

In early 2015, I was approached by the MP for North East Hampshire, James Arbuthnot, to discuss an issue due to come in front of the committee later that month. We met for coffee in Portcullis House one afternoon and he told me the story of a man named Alan Bates, who'd become a subpostmaster in Craig-y-Don in North Wales in the late 90s.

In 2001, Alan had realised that the software system used to tally his daily finances failed to tie up with the money in his cash bag. Over a two-year period this happened many times, and despite contacting the Post Office on hundreds of occasions, he was repeatedly told that no other subpostmaster had ever reported the same problem and the fault must be in his own calculations. In time, internal Post Office documents would reveal their appraisal of Alan as someone who 'struggled with accounting'. These discrepancies, they said, would be marked against him as a loss and he'd be personally liable to pay back the missing funds. Absolutely certain this was not an error of his making, he refused to both hand over the money or take responsibility for the losses. In 2003, the Post Office terminated his contract.

Unbeknown to Alan, subpostmasters all over the country had indeed been experiencing the same problems but most had handled matters somewhat differently. Many had paid back their shortfalls and consequently re-mortgaged their homes, got into claustrophobic debt or struggled with mental health issues. Some had even been tried in court at the behest of the PO and served custodial sentences as a result of their 'offences'. Each and every one was told the same thing: no one else had reported a problem with the accounting software provided by Fujitsu. Alan Bates eventually gathered a small group of subpostmasters who'd found themselves in similar circumstances and formed the Justice for Subpostmasters Alliance (JFSA) group, with a view to fighting the powers that be. That small group quickly grew until they numbered in their hundreds. Spearheaded by Alan, they then took their complaints to Westminster, where they found the sympathetic ear of MP James Arbuthnot. I'd always liked James. I'd known him since coming to parliament and admired the way he operated. I was not at all surprised to hear how diligently he'd been working with Alan and the JFSA to bring their case in front of the select committee. James had a beautiful morality about him but was incredibly humble with it. A truly decent man, he was not afraid to get into the weeds and get stuff done. He was the kind of person we needed more of in parliament. On 15 February 2015, their case was finally due to be heard and I would be sitting on that committee.

Prior to any such hearing, the clerks prepare a selection of appropriate questions for the members. Having heard what James had to say about this case, it seemed clear something serious was amiss. I felt it would be better to ignore the predetermined questions and go in with an open mind and listen to the testimony from both sides before I decided what might or might not be relevant.

The primary witness that day was a woman I'd not met before: Paula Vennells, then chief executive of the Post Office. Alongside Paula was her sidekick, Angela van den Bogerd, as well as a forensic accounting expert called Ian Henderson from an independent company called Second Sight, who'd been employed by the Post Office to look into the allegations. Ian's delivery that day was straightforward, expansive and wholly authentic. His testimony was not 100 per cent polished but it didn't need to be. It was the truth. He struck me straightaway as a no-nonsense sort. Paula, on the other hand, was a lady with whom I felt almost immediately ill at ease. Ian claimed that, despite repeated requests, the Post Office had failed to provide him with the documents required to carry out the investigation they themselves had ordered. Although he'd been told the principle behind the exercise was 'to seek the truth irrespective of the consequences', his requests for the materials to do so had been met with a series of obstructions: that 'under no circumstances' was he going to be given access to the files requested; that he was 'entitled to the public documents that would normally be available to the defendant if the case had, for example, gone to trial'. Whether, as Paula claimed, this was 'the first time personally' she had heard these things, she had an opportunity now to commit to cooperating without obstruction going forward. However, when I asked her directly, 'Why don't you give those files over? What's the problem?' she prevaricated. 'As far as I'm aware, Mr Zahawi, we have shared whatever information was appropriate ...' 'That,' I told her, 'is not what Ian Henderson is saying.' She persisted in evading the question several more times before finally passing it over to her colleague, Angela, who proceeded to deny any attempt to obstruct Ian's access to the information needed. Over the course of those few minutes it became obvious the situation was an utter shambles and I told Paula exactly that. When I reiterated my question about whether or not she would commit to providing the requested documents, her continued equivocation gave me my answer, which, it seemed to me, was a 'no'.

By 2015, this case had already dragged on for more than a decade. Almost another decade later and things have still not been satisfactorily resolved. Alan Bates and the JFSA are still fighting for an appropriate settlement, and although some compensation has been paid, the one thing they have never received or been offered is an authentic apology or admission of responsibility. To my mind, any apology given has come with caveats and a defensive posture. Paula's ongoing claims of ignorance around various aspects of the case that day told me everything I needed to know about the kind of leader she was. Whatever she had or hadn't known about where the dust was hidden, as chief executive, the buck stopped with her. She didn't need to be infallible or superhuman but, had she been the kind of boss who'd led from the front, she'd have taken the opportunity that day to acknowledge the mistakes of the organisation she represented and committed to a change of course going forward. The fact she didn't was what stood out to me.

In life I have learned there's a certain kind of human being who believes themselves to be above all others. People who cultivate a layer of contrived moral superiority that prevents them from ever truly looking in the mirror and acknowledging their mistakes or recognising they could be wrong or need help. When

I'd pushed Paula that day she finally told me she had the 'reputation of the Post Office to consider'. What, I thought, did that matter when what had happened in its name was destroying people's lives? What did that even mean?

The Post Office scandal – as it would come to be known – was not my fight to win. I was a tiny cog in a much bigger wheel that still continues to turn. In time it would gain much greater traction – particularly after an ITV drama depicting events surrounding Alan Bates et al. – but, at the time, it was one of dozens of inquiries I'd sat on. Anyone whose case had reached that level was at an impasse. What they needed was input and support from an impartial third party, and it was my job to give it. What I valued about my role on these committees was the chance to bring my business experience to bear in a way that could make a fundamental difference. It was exactly what I'd come to Westminster to do.

But my skillset wasn't always wanted or welcomed in parliament. A year or so later, I came face to face with what had seemed like the ultimate opportunity to bring something valuable to the table. My offer of help, however, was met with a very different response.

By this point I'd had over five years as a backbencher to grasp the mechanics of government – at least the part of it that I could see from the back row. I'd seen how Cameron and his chancellor, George Osborne, operated as one entity, and it was an open secret they had an agreement that once they'd won the referendum vote – as they believed they would – Dave would hand the baton on to George, who would carry on the work they'd started. It was exactly what Blair and Brown had done in 2007, but a seemingly more amicable arrangement. In January 2013, Dave had made a public commitment to hold a referendum on our membership of the EU if the party were still in power after the next election. When they were re-elected in 2015 it was time to pay the piper, and the government began to prepare for a vote.

In the midst of all this, I received an unexpected invitation to tea at No. 11. Since George was now gearing up to take over, I assumed he was on the lookout for support within the party. I was an odd choice of target. Alongside Jesse Norman, I'd helped destroy what George and Dave had considered a major plank of the coalition agreement they'd struck with Nick Clegg when we'd led the rebellion against the abolition of the House of Lords. Ever since then, I'd been on George's naughty list. With the pleasantries out the way, he launched straight into flattery. 'You're a very talented guy, Nadhim; you should be doing more in government.' This was lovely to hear but also quite amusing, given it was partly what I saw as his distaste for me that had stopped me from doing just that. I thanked him anyway.

The funny thing was, despite not being part of their gang, when it came to Brexit, I did feel they had the right strategy to reform the EU from the inside rather than make the split. Despite being a Eurosceptic myself, I felt that if they were serious about negotiations, we would be able to make a deal that would satisfy the nation and I'd be able to come out for staying in a reformed EU. It was in my interests, therefore, to do anything I could to make that happen.

I also believed I might be able to help. Although I only had five years in Westminster under my belt, for more than a decade I'd been in operational control of a company whose bread and butter was public opinion. At YouGov I'd made my living from research and data. Like me or not, I felt I was an objectively good player to have on the team for this particular match. As far as I was concerned, these guys were about to crash and burn, and my chat with George that afternoon seemed the perfect face-to-face opportunity to show my support. I opened the conversation with a bid to work with them on the mechanics of the European question. Clearly George did not think very much of this offer. As we sat facing one another, he put his hand out to stop me mid-sentence. 'Don't worry, Nadhim,' he told me, in a voice full of quiet confidence, 'it's all under control.' After promising he would find something else for me to do, he walked me to the door of his office and I left confident in the knowledge that wherever we did or didn't land on Brexit, I would not have played any significant part in the outcome.

I'd be the first to say I've hitched my wagon to a few people with some pretty obvious flaws, but, given the choice, I'd pick fallibility over arrogance any day of the week. I'd much rather deal with someone who is open to the idea they could be wrong than someone who believes they're too clever to need help or advice. Because you know what? They screw up too. We all do. It's what humans do. This was an opportunity for George to take advantage of significant support, tailored to an issue that would have a huge and long-lasting effect on people's lives. I think the reason he didn't accept it was because, with the arrogance of a younger man, he never imagined the result would go in any direction other than the one they wanted. I've met George in more recent years and found him to be a much humbler version of the person I remember from that day in No. 11, but, at the time, I didn't believe negotiations were ever taken seriously enough by either the EU or the Cameron–Osborne team, and I eventually accepted that the only solution for us was Brexit.

When it came to the question of Europe more broadly, I was not ideologically opposed to the notion of integration. As a concept to bring us closer together and create a level playing field over a much greater populace, it was good thing. I wanted Europe to succeed. The reason I became a Brexiteer was because I didn't believe the direction of travel would lead to success. Supporters of the European project have a vision for what they want to achieve, but they have a very different tradition to us. I share their desire for peace and prosperity; what I don't share is the roadmap.

If you look at our country, we have the most successful transfer union on earth. But it only came about after hundreds of years, a civil war, war with the Scots, and England, finally, emotionally buying into the idea of the redistribution of its wealth to its less prosperous regions and the three other nations of the UK via its tax system. We have a sovereign currency – the pound – and the Bank of England stands behind it. Once Europe had decided it would have a single currency – the euro – someone had to stand behind that. What you have to ask yourself is whether the most powerful economy of Europe – Germany – would stand behind that currency and buy into the idea of transferring their wealth for the next century to the less prosperous parts of the European Union. The West Germans did it for the East to reunify their country after the Nazis ripped it apart, but it cost them a trillion euros. It was easier for them to buy into that emotionally because it was their own country. I simply don't believe the German people would agree to the transfer of wealth to another country without also having control over that country's budgets. Conversely, if you're the leader of a European country that needs financial support, are you really going to win an election by telling your electorate that your budgets will effectively now be set by a German chancellor? A small country like Greece had had to take the pain in this way during their financial crisis, but I just don't believe that construct is sustainable in the long term. At some point it will fracture and, when it does, I'd rather we were on the outside. Ours is a significant economy. We'll do well enough on our own. Once the EU gets over the hurt of us leaving, a new generation of politics will emerge, with new people who will want to work with us, but once again we have to take the long view.

After the referendum it no longer mattered what Dave or George thought of me or my expertise. When things didn't go their way, Cameron stepped down and any hope George had entertained of moving into the big office went with him. A leadership contest ensued and it was down to the winner, Theresa May, to clean up the mess.

As a junior minister, my dealings with Theresa were pretty limited. Added to that, she was a woman of few words and someone I found fairly difficult to read. The closest we got to any real interaction was in the dying days of her administration. Despite her determination to deliver on Brexit, she'd allowed herself to be surrounded by people she trusted but who fundamentally did not want the same thing. What they wanted was a rerun of the referendum. Sadly for Theresa, this meant losing not only the parliamentary party but also the party membership and, ultimately, the country too. Alongside fifteen or so other junior ministers, I'd organised a meeting to tell her the government was paralysed and the situation couldn't go on. In the event, she stepped down of her own accord so there never was a need for our meeting. She was a decent woman and I didn't envy her having to clear up after the vote; it was a thankless task.

Under Theresa's tenure, I finally progressed. In 2018, I was made children and families minister in the Department of Education – a department I would later go on to run. The work I did there as a junior minister was some of the most rewarding of my career, but it would take the reappearance of a familiar face on the horizon before I was asked to get involved in something that would change not only my life, but the world as we all knew it.

CHAPTER 20
THIS IS NOT A DRILL

HOW TO BE NIMBLE

By 13 February 2020, I'd moved into the Department for Business, Energy & Industrial Strategy (BEIS) and was serving under Alok Sharma. That Thursday I was asked to represent us in a mock pandemic preparation COBRA meeting alongside ministers from every other department. In the chair was health secretary Matt Hancock flanked by the chief executive of the NHS, Simon Stevens, and the chief medical officer, Chris Whitty. Each of us was given a confidential deck and shown a presentation about what might happen if a flu pandemic hit the UK. Chris showed us charts on rising cases and the percentage of population killed, and we talked around the manifold issues we'd be faced with in such a scenario. The moment we went into demo mode, no one was to 'break character' until it was over. The simulation hypothesised people were dying in droves, the nation had been told, and it was our job to manage the crisis and do our best to balance the needs of our various departments.

Among other things, we discussed the option of turning the Royal Parks into temporary morgues to accommodate the rising number of bodies; how we could ensure the safety of soldiers in charge of our national defence; how our nuclear weapons and power stations could be protected and our energy supplies maintained. And what about our transport systems? Could they stay open? The same for schools, universities and local government? And banking? Do we shut the City down and, if so, what would that do to the economy? From every angle there were conflicting positions of arguably equal importance. The number of decisions was endless and none of them easy.

Unsurprisingly, a huge part of the discussion centred on protecting the NHS. I asked whether we could create more field hospitals, but Simon said essentially that was a rounding error: with half a million deaths a year, it doesn't matter how many new hospitals you build if you can't staff them. We talked about the moral and ethical decisions that would inevitably arise: who not to treat if the situation reached that point. The elderly? The frail? The terminally ill? And who would make those decisions? The politicians or the clinicians? We all agreed the latter. A body of physicians, chaired by Chris, would draw up a list of criteria on how to prioritise treatment. A completely impersonal, dispassionate checklist for every hospital to work to.

When the day finally ended, I left the building utterly shell shocked. If that ever happened, I thought, we are properly stuffed. How would we ever explain those kinds of life-changing decisions to the public? I didn't think for one minute it would ever become our reality. Like everyone else, I went back to my department and got on with my day job.

Unbeknown to me, three weeks earlier, Matt had chaired another COBRA meeting about a potentially worrying new pathogen spreading through China but it was concluded the risk to the UK was low. Over the course of the next few weeks, the world began to hear rumblings about people falling over in the street and the Chinese government insisting that whatever was responsible for these incidents was under control. But of course it wasn't. Six days after that first COBRA meeting the first two cases of this new virus were confirmed on our shores, and it wasn't long before I found myself back in 70 Whitehall to talk about what the world was now calling the coronavirus.

LOCKDOWN?

I wasn't yet in cabinet or part of the Department of Health so much of this had gone over my head. I was unaware, for example, that by the middle of January NHS England were having daily operational meetings about this new pathogen. My role at the meetings I was called to was to represent the interests of BEIS, which was responsible for 80 per cent of the economy – covering, as it did, everything from foundation industries such as steel, all the way to nuclear, construction, life sciences and professional services. The COBRA meeting I attended on 19 March was a chance to take soundings on a possible 'non-pharmaceutical intervention' – a.k.a. lockdown – and my first question was, 'Are we sure we want to do that?' If the evidence was that the virus was more severe for the elderly and the vulnerable, why not spend the billions it would cost locking down protecting just those groups instead? It was primarily Chris Whitty and Jonathan Van-Tam, the deputy chief medical officer, who coordinated thoughts around this, and the equation was a fairly simple one: was the possible damage of asking people to stay at home worse than the risk of them mixing, and the answer was deemed to be no. Early transmission rates were 20 per cent, so not mixing was a practical way of curtailing the virus. Today there are those who question why we didn't opt for the bell jar approach – locking down the most vulnerable groups and letting everyone else get on with their lives. The truth was, in the early days, we had no clear idea what the mortality rate was or much about how it was transmitted, so our only real option was to plan for the worst-case scenario. You have to remember, there was no blueprint for something like this – certainly not in a highly mobilised world – and very little information to go on. What we really needed to know was how quickly the coronavirus would mutate. Over time, viruses become less dangerous but more infectious. If they kill their host they've essentially failed because their job is to replicate. The most successful are those with the strongest transmission mechanism. At this point, we didn't know the periodicity of ours and consequently, how long it might go on for. More important than that, there was no sign of a vaccine on the horizon, so its growth rate would be exponential because we had nothing to stop it in its tracks. This wasn't just a question of how many people it might kill but whether it could break the NHS in the process. Our determinant was how many intensive care beds we had and the answer to that was, not enough.

I was still only a junior minister when the pandemic hit – too junior to hold any real sway in a meeting of this nature and not yet part of cabinet discussions. I'm sure, however, there must have been conversations around the idea of just letting the virus run its course. In that scenario, people would die but, equally, by locking down, there would be serious consequences for the economy, education and people's mental health in the longer term. The fact was, at the start of the pandemic, mortality figures were projected to be half a million. I don't believe the public would ever have accepted the idea of allowing those deaths to happen if we had the option to try and prevent them, even if we *could* have demonstrated the higher possible long-term costs of a lockdown. We were juggling with people's lives; not many would be brave enough to take that kind of a risk – especially in the face of near unanimous scientific recommendations. The summing-up at COBRA that day had little to do with our soundings. It was clear the decision had already been made. It wasn't what anyone wanted but, until we had a vaccine, there was no other lever to pull.

I walked out of the building and along Whitehall towards my office on Victoria Street. It was a beautiful sunny afternoon and Parliament Square was heaving with tourists and commuters. The steps to the underground were a sea of bobbing heads, all completely unaware of what was about to happen. One part of me felt like I'd been dropped into a scene from the film *Contagion* – the virus silently passing from person to person as they jostled alongside one another. It's easy to be more relaxed about it with hindsight, but I remember the very real fear this was going to kill us all. Equally powerful was the belief that everyone around me now was going to go nuts at the news. How on earth would we explain to them, the public, that in a few days' time all our lives were going to change forever? Even now the thought of that moment brings me out in goosebumps.

Four days later, Boris made an address to the nation. He did what had seemed inconceivable in that dummy run less than six weeks before and sent nearly 70 million people into lockdown.

THE VENTILATOR CHALLENGE

In the early days we thought intubation – and consequently ventilators – were the big thing. The modelling suggested the NHS needed an estimated 30,000 more machines, but our two primary manufacturers were only producing a combined total of about sixty a week. At that rate it would take a decade to hit our target, and we only had twelve weeks. There had to be an alternative.

In May I was asked to dial in to a call with the PM and the CEOs of sixty-five of Britain's biggest industrial companies to discuss how we could either step up production of existing devices or design new ones from scratch. Airbus, JCB, Ford Motor Company, McLaren, Dyson – you name it, they were on that call. Boris did what he did best and went full Churchill. 'I need you,' he told them. 'The NHS needs you.' It did the trick. I left the call in no doubt that some of the most innovative companies in Britain were about to put their intellectual and commercial weight behind solving what was dubbed the 'Ventilator Challenge'.

After any call like that in government, someone has to follow up with any sweeping necessary to get the project off the ground – following up with action points to translate what's been discussed into results. In layman's terms, to get stuff done. Ultimately it would be BEIS that would operationalise the programme, so in this instance that sweeper was me. Luckily, if you put the word 'challenge' after anything, I'm like a dog who's just noticed his owner is holding a dirty tennis ball. Inside I'm jumping around manically just waiting for him to raise his arm and throw it. I was in my element.

On the other side of the project, representing the NHS, was someone I'd come to know as an absolute powerhouse of a woman: Emily Lawson. Emily had become the NHS national director for transformation and corporate operations before being promoted to chief commercial officer in 2020. In November 2020, Boris had drafted her in to stabilise the PPE situation and, once she'd handled that, she'd moved on to work on the Ventilator Challenge. Throughout the pandemic, government and the NHS worked in tandem, and Emily was the one with her ear to the ground on all matters outside Whitehall. Professor Ramani Moonesinghe was the clinical director for respiratory medicine in England and told us what needed to be the case for a ventilator to be a safe piece of medical equipment, and this formed the baseline of the spec we gave to everyone involved in the challenge.

Running alongside all this, Emily and the NHS were anxiously plotting the number of patients on ventilators to see at what point they'd reach their limit, and Patrick Vallance, chief scientific officer, and Chris Whitty were attempting to design the lockdown around this variable. On the commercial side of things, Gareth Rhys Williams – the government's CCO responsible for any contracts we took out – liaised with Emily to decide the kind of numbers of machines needed to prevent the NHS collapsing. I sat below all this in the department responsible for working out how we'd make the machines they needed, and the guy that oversaw *that* was Dick Elsy.

Dick is a brilliant engineer who ran the High Value Manufacturing Catapult for the government – a non-profit, independent organisation that promotes and supports the research and development of new products. Dick had been drafted in by Boris to oversee the consortium of manufacturers willing to try and address the issue of our ventilator shortage. In his day job, Dick was used to companies sharing innovation and working together for the best possible outcome, so was the ideal ring-leader for the project. The reputation of Dick and the Catapult was part of what made these companies feel comfortable taking that kind of corporate risk. In the end, it was he who told me we had no hope in hell of making 30,000 ventilators in twelve weeks if we were going to design and manufacture them from scratch.

The main obstacle was that any machinery, especially anything related to medical equipment, has to go through the regulator, who would not be able to test and approve anything in less than four to six months. Even with all this talent onboard, delivering in twelve weeks wasn't going to be possible, but Dick had a backup plan. In the UK, we had two designs already approved by the regulator: if we took these and paired them up with a big manufacturer it would be quicker and cheaper to modify and scale up their production lines than produce new models from scratch. And so it was that Smith Industries and Penlon were matched with Ford and Airbus, and production of our new ventilators began. In the end, we needed less than half the estimated 30,000 machines, but by July 2020 the consortium had turned out 13,137 units for approximately 50 per cent of the usual cost. It was an unmitigated success, and a demonstration of Britain's innovative capabilities and industrial capacity.

One of the greatest things about the Ventilator Challenge was how nimble we were able to be. The crisis necessitated cutting through red tape and bureaucracy. That isn't to say the process lacked checks and balances; these were highly sophisticated pieces of equipment, so ensuring they adhered to regulatory standards was paramount. What it did mean was that everyone involved was inspired, motivated and – crucially – empowered to work to the absolute best of their abilities unfettered by unnecessary restrictions. It was what Dick called the 'stop-at-nothing culture'.

Like me, Dick would tell you there were huge lessons to be learned from the way we ran the challenge, that bright minds excelled in an environment where they could let their imaginations guide them. 'When you set the right environment up, empowering people to do the right thing, minimal bureaucracy and no heavy-handed oversight, it is amazing what you can achieve.'* It was a concrete lesson in how we could work together for better outcomes going forward.

* https://catapult.org.uk/dick-elsy-reflects-on-his-journey-as-ceo-of -high-value-manufacturing-catapult/.

CHAPTER 21

THE MOONSHOT

THE VACCINE ROLLOUT

While I'd been busy on ventilators, Patrick Vallance had convinced No. 10 we needed a Vaccine Task Force (VTF) to try for a moonshot, and in May 2020, Boris appointed a venture capitalist called Kate Bingham as an advisor to chair it. A standard vaccine took around ten years to produce, and while the team felt they could reduce that considerably, they still hadn't expected to be vaccinating people until Easter 2022.

Since the Department of Health was already massively overstretched, it was agreed the VTF would function as a separate entity and would sit, fortuitously for me, within BEIS. What Boris wanted now was a dedicated point person within government to concentrate on deployment when the time came, and that's when he called me.

Before the Ventilator Challenge, I don't know that the role of vaccine deployment minister had even been thought of, but my work on the former effectively formed the basis of my 'interview' for the latter. Evidently, I'd passed the test because Boris was back on the phone and now *I* was getting the Churchill treatment. 'I need you,' he told me. 'Your country needs you.' As luck would have it I was in full-time excited-dog mode, so this was music to my ears.

At this point, my relationship with Boris inside Whitehall was still that of PM and junior minister. I had a history with him from the early days of YouGov and we knew each other well enough to be honest with one another, but, as a junior minister, my view of him as leader was restricted to the cheap seats. Even so, from what I could see, he was pretty bloody dynamic in this environment. It was quickly becoming obvious our country was at war and this outwardly bumbling, slightly chaotic man had stepped unexpectedly into the shoes of a wartime leader. I'd served under two other PMs and, for all his flaws, Boris was by far the most decisive and commanding of the three. It was clear to me that, as long as you delivered, he'd back you and let you get on with it. The things Boris has done wrong are easy to list, but what many miss is the huge amount of energy he exuded in a situation like this. There was an extraordinary sense of possibility when working around him: an innate feeling you could get things done. He was one of the few people I'd worked with in government who had this quality, and, for me, it was this that made him a powerful leader. If there were ever any obstacles during the rollout, Boris was not one of them.

When he called to ask whether I'd take on the role I said, 'Of course, boss.' If I'd learned anything from my dad's entrepreneurial streak it was that this was one of those things you didn't say no to. You agree first, and worry about how you're going to do it after you put the phone down. Nevertheless, my acceptance came with a caveat: I could only do the job if I could speak with his authority. I knew there'd be gatekeepers around him and I didn't want to be waiting days or weeks on critical decisions. Decisiveness and the ability to act were key to success in a situation like this, and I knew I'd need to be properly empowered if I was going to do the job to the best of my ability. The response was a typically Boris-esque, 'You've got it.'

THE MOONSHOT

Back in BEIS, my own team were brilliant about the fact I'd be dropping my ordinary responsibilities. Gerry Grimstone and Paul Scully took over most of my portfolio, and Alok Sharma was equally supportive. 'You're gonna make history,' he told me. Having seen how badly PPE had damaged Matt Hancock's reputation, whether I failed or succeeded, I was in no doubt about the truth of Alok's statement. The move was a gamble. My friend Jamie texted immediately with the message 'It's a poisoned chalice' and the journalist David Aaronovitch – whom I very much admired – tweeted that Boris was a fool for appointing such a lightweight to the role. Neither of these comments filled me with hope but my country was at war; I had no intention of missing the opportunity to make a difference.

HOLDING ON TO RISK

By trade our VTF chair, Kate Bingham, was a venture capitalist who specialised in healthcare. Kate was married to my colleague Jesse Norman, so we'd been friends for many years and I knew her to be a hugely accomplished, competent, straight-talking woman. Had she not been willing to chair the VTF pro bono, I doubt we could have afforded someone anywhere near as accomplished. Kate's job was not just to identify and source a viable vaccine but to get the public to buy into it, and I'm not sure which was the bigger hill to climb. However effective a vaccine turned out to be, if we couldn't convince people it was safe, we were stuffed. Kate had an almighty task on her hands, but I could not think of a better person to tackle it.

Like me, Kate came from a world that relied on risk-taking and creativity, where you rose to the top – at least in part – because of your willingness to try something new. She was used to taking responsibility for the success or failure of her actions and understood error was a legitimate part of the path to success – especially in a high-stakes operation. This was not standard practice in Westminster. As a new minister back in 2010, I'd found it odd that senior politicians were surrounded by gatekeepers trained to subcontract risk out to someone or something else, to hold it at arm's length from the very person put in place to hold it. There are some brilliant civil servants in Whitehall, but the shock, horror, 'gotcha' drive of the twenty-four-hour news cycle has undermined their desire to take chances because the UK media does not allow for failure. The net result is that we've normalised the idea that a minister should be protected at all costs. That it's better to take the safe route than expose them to any possible criticism. That under no circumstances should the blame ever land at their door. This ethos was as alien to me as it was to Kate. In any working environment of course you aim to minimise mistakes – and learning from them is critical – but if the only thing you're focused on is the avoidance of criticism, your output will be correspondingly narrow. To my mind, a good minister should get used to holding risk because, when you're shielded from it, it comes back and takes your head off anyway.

Jeffrey Archer always said that Thatcher loved a crisis – that it brought out the best in her – and I was the same way. Whether it was covertly flicking chalk at the blackboard behind the teacher's back or escaping the police outside White Hart Lane, I thrived on adrenalin. That I could use this aspect of my personality now in my job was just a very happy coincidence. I also believed I had one other advantage over many of my colleagues during the pandemic: I was quite used to working in situations of extreme stress. Fleeing Iraq aged twelve turned out to be the first of many intense situations I'd need to process. From snowbound mountains in war-torn Kurdistan with Jeffrey to the Republican Palace with my dad and the US army – these scenarios required an ability to drown out the noise, stay focused and make decisions with clarity and confidence, and they served me well in my new role. Our country was at war and I quickly found I was very comfortable fighting in the trenches.

READY FOR PRIME TIME

The list of people who worked on the vaccine is awesome in the truest sense of the word and I couldn't possibly hope to do their work justice in the space I have here. Suffice it to say, the 'government's' response to this national emergency was actually a combined effort of many thousands of hardworking people who stepped up for their country in a time of need. I was just one of a handful of front-facing players you may have seen on TV or read about in the papers, but behind the scenes there were many, many others doing their part to make a coherent, efficient whole. If you were in the trenches with any of these people, you'd be amazed they're not now household names. We owe them a huge debt of thanks for what they did. There are undoubtedly lessons to be learned from the pandemic about preparedness and the need for early, decisive action, but this should not detract from the gratitude owed to the thousands of people who put their own lives on hold for the sake of the nation and who walk among us every day without recognition.

Under the 'executive' tier that included Boris, Matt, Rishi, Michael Gove and Dominic Raab, the VTF represented the supply side of the equation and was a rainbow team, pulled from all walks of life to ensure the greatest range of experience and skills. Each person brought a different perspective to the table, making for more effective problem-solving. In all, there were seventy-six people on the core team* – about a quarter of the number overseeing this area of government now. It was pretty astounding what they managed with such small numbers but in part, I believe, this was because Covid was apolitical. Just like the cross-party select committees I'd sat on, there was no room for game playing or egos, which, to my mind, always made for better results.

Kate's director general and SRO within the VTF was another remarkable civil servant, called Nick Elliott. As well as handling all interaction within government, Nick put everything Kate thought of into action. With the product sourced and optioned, he and Kate went back to their day jobs, leaving Clive Dix to take over as chair. Under him was another formidable woman, Maddy McTernan, who stepped into the role of SRO and negotiated internationally to secure our vaccine supply. Maddy was a master negotiator whose kind face and infectious smile would have made her an excellent baby-faced assassin. She expertly navigated some fairly choppy waters and kept the vaccine flowing from Europe. Alongside Maddy was Ruth Todd. Ordinarily responsible for the contractors supporting our nuclear submarine fleet for the MoD, Ruth became our logistics and supply-chain supremo, making sure everything got made and came in on time. Not only was she competent and efficient, but, because you knew she understood every step of product development, manufacturing and regulation, it was also impossible to pull the wool over her eyes. The fact she had a brilliant sense of humour made my day-to-day job even better.

---

* The full VTF was about 200 and included the team looking after efforts internationally and the teams dealing with strategy and HMG policy.

NEEDLES IN ARMS

Thanks to a mixture of innovation, dedication and dogged hard work on the part of many hundreds of people, by November 2020 the vaccines had been sourced and approved, and the team were getting ready to protect the nation. While Kate and Nick had managed the selection and supply of vaccines from the pharmaceutical companies and seen them to the point of regulation, the manufacture and supply were still very disrupted and needed lots of care, attention and support to make them routine. As with many product launches (especially with such a new product), there were lots of opportunities for things to go wrong. From the government's side of things, my job was to take up the reins from where Kate left off, and operationalise and regularise the work she'd started.

Although I was officially seconded to work on deployment, that arm of the system depended for its success on supply, so, in truth, I sat between the two divisions. My job was to kick the tyres for Boris. 'You're my Beaverbrook,' he told me. It was a classic piece of Boris flattery; Beaverbrook had mobilised industrial-scale resources during the Second World War for Churchill. His comment did the job nicely. I was primed for the challenge, locked and loaded. If it looked like bureaucracy might be about to get in the way and make it difficult for anyone on the delivery team to do their job, it was my responsibility to head them off at the pass. If the team was in any way faltering or uncoordinated, it was my job to fix that too. In short, as the minister given responsibility for both sides of the equation, I was the bridge between the two.

I was not the only person in Whitehall to be repurposed in 2020. There was a huge amount of movement among public servants, with many who stood out in their field being seconded elsewhere for the war effort. This was standard practice when one part of government needed reinforcements, and it was the job of the perm secs in each department to identify the right people for the task at hand and shift them to the area of most need. None of these people were paid anything other than their normal salary and, in a few instances – where people such as Kate were drafted in from the private sector – they worked for nothing at all.

On deployment, the chief executive of the NHS, Simon Stevens, was 'The Experience', and there wasn't a nut or bolt in its plumbing he didn't understand. Simon once again drafted in Emily Lawson of PPE and ventilator fame to work her magic and make sure the plan was fully integrated and ready for prime time. Alongside Emily we also got Brigadier Phil Prosser, commander of 101 Logistic Brigade. Phil was the guy within the armed forces who was responsible for delivering combat supplies, including medicines, to British troops on the frontline in time of war. He was just the man we needed now.

Emily hit the ground running and did what she did best: identify the flaws in the plan and work out how to fix them. When she was told she'd be getting a new vaccine deployment minister, her response was that she'd really rather no one else interfered in what she was doing, thank you very much. Knowing her as I do now, that doesn't surprise me at all. Emily was a person who could easily have turned around any FTSE 100 company but had chosen instead to devote herself to public service. I would soon learn she was someone who never, ever took her eye off the ball, and our partnership would prove as good as anything I'd done with Stephan at YouGov. Although she was eminently capable of handling the rollout for the NHS, where NHS and government operations met we needed a dedicated point person in Whitehall to facilitate the conversation in both directions. I may only have been a junior minister, but the advantage of my time on the backbenches was that I now had ten years of wide-ranging political experience under my belt as well as another twenty years in sales and operations. I'd been waiting a long time to put my skills to good use, and this was my chance. While Emily knew the NHS inside out, I knew how to navigate the corridors of political power, and both areas were of equal importance when it came to realising our goal. Together, I felt, we were greater than the sum of our parts.

A great example of this belief came on my first day in the post when the patient group directions (PGD) threatened to derail Emily's plans to get needles into arms. A PGD is the legal certificate that allows a nurse, rather than a prescribing doctor or nurse, to administer a vaccine to a member of the public. Ordinarily, getting one of these signed off would take twelve weeks. In an environment in which hours and minutes could mean the difference between life and death, such a lengthy time frame was untenable. Emily was stuck because this was an issue that sat somewhere in the grey area between her 'shop' and mine, and the problem required a bit of diplomatic footwork. Fortunately, this was exactly my area of expertise. As soon as I left our first meeting I was on the phone, wheeling and dealing in Whitehall to try and find another, quicker route to our destination. Jonathan Van-Tam, deputy chief medical officer for England, was the key to my success. Prior to this, Jonathan had worked across academia and corporate pharmaceuticals, and there was nothing he didn't know about the world of medicine. Within twenty-four hours we'd worked out how to reduce the approval process to a matter of days, which meant very capable nurses weren't sat twiddling their thumbs because of a piece of paperwork. Emily is a pretty formidable woman – and by that I mean intimidating – so I was very pleased to have resolved the very first problem in both her and my path in such a short time. It was a happy start to our relationship and one that I hope gave her faith in this minister's ability to do a good job.

SPACE TO DELIVER

In situations that require a complex and coordinated approach, it's also common to set up an operational HQ to ensure every facet of the bigger picture sits under one umbrella, easily visible to and accessible by the government. The rollout was one such scenario, and it was agreed the deployment team would be embedded inside NHS England headquarters at Skipton House, a mile and half away from Downing Street, just over the river. The NHS now sat alongside the police, military, and fire and rescue – just like a war room.

By the time I reported to the Department of Health in November 2020, Emily had already been there three weeks and had made significant headway. On her arrival, bits and pieces of the rollout plan were in place but the NHS was stuck in the complexities of not knowing which vaccines would be approved or when. It wasn't until the week she took over that we received clinical data showing Pfizer's 95 per cent efficacy rate, meaning we were finally able to move forward in the knowledge we had a viable vaccine on the table. And then there was the Treasury to contend with. Despite the fact we started vaccinating in December 2020, they'd still not signed off the money to fund the operation. In fact, the business case wasn't approved until New Year's Eve that year, so services and products had been ordered from DHSC funds prior to a decision about who was going to pick up the bill. It was a pretty nailbiting time and the job Emily had been tasked with was an extremely complex one to say the least.

KEEPING THE FAITH

In the first instance, I think it's fair to say there was a lack of trust from government towards Emily's team: a fear that this was going to go wrong just like everything else. After Test and Trace and PPE, Boris desperately needed to maintain public confidence in the rollout and was understandably nervous about falling on his face. Throughout my time in the post, he'd call every evening around 11 p.m. to debrief, and I soon sensed he was in a panic about the team's ability to deliver. This was best demonstrated by the fact that Emily spent twenty-four hours in assurance meetings in her first week alone. One of my biggest concerns was her diary and making sure she had the space to deliver. To make matters worse, anyone who had Boris's number was now calling with their hot take on things. When we were weeks, if not days, away from deploying the biggest peacetime mobilisation in history, I wanted to tell them that if we were still thinking about how to move or store the vaccine, we really were in trouble. The press – either panicking or looking for headlines or being slow to share vital information when a better story came up – were an additional pull on our resources. Oddly, despite being in the middle of a global pandemic with its attendant logistical nightmares, the noise was one of the greatest challenges of my job, and all this armchair analysis was in danger of unnerving Boris and destabilising the team.

It very quickly became clear that one of my biggest challenges was to change people's attitude in No. 10 and the Cabinet Office towards the team. Someone like Ruth, for example, had thirty-five years' experience doing stuff like this but was regularly having to explain to senior advisors and politicians how you make and produce a vaccine at volume. This was time that could have been better spent elsewhere. Individually, the people running the rollout were all at the top of their game. In isolation, they were capable of great things, but when you pulled them together and took them as a whole, they were superhuman. In layman's terms, they were the Avengers, but with a highly contagious, acute respiratory disease rather than Thanos as their enemy. It was a crack team even Tony Stark would have struggled to pull together. What they needed now was for everyone to trust in their abilities and let them get on with their jobs. Flicking that switch was one of my primary tasks.

Personally, I had no reservations about either the procurement or rollout teams' abilities to deliver. On my first day in the post, Emily had invited me to sit in on their daily meeting and it was clear she ran an extremely tight ship. She took me through the strategy and I could see it was watertight. Nevertheless, despite knowing the implementation was pretty much all in place, it was still a huge task to keep people believing in us, and I'd estimate a third of my time was spent responding to questions from both No. 10 and MPs – 'Have you *really* looked at every possible way of maximising needles in arms because every day matters?' 'Is my constituency going to get its fair share of doses?' They were varied and unending. Communication was vital, but ensuring the team weren't distracted by the noise was a constant battle. No. 10 needed reassurance that their concerns weren't just disappearing into the ether because they were answerable to the public and, while the team did need space to deliver, they also had to make sure the necessary information was fed back to No. 10 – or the executive as I liked to call them. That's where I came in.

Emily and I had an unspoken agreement: she'd make sure I was well briefed and able to speak with confidence to government and the media, and I, in turn, would do my best to create the calmest, most productive working environment I could for her team to get the job done. In an effort to quieten some of the noise from No. 10 and reassure the PM, she and I eventually colluded to bring Phil Prosser to one of our meetings so Boris could get a sense, first hand, how the Avengers and their war room operated. There was something incredibly reassuring about Phil. He spoke with such authority it was like a shot of Valium in the arm, and I saw Boris visibly unwind in his presence. On the back of this, I suggested getting Phil up on screen at the next press conference; if the public could see how composed he was it would calm them, just as it had done Boris. Phil eventually appeared next to the PM on the podium in the press briefing room at No. 9 Downing Street and spoke to the nation. I sat and watched like a football manager who'd had the instinct to put his best player on the pitch and was now seeing him deliver. Internally, I was punching the air with joy. I don't think it's an exaggeration to say that Phil was part of the reason No. 10 were so successful in delivering their message around the vaccine. It is no surprise to me that he has since been promoted even further to the rank of major general.

The executive weren't the only ones who needed reassurance around safe delivery of the programme. By the time we got to December we were fielding something like thirty MP inquiries a day, as well as hundreds of questions from GPs and other community practitioners. Clearly these people all needed answers, but the way we were managing the responses was an increasingly poor use of our time. With this in mind, I decided to set up a weekly Zoom call and invited all 650 MPs to join. This was the best way I knew to communicate our message to the whole of the Commons and take on board their concerns based on what they were hearing on the ground. Often these calls would include Emily and the medical director of primary care, Nikki Kanani, who was the clinical lead on the programme, as well as two brilliant members of the NHS – Dr Jonathan Leach and Professor Anthony Harnden. MPs were my main conduit back to their constituents, so when someone said they had pregnant women in their community or parents worried about children, these professionals could share the evidence they had and reassure the MPs about the choices we'd made within the programme. It was a hugely important factor in transmitting the confidence I had in Emily's team to MPs and, by extension, the public. Every single person on those calls set aside their political differences and, despite regularly having information before it was publicly announced, there was not a single material leak during the lifetime of the programme. It was extremely refreshing to work in this way and gave me renewed faith in my profession.

THE DATA

Part of the stress during the pandemic was the fact that so much of it was out of our hands and we'd never had to deal with anything like it – on this scale – before. My approach to this lack of control over our circumstances was a reliance on the data. From my earliest days in business, it had been my go-to source of reassurance; it drove everything I did commercially. It was what allowed me to get confident holding risk. Part of the success or failure of most businesses rests on whether you're able to keep pace. Every morning when you wake up there are decision points. Knowing what to take on board is as important as what to ignore or table for a later date. The key is being able to identify what's material to success and knowing how to drown out the rest. The only difference with the pandemic was that failure to make the right decisions would mean more people died, and knowing which way to jump was not always easy. We were swimming in deep water and the data, for me, was like sonar.

A great example of this was the Joint Committee on Vaccination and Immunisation (JCVI) – the body tasked with deciding who to vaccinate and when. The entire thing was run by medics under the leadership of Professor Wei Shen Lim, who was a certified genius. We looked at everything from ethnicity to profession, and all the evidence demonstrated age to be the greatest determinant of outcomes for the virus. Given the NHS had the address, gender and birth date of everyone in the system, if you wanted to protect at scale and pace, there was no quicker way to do so than by age. Despite this, the buffeting soon came – not just from the press but the unions and Opposition too, who were pushing to vaccinate teachers and frontline workers first. Once again, there were no easy decisions, but if we stopped to ask whether these people were teachers or assistants or just working in a school, we'd delay the process for months, during which time we could have vaccinated another five or ten million people *including* the most vulnerable teachers and frontline workers. The data was what allowed us to make a clear-sighted, logical decision in the face of a very emotive topic. With hindsight, it's easy to see that the countries who yielded to the noise and deviated from the plan were the ones who screwed up their programmes. For me, it came down to the data every time.

At the height of the roll-out, the data came in at breakneck speed. We'd chosen US firm Palantir to work with us on the tech side of things. From their platform, Foundry, they developed a management information system that enabled us to see daily figures on who'd been vaccinated, as well as when and where. I could cut and slice it whichever way I needed, which was critical for both my understanding of things and my ability to share it with the executive and the public with complete transparency. A huge part of the programme's success hung on confidence, and the data was a critical part of that equation. At first, the NHS was only updating the public once a week on the stats, but my instinct from my time in YouGov was that we needed to be more frequent and more granular with the data. When I first suggested we share the stats daily, I was told it would be too difficult – that it was resource-hungry – but, with Palantir's approach (which took imperfect data and made it tell sensible stories) it was easy, and the NHS quickly accommodated the shift. When I moved into the DfE less than a year later, I did the same thing. I went before the Education Select Committee and said I was going to publish our key decision and delivery points for the next two and a half years. My civil service team were nervous. If we missed a target, what would happen then? But that, I said, was the whole point. We'd hold ourselves to account, and if we missed a target we could explain why. The rollout was no different.

Out of all the countries in the world I think we did the best job in terms of vaccine confidence. We faced many hurdles but worked creatively with communities to try and resolve them. The best example of this for me was Tottenham. Fairly late on, we still only had a 24 per cent uptake in vaccination among the Afro-Caribbean population. Our initial thought was, perhaps the community were uncomfortable making appointments over the phone or online and that we needed more walk-in centres. A look at the data showed there were more centres within five minutes of those postcodes than in Stratford-upon-Avon, which had an 80 per cent uptake almost immediately. Without Palantir, we could easily have spent half a billion pounds trying and failing to rectify the problem with more walk-ins. In fact, the issue turned out to be a cultural one. Many of these communities were first-generation immigrants with a mistrust of government because historically, big pharma in their country of origin had done some dreadful things to their communities in the name of medicine. These fears were understandably deep rooted. What these communities needed now was the equivalent of a Phil Prosser, someone they trusted who could speak to them with confidence and make them feel safe. The solution came in the form of local ambassadors; people of the same ethnicity from the community – often practitioners themselves – who'd already been vaccinated. These ambassadors went door to door to reassure communities about the efficacy and safety of the programme and talk through people's fears without judgement. Our plan was a success and the uptake in vaccinations rose accordingly.

In retrospect, I know Whitehall did its best to give us space to deliver but the truth was, they were looking for reassurance because they felt out of control too. Just like every other person on the planet. Even with all the information at my fingertips, I woke up every day just as scared as the next person and went to bed wondering what would happen next. I'll never forget walking along Piccadilly one evening. The shops were battened down and the road so empty I was able to walk right down the middle, completely unimpeded. I was the only human being there. Six months before I'd watched as swathes of commuters funnelled into Westminster tube and wondered how we were ever going to tell them their lives were going to change; now, here I was, wondering whether life would ever return to normal. I didn't know if the vaccine would solve our troubles or whether this would be the place where another life form would one day land and say, 'That's where they used to live.' People in Whitehall felt no different from anyone else.

My time on the rollout was undoubtedly pressurised but it was nothing compared with two months' home-schooling an eight-year-old. Despite the fact my wife and I are both well educated and we had two sons in their twenties on hand to help, online schooling was the hurdle at which we fell. As soon as Mia worked out she could play Roblox at the same time as being signed in to a maths lesson, it was game over. I take my hat off to teachers everywhere and their ability to do it day in, day out. The one saving grace was that I still had a job to go to – even if that only meant walking into the spare room that I'd converted into an office. During the rollout, I was on TV most days presenting the data. The bookshelf backdrop option was far too pretentious for me, so instead I went for closed curtains and a Union Jack I'd purloined from the office to make sure foreign diplomats knew I was broadcasting from London. Little did they know that under my desk it was only ever bare feet and shorts. My allegiance to those was still just as strong as it had been in 1970s Baghdad.

For a few hours each evening we attempted to regain some sort of sanity as a family and ploughed through all eleven seasons of *Curb Your Enthusiasm*, followed by a back-to-back binge of *The Sopranos*. Boris would call religiously between 10 and 12 for a catch-up and then it was back to the box set. In the end, we were averaging three episodes a night and I was going to bed at 1 a.m., despite a seven o'clock start. It was a relaxing but addictive outlet. The violence was just a sideshow to Tony's vulnerabilities, and I was almost as invested in him as the rollout. No doubt Dr Melfi would have had something to say about the significance of that …

CHAPTER 22

A HOMEGROWN SUCCESS

OXFORD ASTRAZENECA

In the sourcing phase, Kate Bingham had gathered data from around 130 labs that were developing vaccines. She and her team decided which ones had potential and which made no sense to explore. After whittling them down to a shortlist of around nine, Maddy McTernan began supply negotiations and they eventually settled on three, which were optioned and contracted.

Oddly enough, the first supplier I met with was someone I'd had dealings with in 2014 on the Business, Innovation and Skills Select Committee during a proposed hostile takeover of AstraZeneca by the American Goliath, Pfizer.

AstraZeneca was run by a lovely guy called Pascal Soriot, who was convinced Pfizer were trying to devalue his company in order to swallow it up. Pfizer's CEO had more or less been given the nod to do that by No. 10 and consequently came to the hearing with more swagger than John Wayne. Convinced he was going to walk it, he was arrogance personified. Pascal and his team, conversely, were superb – largely because they were completely authentic and honest. The committee took Pfizer down question by question until it was clear they weren't looking to buy AstraZeneca to make the world a better place. They just wanted to smash the two companies together to consolidate costs and were looking to buy it at a fraction of what it was worth. Under our grilling, it was impossible for Pfizer's CEO to hide his true motives and it was an absolute pleasure to see this guy's flimsy case fold in two. Given Pascal's operation is now one of the most valuable companies on the Footsie, it was one of the best decisions we've ever made. A British asset now worth about £140 billion remained independent. Pascal was pretty thrilled to have won, and nearly ten years later when I called him to talk vaccines, I wondered if he'd remember me. 'Of course!' he said. 'You saved my company.' And boy was I glad we had ...

But it wasn't Pascal who developed the vaccine. In January 2020, a professor of vaccinology called Sarah Gilbert at the University of Oxford had read a report about four cases of a strange kind of pneumonia in Wuhan, China. Within two weeks, her team had designed a vaccine against this new pathogen and within eleven months it was approved for use in the UK. Sarah's was one of the 130 labs who'd responded to the PM's call to action. What she hadn't had was the ability to scale up, so Maddy and Matt Hancock teamed her up with Pascal and the Oxford AstraZeneca vaccine was born. Pascal's board agreed to provide the vaccine at cost during the pandemic, so made no profit at all in those years. Of course they'd go on to profit from the fact they now had a fast-tracked vaccine, but we, likewise, benefited from their ability to provide us with it. The civil service is a fantastic piece of infrastructure but there's no one out the back with a Bunsen burner knocking out life-saving medicine. Without Pfizer, AstraZeneca et al., we'd have been up the creek without a paddle. As of January 2022, 2.5 billion doses of the Oxford AstraZeneca vaccine had been produced and distributed to over 170 countries globally. Not bad for a university town with fewer than 200,000 people, and a brilliant example of what we can do as a country when we invest properly in our research and development.

At the height of the programme, demand reached the stage where governments – including ours – were seriously discussing the option of dropping in special forces abroad to get their shipments back home. During the PPE crisis, there'd been all sorts of shenanigans around supplies. Intelligence agencies were allegedly stopping planes in Asian airports to bribe pilots to divert cargo away from its intended destination. It was clear we were operating in a world no one recognised. Police and security services did amazing work to keep things moving and theirs is a part of the story that will never fully be told. Everything from petty theft to the highest-level threats from hostile states had to be mitigated, and the most incredible thing was how tight our control was over the product. Right at the start, Emily looked at the distribution of the vaccine as if we were building a medium-sized supermarket and transporting gold. We needed to know where every single dose was at every single point. Which lorry it was on; when it was arriving at a distribution centre; when the box was defrosted; when the dose went into someone's arm and who that person was. If there were any unexpected side-effects, we had to be able to track the exact vial responsible. The data system Emily and the team had built with Palantir was able to track all this and, from day one, we were able to see overnight data for every single dose administered by hour. It was so granular and our traceability so good, the day two single vials were stolen, we knew immediately they were gone.

Making a vaccine like the Oxford AstraZeneca one isn't like making an alarm clock or a trampoline. It's a living entity, and all the money and angry phone calls in the world weren't going to make it grow any faster. Just as with the ventilators, more than one 'model' had been optioned because no single lab could manufacture the volumes needed in the required time frame. A brilliant company called Oxford Biomedica produced 80 per cent of our Oxford AstraZeneca jab, and we were helping a factory called Halix in the Netherlands manufacture the other 20 per cent. Anything beyond that would go to help Europe's own production. I say 'helping' because the Oxford AstraZeneca vaccine technology is not that easy to transfer. It's a really fragile cell structure – a biochemical reaction – and the correct conditions to produce it in are extremely difficult to emulate. If you get it wrong, it doesn't multiply and you end up with nothing. In the end, we sent our own engineers from across the UK bioindustry to Halix to make sure they got it right.

Just as Boris was pressing for greater scale and faster deployment, I got a well-timed call from a crossbench peer, Karan Bilimoria, then president of the Confederation of British Industry (CBI) and a hugely successful entrepreneur. The world's largest vaccine manufacturer was a company called the Serum Institute of India, and Karan told me its founder, Cyrus S. Poonawalla, thought he might be able to help us out with additional vaccine doses. Serum had already manufactured 25 million doses of the Oxford AstraZeneca vaccine, but the developing world wasn't yet ready to deploy. We were fairly mature in our distribution mechanisms and therefore in a position to make a deal with Cyrus to take 4.5 million of his doses – doses that would otherwise have expired before he'd had the ability to use them. But, when it came to supplies from India, there was the issue of the regulator to consider. Kate Bingham and her team weren't sure the facilities in India would be suitable because the Medicines and Healthcare products Regulatory Agency (MHRA) didn't have a history of regulating those factories and the UK doesn't buy medication from anywhere not approved by its own regulator. That process could take six months, but if we could reduce it, Cyrus might just be the answer to our prayers. I asked him to give me twenty-four hours to try and work things out, and immediately got June Raine on the phone to see if we could pull this off.

June was the head of the MHRA, an incredible academic and whip smart at her job. During Brexit negotiations, one of the primary issues within BEIS was that many manufacturers were considering pulling out of Britain in the belief the UK would not be able to regulate in the way the 800 lb gorilla of Europe could. They feared Europe would dominate the manufacturing market and the UK would be left behind. June had worked tirelessly to transform that perception and demonstrate just how safe and nimble we could be as a nation, so I knew first hand how good she was at her job and that I could speak to her without frills. 'If you had to inspect a factory in India,' I asked her that day on the phone, 'how long would it take?' Her answer was the same as the one I'd given Cyrus. 'Give me twenty-four hours and I'll find out.' True to her word, she was back on the line the next day. Provided we could get her team of inspectors vaccinated, she told me, she could do it in three weeks. I'd have to supply each inspector with an individually named letter, by decree of the government, to hand over at the vaccination site, but for the sake of 4.5 million doses it seemed like a pretty fair deal.

Our next hurdle was Pascal. Although AstraZeneca had licensed the vaccine to Cyrus, that was only for sales to a pre-defined market; he couldn't sell to us without AstraZeneca's approval. Fortunately, Pascal and I had developed a great relationship by then and he duly approved the contract. He, however, was now having his own issues in Europe, with French President Macron publicly attacking him for late delivery of stock. In fact, AstraZeneca wasn't late with anything. We'd just negotiated our supplies with them six months before anyone else, and my guess was they didn't like being behind us in the queue.

Pascal was now living in Australia and was good friends with their PM, Scott Morrison, who, like everyone else, was desperate for his own supplies. Unfortunately, the 700,000 doses due to come to him from AstraZeneca were being manufactured in Italy and blocked by the EU for export. It was now Pascal's turn to ask me for a favour, and I relayed the details of the deal he and I struck back to Boris in the traditional way: 'The good news,' I said, 'is that we've got 4.5 million doses coming from India. The bad news,' I continued, 'is that 700,000 doses of our Oxfordshire supply have got to go to Scott Morrison.' I explained we'd still be 3.8 million doses up but that it would mean letting go of our 700,000 *before* taking delivery of Cyrus's surplus. There was a sharp intake of breath on the other end of the line before a typically understated Boris inquiry: 'Are you sure?' He was understandably nervous but I told him I'd kicked the tyres. 'Don't worry, boss,' I told him, 'trust me. This will work.' By now Boris had given me a nickname and, after a tense five minutes, he agreed to Pascal's deal: 'Okay, Maestro. Let's do it.' Not long after that, Scott Morrison stood beaming on live TV as the first person in Australia was given the Oxford AstraZeneca vaccine. I later learned the EU had sent envoys to investigate how these doses had been 'smuggled' out of Italy. The fact was, vaccine nationalism was a serious business and it would not be an exaggeration to say that, at one point, it threatened to derail our whole programme. If you couldn't navigate the waters, you were out of the game.

PLAN, PLAN & PLAN AGAIN

Planning and rehearsal were the key to much of our success during the rollout. It didn't matter whether the product was colour-change T-shirts or liquid gold – as we came to call the vaccine – it was all about the logistics. Transporting it was akin to moving the crown jewels but with life-threatening consequences if you got it wrong, and Ruth and I had done a huge amount of work in the background to stay ahead of the curve on this front. Her philosophy from the start was, 'What might go wrong and how can we stop it?' The team rehearsed repeatedly on paper and by talking it through to make sure they were as operationally ready as possible. Despite all this, it was sometimes the simplest things that threatened to trip us up.

On 2 December 2020, Matt Hancock – as secretary of state for the DHSC – gave temporary regulatory approval for the Pfizer–BioNTech Covid-19 vaccine on the recommendation of the MHRA. It would be another wait before we received our main shipment but, on 3 December, we received a few hundred thousand early doses to administer to the most vulnerable.

In the second week of December, a single box made its way to the Welsh NHS in the back of a white Transit van. Somewhere near Swindon, the driver pulled off the slip road for a pee, braked too hard and was rear-ended by another motorist. Unbeknown to anyone else on the road that day, this particular Transit van was being tailed by a fleet of police and security vehicles whose job it was to protect that little box of medicine. Within twenty minutes, they'd shut the M4, swapped in an alternative vehicle, switched pallets and were back on their way. This little blip demonstrated that, in a supply chain bigger than Tesco's, it was impossible to control every single element. I was reminded of Brigadier Phil Prosser's oft-quoted maxim: the reason you have a plan is not so you can follow it but so you know when you're deviating from it and how you're going to get back on track. If the question was, were the team able to get back on track when we were thrown a curveball, the answer was a resounding yes.

Despite our success in that instance, it didn't stop me feeling nervous when it came to logistics around the big shipment later that month. By 2020 we'd initiated our plans for Brexit, and throughout the rollout we'd treated it as one of our primary risks and were therefore expecting frictions at the border. Fortunately, we had the British ambassador to France, Ed Llewellyn, on our side, so when it came to the smooth movement of our shipments, we had our bases covered. This was lucky because the Pfizer shipment wasn't just *our* first proper doses but the first ones in the world, and I could not afford to have our contracted deliveries stuck somewhere in France. Despite Ed's help, Ruth and I were still on tenterhooks in the days leading up to our primary shipment.

The manufacturer had told us that once you load or move the vaccine, the clock starts ticking and you only have ten days to get it into people's arms. That time frame didn't leave much room to breathe. On the plus side, however, vaccines are small. Each tiny vial held ten shots, so our entire shipment was contained in one lorry. Even so, in terms of transportation, we were still having to invent everything on the hoof. After Ruth called an old buddy at Jaguar Land Rover who'd already been modelling scenarios to minimise the risk of their supplies being disrupted by Brexit, we copied their plans. Our preferred route, therefore, was out of Belgium, through France, into the Channel Tunnel and out into Kent, but I already had a Hercules on the tarmac so we could put the whole truck on a plane and fly it over if anything went wrong. The risk of doing something like that, however, was that we had no idea how the vaccine might respond in flight and we were eager to avoid finding out. Nevertheless, I had everything the great agencies of Her Majesty's Government could offer at my fingertips to aid safe delivery. We were as ready as we were ever going to be.

After months of planning, and supplies arriving in dribs and drabs, on 21 December the world's first major shipment of Pfizer–BioNTech was finally loaded onto an articulated lorry for export to the UK, coinciding perfectly with President Macron's surprise decision to close the border in response to a massive spike in the Kent coronavirus variant. In a twist worthy of an ITV drama, Ruth was also now bedridden with Covid but, with the help of Ed, had somehow found the energy to convince the French to let our one truck through the border as a matter of national security. If she'd not been working for us, she'd have made a brilliant Master of the Dark Arts. With a soaring temperature that prevented her from sleeping, Ruth and I stayed up texting and talking as we tracked the truck together through the night. An hour before the border was closed our magic lorry passed through customs, and I flopped into bed at 4 a.m. My briefing to relevant members of the cabinet next morning was predictably frenzied, but just as the room was about to reach fever pitch I got a typically cool and collected 'Lorry's just arrived in Haydock' text from Ruth. The team's fears around Brexit had meant we were weeks ahead of the issue, which meant my 'Good news, everyone ...' was met with a fairly satisfying thirty seconds of absolute stunned silence. It was good to know all that planning had paid off.

On 8 December, at University Hospital in Coventry, ninety-year-old Margaret Keenan became the first person in the world to receive a Covid-19 vaccine outside of a clinical trial. To this day, Ruth has the front page of the *Daily Mirror* on her wall with the photograph they managed to get of our precious cargo. After everything we'd done to protect it and maintain security around our processes, she was understandably absolutely livid. My old friend Mary Archer, in her role as chair of the Science Museum Group's Board of Trustees, asked me to get hold of the syringe and vial used on Margaret Keenan to keep as part of their exhibit at the museum, where they'd been meticulously documenting the pandemic. A tiny reminder of what we'd been through as a nation.

CHAPTER 23

A PLACE AT THE TABLE

INTO THE CABINET

During the rollout there'd been no blueprint for the team to work to. They'd had to design the programme, work out how we were going to deliver it and then make it happen. Everyone involved had to be prepared to think on their feet and remain open to new possibilities if there was a chance those ideas could lead to better, quicker outcomes. No avenue could afford to go unexplored. The key to problem-solving, I'd learned, was being prepared to investigate all angles and, in Ruth's words, 'not get your knickers in a twist' if the successful plan wasn't the one you came up with. November 2021 was a very good example of this maxim.

Two months before, I'd finally got my *Blue Peter* badge and been inducted into the Political Hall of Fame as a member of the cabinet. My work on the rollout had proved I was ready for more responsibility and, as a reward for my work, in September that year I was appointed secretary of state for education – a department very close to my heart, given my time as minister for children and families. The pandemic carried on semi-quietly in the background, but we were over the worst of it. Or so we thought. Strictly speaking, in my new role I was no longer involved in the vaccine deployment programme but, having spent twelve months of my life living and breathing it, I was heavily invested in its long-term evolution. When a brilliant epidemiologist called Dr Raghib Ali from the University of Cambridge reached out to chat, I was therefore very interested to hear what he had to say about the stats the government had amassed during the pandemic. Like me, Raghib was a data freak, and despite neither he nor I being officially engaged in the programme, I kept up a dialogue with him in my own time to satisfy my own curiosity.

When the Omicron variant hit in late November Sajid Javid was then health secretary, and he came to that week's cabinet meeting adamant we were heading for another disaster. Unlike the original strain at the start of the pandemic, this one had a 70 per cent transmission rate, so he was understandably nervous about where this was going. It was indeed a frightening statistic, but the fact remained this *wasn't* 2020. The virus had now mutated and done exactly what the virologists had predicted; it was more infectious but also less deadly. Added to that, a significant percentage of the population had been vaccinated or already had immunity from infection. We were in a much better position to handle things than we'd been in 2020.

We also had the benefit of historical data. If we took our own numbers and looked at where they'd landed in the real world, they'd overestimated the lethality every time. My conversations with Raghib had convinced me that our models had been more pessimistic than the reality, and I was now, therefore, against another lockdown. But Saj was not convinced. 'The country will never forgive us for breaking the NHS,' he said with a fist to the table. What followed was a series of very challenging cabinet discussions about the right way to proceed.

I didn't believe we'd done the wrong thing with previous lockdowns: there were legitimate arguments supporting each one. In the first wave, with no vaccine in sight, we'd had no choice but to plan for the worst. When the Kent variant hit, we'd only just begun the rollout and the nation was still completely exposed. Now, though, the picture was different. To my mind, if the NHS wasn't going to break under Omicron, the long-term effects on the economy, people's mental health and education had to now take precedence. But there was a mix of voices in those conversations – every one of them arguing for what they believed to be best under extremely testing, stressful conditions. Once again, it was a hugely emotive topic with complex questions around morality and responsibility. For me, as always, the best way to make a decision under those sorts of circumstances was with the help of the data, because data is completely dispassionate – like having a member of cabinet with no hypothalamus, able to make a decision unimpeded by fear, emotion or guilt. For my part, Raghib's interpretation of the statistics gave me the confidence to make the point to Boris that even the worst-case scenario for Omicron would not break the NHS and therefore not necessitate yet another lockdown.

But it wasn't just the historical data that helped me argue my case. Something else had also changed since 2020. I was no longer the lightweight junior minister David Aaronovitch had criticised Boris for hiring at the start of deployment. In April 2021, when I'd reported vaccination rates of over 50 per cent of the population with at least one dose, David had tweeted a very magnanimous apology: 'I'm eating my words now,' he wrote. 'He's done a great job along with a great team.' My voice in cabinet did hold more weight than before, but not just because of my new title. I had survived the last twelve months and helped make the deployment programme a successful one. I'd come through the war without injury, and my experience meant I was better prepared for the next battle and better equipped to comment on the matter.

When the pandemic had hit in 2020, I was still only a parliamentary under secretary – or PUS. Given the level of responsibility

Boris had just handed over, I thought it the ideal time to ask for a promotion. Frustratingly, his answer had been a 'no', but his response was one of the best pieces of advice I've had to date. 'Nadhim,' he'd told me, 'it's not the office that makes you; it's what you make of the office.' He rightly pointed out that no one remembered or cared what roles he'd had when he was first in parliament. It wasn't the title that mattered, he said; that was just a label. And so it was, I carried out the vaccine rollout as a PUS and Boris was absolutely right; no one cared less about my job title. And actually, by then, I didn't either. What you did with the job was what mattered, and I felt like I'd given it everything.

The vaccine rollout was the largest mobilisation in peacetime. We had 250,000 people volunteer to be part of the campaign. If anyone was worried about how liberal democracies would respond to the pandemic, that was your answer. It was a demonstration of how we could work together for the better when we really needed to. The government and the people were forced to treat one another with respect, get in a room together and talk. And you know what my mum would say about that.

Ruth will tell you the person I was at the end of the rollout was not the same one she'd met in those early meetings. That at first I'd been excited and deferential – sitting in the right place; saying the right things; looking at people in the right way – but that over the space of six months, she'd watched as I found my feet. I think that's probably true. Each time I succeeded in delivering on an aspect of my job, I gained confidence. As cabinet saw what I was capable of, I saw it reflected in their demeanour – and I felt it too. It was not so different from the way I'd felt all those years ago working with Jeffrey. When someone recognises you for your mind and effectively tells everyone else about it with their endorsement, it's hard not to feel flattered. After ten years in parliament, I'd finally been given a place at the table and I was happy to have earned my slot. It was an incredible chapter in history to have been part of.

Just like the rest of the world, many of us on the rollout had been operating remotely, conducting the whole thing from our little techno pods, never actually meeting in person. These were people I'd trust now with my life but whose faces and voices I'd only ever seen and heard through the screen of my computer. It was an odd, Orwellian experiment to have been part of, but one that demonstrated unequivocally that humans will always need other humans. I doubt any one of us will ever forget the visceral nature of the days and nights we worked together or the low-level trauma I'm sure many of us felt coming out the other side. To an extent, none of us were the same people that went into the project. At the end of July 2021, I finally got the chance to meet some of the team face to face for the first time. Ruth called us 'a group of ordinary people who'd done an extraordinary thing,' and that felt about right. Part of the greatness of our nation is that, when you really need them, there are lots of Kates and Emilys out there if you know where to look. My feeling is, let's get them into government.

As a very young man considering entering politics, I'd gone to lunch with Michael Portillo and had never forgotten what he'd said on the subject of power and responsibility. 'Always remember,' he said, 'everybody's an outsider.' Even as a secretary of state under Thatcher, he told me he'd always felt there was someone above him making the 'real' decisions, that perhaps there was a door in the corner of cabinet that led to another room where all the really big issues were being thrashed out. In all my time in parliament, I felt the same way. That there was a group of more experienced people out there somewhere, taking charge. What I learned from the pandemic was that cabinet was the last room in the building, and if you were part of that 'first' team you just had to do your best and hope it was good enough. There were no superhumans inside. I'd like to think that when I got to cabinet myself, this same thought gave me a sense of humility. We were all just human beings doing our best and, as Peter Dubens always said, the true mark of success is to be open to the idea you could be wrong. That you don't, in fact, know it all. That we make mistakes every day, and understanding how fragile things are is a good thing to keep in the back of your mind when you next make an executive decision.

There are moments after a crisis when a new kind of politics can emerge. During the pandemic, the government started treating people like grown-ups, and the nation, in turn, got used to it. People saw Chris and Patrick sharing the data and understood that, in a situation like this, there were no easy decisions. It gave me hope that if we could all get onto the same page, we could have a proper debate about how to fix our problems – whatever the issue. Despite the obvious negatives of the pandemic, our collective response felt like something of a reset and I grew hopeful we could build a new future on the back of it.

CHAPTER 24

THE LETTER

CHANCELLOR OF THE EXCHEQUER

It didn't take long, however, for things to sour. Within eighteen months, it was business as usual, except things seemed to have deteriorated even further. My hopes for a post-pandemic regeneration were looking unlikely. At the heart of it was Partygate. Many mistakes were clearly made, but the video of Boris's press secretary making light of the situation, combined with Dominic Cummings's twisting and turning to try to justify his trip to Barnard Castle, escalated the situation to a whole other plane; it was Boris's 'Let them eat cake' moment, and there was no way he could recover from such a flagrant disregard of people's feelings. On top of this came further public outrage at his handling of Chris Pincher's inappropriate sexual behaviour, which tipped things over the edge. The seeds of dissent, however, had been sown way before that.

Where many aspects of the pandemic had united both society and government and we'd had a brief respite from the noise, we'd now returned to an insane level of political backbiting and an accompanying stream of fury in the press. Even under the coalition we'd managed to get things done in government, but now we were virtually paralysed and the machine was in danger of grinding to a halt. While MPs had understood furlough during a national emergency, post-pandemic they struggled to see a clear economic strategy they could convey with confidence to their constituents. How would we get out of this difficult place on inflation? How would we help constituents with the cost of living? If you were a small business, what was the government doing to help you? What was our *leader's* economic vision for the country? What did Boris – not the chancellor, Rishi Sunak – stand for? Additionally, I didn't feel we had been sufficiently clear that we were now living in a post-war, post-pandemic economy and that there were inevitable hardships that came with that reality. There appeared to be no clear agenda and it was unsettling for everyone involved.

During the pandemic there'd really been two Borises: the one in small meetings who asked all the right questions and was thoughtful and considered, and the one in bigger meetings who was prone to a bit of showboating. Both modes had their uses, but one of his flaws was that he didn't do serious well enough, and even when he'd spoken eloquently in a private meeting, he could struggle to articulate his strategy outside of that small room. The problem is, backbenchers rely on the frontbench for a plan but they couldn't explain government policy clearly enough to their constituents because they didn't understand it themselves. In fact, even in cabinet it became obvious that we weren't clear on it either and there was a sense the ship wasn't being properly steered, that nobody really knew what we stood for. The fact MPs didn't understand where Boris was heading manifested itself in unpopularity among Conservative colleagues.

The Pincher situation was serious and should undoubtedly have been dealt with more decisively than it was, but it was really just the straw that broke the camel's back. Boris's superpower was loyalty but it was also his kryptonite. His desire to stand by Chris prevented him from being decisive. To the outside world, it looked like the PM had failed to take ownership of the problem and had instead chosen a path of denial. As a consequence, the public switched off. The danger for us as a party was that once people stopped listening, it wouldn't matter what we said. Whether it was good, bad or indifferent, it would fall on deaf ears and governing under those conditions would be impossible.

By Tuesday 5 July 2022, things had deteriorated significantly and there was a palpable feeling of disquiet in the parliamentary party. As I left cabinet that morning, Sajid Javid pulled me aside and asked for a word. I'd known Saj since the days of Jeffrey's mayoral campaign so it wasn't unusual for us to chat privately. When he led me along the corridor to the chancellor's office, however, I knew something was amiss because the chancellor wasn't in it. Rishi was out, Saj explained, but he knew Saj and I were meeting. When he said the two of them had been talking and that he was thinking of resigning, the location made much more sense. I had hugely mixed feelings about what he'd just said. Standing in 11 Downing Street with the prime minister a stone's throw away at the other end of the corridor made it one of the more surreal conversations I'd had in that building. Saj was a great friend and someone I considered to be a very decent, principled person, but I've always been of the view that when you play for a team, whatever you think of the coach, you put the jersey on, go out on the pitch, play the game and do your best. I understood his aims and respected his principles, but I also knew he'd been health secretary at an extremely pressurised time. I'd watched as he'd been put through the mill in cabinet in recent weeks over his strategy for the NHS, and wasn't sure how much of his thinking centred round this and how much was down to his issue with Boris's moral compass. Whatever the motivation, I told him if we acted now, we risked destabilising the entire government – something I had no desire to do. It was clear from our conversation that I had no intention of joining the rebellion against Boris and he let the subject drop, saying he'd think about what I'd said. At

6.02 that evening he resigned from his post as health secretary, followed nine minutes later by the chancellor of the exchequer, Rishi Sunak. I texted Lana to say I was on my way home.

These positions were not the kind that could be left vacant for any length of time, and since my name had been included in press speculation about possible replacements, I was not too surprised to get a call later that night asking how soon I could get back to No. 10. Lana drove me to Westminster and dropped me at the gates of Downing Street with a horribly prescient, 'Be careful.'

When Boris said, 'I want you to be my chancellor' that night, I accepted. As far as I was concerned, he was still my boss and I wanted to support the team, but, just as when he'd asked me to oversee vaccine deployment, my agreement came with a caveat. I told him what I believed lay at the root of current frustrations within the parliamentary party; that we'd moved from a global pandemic to a national economic emergency, and that nobody had a clue what his plan was now. Boris did what he did best and showered me with stardust. 'I agree with everything you've said,' he told me. That between us, he said, we could deliver on the economy just as we'd done together on the rollout. It was hard to resist in the face of his enthusiasm.

It would be ridiculous to say there wasn't a little bit of ego involved in my acceptance of the job, but it wasn't the same as being offered the position under traditional circumstances. If Boris went down, I'd probably go down with him, but if I didn't step up, where would that leave the country? I understood what Rishi and Saj were doing but equally, we had to have a functioning government. Keir Starmer dubbed those who remained in cabinet 'the Light Brigade', which was easy to say from the sidelines. I've always tried to put country before my party. In this instance, I believed that what we needed to do now was demonstrate a clear economic strategy to the people and I felt confident

I could do it. It was the same way I'd felt in 2010 when I'd first entered parliament: the country was in crisis and I believed I could help, so I took the job. I didn't imagine anyone would be handing round cakes and champagne. Becoming chancellor now wasn't about political gain, it was about survival.

Being sworn in to cabinet is a fairly lengthy process, and I finally got home around nine o'clock to be met with a barrage of hugs from Lana and the kids. Nothing matched the enthusiasm of my ten-year-old daughter, however, who is hands down my most loyal supporter. My phone exploded with messages, and responding proved a good distraction from the onslaught of thoughts about what the next day might bring. I got into bed at 2 a.m. and lay staring at the ceiling. Lana periodically rolled over and told me to close my eyes so I didn't die from an adrenalin overdose, and I drifted off for one unsatisfactory hour.

At 3.30 I finally gave up, showered in silence and changed into my suit. While the house slept, I sat alone downstairs and started on the briefs, which fortuitously sent me off for another forty minutes. At 5.30 it was time to prepare for the media round – not something you ideally want to face on less than two hours' sleep. The first interview kicks off at 7.05 with Kay Burley and is followed by a further nine, back to back, to cover all the broadcasters. At 9.30 you finish with ITN, and in between there's everyone from the *Today* programme to *Good Morning Britain*. One wrong sentence, and that's the day's headline. At this level all these people are good at their job, but the ones who can't hide their own prejudices are much easier to deal with than those with a less obviously anti-Conservative slant. When it comes to media more broadly, Andrew Neil is hands down the guy you don't want to go up against. Much like Piers Morgan, Andrew has the edge as an interviewer in that he's able to put his own views aside and ask you the question you'd ask yourself if you had half a brain. I admire all these journalists, but I couldn't tell you who was the 'nicest' because words like that just don't come into the equation when you're the one under the spotlight. Thankfully, I've never had a really bad interview but that doesn't mean you don't worry about slipping up before each and every one. Thanks to the internet, a 'gotcha' moment that turns into a meme will float through the atmosphere for all eternity. They're non-biodegradable and every politician wants to avoid having one out there with their name on it.

I managed to scrape through the media round that morning without putting my foot in my mouth, then headed over to the Treasury. I was greeted on the steps by permanent secretary Tom Scholar, who very kindly told me, 'The only position in government that matters at a time of instability is the chancellor. You've done the right thing.' Apparently I'd broken a world record by being the first chancellor to do the media round before stepping foot in the building, but it didn't seem like the kind of record you'd want to brag about at a party. It was just another horrible reminder of how chaotic things had become.

My plan going in as chancellor was the same as in any other job I'd had: surround myself with talent and listen to what they've got to say. The great thing about the Treasury is it's full of very talented people. We gathered the team, looked at the options, worked out where we wanted to land and made a plan. Our deadline for an announcement was what should have been the Boris/Rishi reset speech, which had been planned for a fortnight's time. It would still go ahead, but now it would be me in the hot seat. The range of options on the table suggested to me the timeline for the announcement was tight but doable, and I left the meeting that day feeling unexpectedly buoyant. Boris and I would stand up in two weeks' time, I'd present our economic vision, and the public would be able to see their government was focused and able to deliver. I felt confident we'd crack it. There was a clear path forward.

Even so, I knew we were lining up for a difficult time ahead. Boris had lost both his chancellor and health secretary, which was no small thing. If, however, we could limit the resignations to one or two more among junior ministers and PPSs, he could potentially survive until the day of the speech. We'd have our big economic moment; MPs would begin to see a way out and we'd be clear of the storm. All we needed to do was hold on. But by four o'clock that afternoon, it was clear this was now a stampede, with junior ministers resigning by the half-hour. I texted the chief whip, Chris Heaton-Harris, to say I was coming to No. 10 to talk.

While Boris was being grilled by the cross-party liaison committee in parliament, ministers were pouring through the cracks in the leaky boat at a rate of knots. I told Chris that the situation was now untenable, and he agreed. We knew there was a group of ultra-loyalists who'd want to fight for Boris, but there were also plenty of others baying for his blood, and I felt it was our job to protect him. Whatever he'd done, I didn't want him to be humiliated. I now recognised it was impossible to save the government, but hoped he could go with as much dignity as possible. A few other cabinet ministers joined us in the upstairs small dining room of Downing Street, and we agreed to go and talk to the PM together. When he returned to No. 10 later that day, however, we were told by his inner team that he wanted to see each of us individually instead, and I was first up. As we sat together in the cabinet room, Boris was calm and reflective but, on the back of his pummelling from the committee, he looked absolutely worn down. 'What do you think?' he ventured in an uncharacteristically subdued voice. I said, had he asked me the same question that morning, I was punching the air; that I'd had a solid economic offer to deliver in two weeks' time. The problem was, I said, I no longer believed we'd survive until then. 'The herd is stampeding, boss,' I told him. 'They're going to humiliate you.' I'd known this man for nearly twenty-five years and couldn't bear the thought of watching while they dragged his carcass out into the street. 'Really?' he said, probing further. 'Yes, boss,' I told him, 'that's what I'm seeing.' But he just wasn't ready to accept it. 'Can't we just try one more time?' he asked. He said he'd been 'held back for the past year' and that he 'should have made these changes sooner'. He told me that I understood business and the economy and could pull something out of the bag. I told him I thought it had become impossible to form a functioning government but he pressed me to go back and work on the presentation. Out of loyalty, I said I'd do my best, despite knowing it was over. I promised I'd try to get the work done early and pull the speech forward by a week. It was an absurd undertaking and I knew he was clutching at straws, but it felt inhuman not to try.

Had you asked me what was at the root of his doggedness that day, I'd have said survival. The people who hate Boris see him as a superficial construct; someone with no feelings. The guy I knew was really not like that; he'd always been his authentic self in the moment. I knew he genuinely cared about the fate of the country and that this was why he was so desperate to hang on. He wanted to try and fix things. I suspect part of it, though, must have been pride too. He'd delivered the biggest victory our party had seen since 1983, so on one level I understood why he was struggling to comprehend why they were kicking him out now.

By the time I got home that evening, someone from Boris's inner circle had already briefed out that he and I would be making our big economic speech the following morning. This was absurd and annoyed me greatly. I'd been chancellor for less than twenty-four hours, so it seemed unlikely I'd be able to deliver a convincing rescue plan for Britain's economy in another twelve. Any such speech would not only have made Boris look ridiculous, but would have wrecked my own reputation in the process. I understood that someone in his team must have believed the only way to salvage this ever more chaotic situation was with a big moment, but I could not in good conscience be part of it. I knew it wasn't in the best interests of my own career but, more importantly, it wasn't in the best interests of the country either.

At 7 a.m. the next day I got a call from Steve Barclay MP, who evidently felt the same way as me. I knew there was no point in going to see Boris again. We were beyond that now. The only option left was to write to him formally. That way he'd either have to sack me or resign himself, but one way or another it would be over. I sat at the desk in my bedroom and drafted a letter over the phone with two brilliant young guys in my team – Tom Kennedy and James Price. We batted the text back and forth in an effort to hit the right note. The final line in their version had said that if Boris didn't resign, I wouldn't back him in a vote of no confidence. But that wasn't me. That's not how I felt. When someone's already down, you don't put a bullet in his head. You hug him and let him sleep peacefully, right? I changed the wording to something I hoped he'd come to understand in time. *'Prime Minister, you know in your heart what the right thing to do is, and go now.'*

That afternoon the prime minister announced his resignation on the podium outside the doors of No. 10. Not long after, I got a telephone call from my friend Boris. This time he was more his old self: 'I wish you hadn't written me that letter,' he said, in a somewhat bruised voice. Even though I knew it was the only viable outcome, after the trauma of the day it was still my instinct to try and comfort him and give him a way out, 'You know,' I started, 'I think maybe some of the people around you last night were delusional and ...' but he cut me off before I could finish. 'No,' he said, 'it was me; I was in denial. But I've done the right thing.' It was a relief to hear he'd come to terms with his lot. 'I want you to stay on as chancellor,' he said, 'and continue with the plans we've started.' To deliver on his legacy. 'Of course I will,' I told him. Boris was a flawed individual, but he had been powerful and decisive in his stewardship of the country at a time of incredible pressure. When there were hard decisions to make, he'd made them; but now, on the other side of the emergency, people expected him to be more orderly. In essence, he'd fallen foul of the same thing as his hero Churchill: he'd been a great wartime leader, but in peacetime his management style didn't stand up to close inspection. If I had my time again, though, I'd still have chosen him to have steered the ship through those waters. Not many could have kept the boat upright in such treacherous conditions. There have been several formidable leaders since Churchill but none had to deal with our divorce from the European Union, a once-in-a-century deadly virus and a war on our continent in quick succession. To my mind, Boris Johnson will be remembered as the most consequential prime minister of his generation.

The 'coup' against him had been a painful lesson. Just like Jeffrey and my dad, he'd struggled to confront his own truth and now it had smashed into him. He knew what an error he'd made, but with speculation about his resignation removed, the whole place calmed down. Boris 2.0 was more focused than I'd seen in months and we achieved an enormous amount in that very short time. In the space of eight weeks we secured extra funding for Ukraine, prepared all the options for the forthcoming winter energy support package, saved the Advanced Research and Invention Agency (ARIA) from bureaucratic capture, pushed forward Britain's nuclear energy industry and agreed an oil price cap alongside the United States to hamstring Russia's economy. In layman's terms, we were getting stuff done and it felt great to be working without the noise.

I've always been a great believer that people can be both flawed and brilliant. Right from the early days at YouGov, I knew Boris came with caveats. He was a fantastic wordsmith, but his work was always late. He had a wonderful mind but was easily distracted, and getting him to focus was the biggest hurdle if you wanted to get the best out of him. His energy and mental capacity were difficult to harness, but when you did they were incredibly powerful. Boris showed who and what he was very early on in his career, and people bought into that person. They voted him in with a huge majority. There was no reason to think he'd transform himself into someone else just because he was appointed to high office. It wasn't Boris that changed, it was us. My dad had been the template for my relationship with this type of persona – the powerful, risk-taking, blue-sky thinker – so I was very used to admiring a person I knew to be imperfect. What I'd learned during this crisis was that those types of people sometimes needed boundaries, and one day it might be me who had to set them. It was a skill to get people to like you, but another test altogether to be the bad guy and still retain people's respect. If I had to identify a flaw in my own character it would be my distaste for confrontation; when the time came, I knew I had to write Boris that letter, but I'd hated doing it.

CHAPTER 25

THE RACE

A NEW LEADER

It was originally my friend Brandon Lewis, secretary of state for Northern Ireland under Boris, who suggested I put myself in the running for leader after Boris's resignation. There are very few politicians who set out with a plan *not* to become prime minister, so I can't say the thought had never crossed my mind. Even so, the decision to do so would be a huge step, especially under such toxic circumstances. I knew that winning would be more pyrrhic victory than cause for celebration and whoever came out on top would need to shoulder the weight of a post-pandemic government as well as a horribly divided party. When it was suggested the 1922 Committee might change the rules to allow for a second confidence vote after Boris defeated his naysayers in June 2022, I'd discussed the possibility of standing with close friends, but the idea never moved beyond casual conversations over dinner. I told Brandon the person I'd really need to discuss it with now was my wife. Lana and I were quite close to Brandon and his wife Justine, and they came over that night for drinks to talk it over. After they left, Lana and I stayed up late with the kids. I told them honestly that the campaign would be awful. That I'd be pummelled, that the press would personalise it and that they'd attack my family too. There'd be photographers outside the house constantly and our lives would become very public. If I got the job, it would get even worse.

My wife has always been very private and we've purposely kept our home life separate from my work, so she was understandably cautious. My sons felt the same way – a mixture of excitement and trepidation. Predictably, the only person who was fly-by-the-seat-of-your-pants gung ho about it all was my daughter Mia, who said, 'You have to do it, daddy! You have to win!' I didn't know whether to be proud of her or really worried about her future. For better or worse, at the end of that evening we agreed as a family that I'd give it a go, and the next morning I called my good friend Mark Fullbrook. Mark was a brilliant campaign manager and would later go on to become Liz Truss's chief of staff. He and I had talked a couple of times over the previous few months about the possibility of my running should the situation arise, but we had absolutely nothing in place. My entire campaign therefore had to be pulled together in the space of three days, and on 9 July 2022 I officially threw my hat into the ring.

When a person runs for the leadership of a political party, especially when winning that race entails becoming prime minister, they are properly subjected to a level of scrutiny they have almost certainly never experienced before. I should have had that in the forefront of my mind when I decided to run, but my focus was on my policies and the mechanics of my campaign. You can never prove to anyone what is in your heart, but I genuinely felt I had nothing to hide. More fool me.

Ironically it was Jeffrey who told me to make sure that if I had any dirty laundry to air, I should do it myself before the press had a chance to do it for me. If you run for leader, he told me, there will not be lovely, glorious stories about how you've come over here as an immigrant and conquered the world and isn't it amazing? The press and your opponents will search for something negative, and you must now search for that yourself. I told him there was nothing. He said he didn't know a single person with nothing to bury and warned me it was always the cover-up that killed people, not the act itself. If I had anything to hide, he said, now was the time to put it out there. But there was nothing. Or so I thought.

The moment we announced my candidacy, however, the media chucked everything they had at me. It was a no-holds-barred character assassination and the 'millionaire gets tax payers to heat horse's bedroom' stories were rolled out once again. Every good journalist knew the truth of that one but, for the sake of posterity, I should probably take a moment to explain it. When I became MP for Stratford-on-Avon, we bought a house in my constituency with riding stables attached. Since there were two separate electric meters – one in each building – I assumed they'd generate two separate bills. I was wrong. Unbeknown to me, the electricity company aggregated both meters and generated a single bill for both. My secretary, meanwhile – still relatively new to the job, nearly 100 miles away in parliament and unaware of these two meters – simply carried on paying the single bill in the belief it was for the house only and therefore a legitimate expense. It wasn't until the press contacted me to ask why I was claiming £5,000 for utilities that we investigated further and discovered our error. As in all such cases, the parliamentary authorities sent an investigator to look into the situation. It only took him a few minutes to realise what had happened, the matter was resolved and I paid back what was owed. This story, however, turned out to be the least of my worries. Now the press had something much bigger to get their teeth into.

A year earlier, in June 2021, when I'd been in the thick of the vaccine rollout, my accountants had received a letter from

HMRC asking a series of questions about my taxes dating back to the formation of YouGov in 2000. Nobody likes to be called in by the tax man, so I was understandably concerned. It was agreed it would be best to address these questions face to face. During an appointment with my accountants, HMRC officials made it clear this wasn't a criminal or tax evasion investigation – a.k.a. a COP9. I left the meeting confident that my accountants could deal with things on my behalf while I got on with the rollout.

That September I'd been appointed education secretary by Boris and joined the cabinet. I hadn't updated my ministerial declarations to reflect the queries I'd had from HMRC that June because they'd told me they were not conducting a COP9 and I'd understood the matter to be queries, nothing more. Consequently, when it came to responding to the question in the declaration about whether I'd ever been in dispute with or under investigation by HMRC, the answer I ticked on the form was 'No'. With hindsight, this was naive and a mistake. Whether or not I believed it to be an investigation, I should have flagged up these queries on my declarations. I appreciate now this fell below my ministerial obligations and wholeheartedly take responsibility for my error.

When Boris had made me chancellor in July 2022, I went through the usual ministerial declarations process again with the Proprietary and Ethics Team (PET). When they'd asked about my tax affairs, I'd told them my accountants were in the process of responding to queries from HMRC. I filled out my declaration two days later and added a note that said, 'I have always declared and paid my taxes in full. I am currently in discussion with HMRC to clarify a number of queries.' A week later, however, I received a letter telling me that HMRC's inquiries were more serious than I'd thought. That although this was still not classed as a COP9, my tax affairs were, indeed, being officially investigated. I informed the Cabinet Office I was now under investigation, amended my declaration to reflect this development and recused myself from further negotiations with HMRC in light of the obvious conflict of interest. Two weeks later, they reached an in-principle agreement with my accountants, which I agreed to pay.

The questions from HMRC had centred around the original shareholding of YouGov – specifically the number of shares given to my dad when we'd set the company up in 2000. After looking into my affairs, HMRC had concluded that, while Dad had been entitled to founder shares given his input of both capital and expertise, the division was too high in his favour. Of the 42 per cent he'd been given, they concluded I should have held 85 per cent and he the remaining 15 per cent. At the same time they discussed my dad's offshore company – Balshore Investments – and concluded I was neither its founder, owner nor beneficiary.

In layman's terms, this meant they didn't believe I was guilty of tax evasion or avoidance but that I should have taken more founder's shares than I had. They classed these errors as careless rather than deliberate but, as with many tax errors of this kind, they came with a penalty. They backdated the capital gains tax I would have paid on 85 per cent of the shares to a figure of £3.1 million, added interest and a penalty of 30 per cent. In all, the bill was just shy of £5 million and we agreed terms for its payment.

My accountants said that had I been a 'normal citizen', they'd have advised me to challenge the ruling. That if I took HMRC to tribunal, they were confident the case would be dismissed or the settlement reduced. In all the time YouGov had existed, HMRC had never once questioned the share distribution. It was a matter of public record and visible to anyone via Companies House. When we floated in 2005, we were subjected to further scrutiny by the bank and lawyers, and again, no one ever questioned my dad's shareholding.

So if I'd done nothing illegal, why accept the ruling? The fact was, I wasn't a normal citizen. I was, by then, chancellor of the exchequer and felt if anything were an abuse of power, it would be to challenge the institution I was now running about my own tax liability. So I settled. With the amount agreed, I informed PET that the error was found to be non-deliberate and thanked them for their guidance in helping me get the matter right. A week or so later, I again amended my declaration to show my tax affairs were now up to date. I never did include more detailed information about the specifics of the settlement on my forms, and, in retrospect, I recognise I could have been more explicit.

That might have been the end of things but, to complicate matters further, even before the settlement had been reached, someone had evidently leaked to the press about my tax affairs. In early July, a journalist called Simon Walters contacted me for comment on an article he was intending to run the following day in the *Independent*, which claimed I had been the subject of an investigation by the National Crime Agency. Since I had never been contacted by the NCA myself, I was understandably pretty taken aback by this claim. In fact, I believe my response was something along the lines of, 'What the hell are you talking about, Simon?' To this day, neither my accountants, lawyers nor I have *ever* been contacted by the NCA. Simon's piece concluded that the alleged NCA inquiry had not led to any action and that there was no suggestion of any wrongdoing by me. Despite this, the story came at just the right time to cast a dark shadow over my leadership campaign.

The article also attracted an additional player onto the field, Dan Neidle. Dan was a tax lawyer at Clifford Chance who got the bit between his teeth about me and began regularly tweeting about my being guilty of tax evasion, setting up an offshore account and being under investigation by the NCA. My lawyers contacted him to try and resolve the matter in private, believing Twitter was not the best platform for the resolution of a dispute of this nature, but he refused, carrying on with his accusations on social media. In the end, I instructed them to politely write to Dan asking for a retraction on the basis he was accusing me of lying to conceal tax avoidance and the more serious crime of tax evasion. By mid-July, I did in fact know the HMRC queries constituted a COP8 investigation – one in which there is uncertainty or disagreement about whether a tax payer has used complex arrangements to reduce their tax liability – but I didn't go into these details online with Dan because honestly, I was angry at the range of misleading and damaging accusations he'd made. He was attempting to conduct a conversation about complex tax matters and reputational damage on a platform that limits itself to 280 characters. Taken as a whole, his allegations were incredibly serious and I responded in a manner that seemed appropriate at the time. I realise now it was my ministerial duty to correct the public record on this and I failed to do so. That did not mean, however, that I was guilty of tax evasion or avoidance.

My biggest issue with Dan, however, was the fact that, as well as being a tax specialist, he was also a Labour activist who'd served on the National Constitutional Committee of the Labour Party. Personally, I did feel there was more to his crusade than met the eye; I believed it was a politically motivated attack and I allowed that to affect my judgement and get the better of me.

A couple of months on and the questions around my taxes would be resolved; a few more still and they would resurface again and form the basis of my political downfall. For the time being though, the noise was enough to throw a serious spanner in the works and, alongside Jeremy Hunt, I was knocked out of the leadership race in the first round. Much later down the line, one of Liz Truss's team told me, 'You were the guy we feared,' which at least took the edge off not having succeeded. But, in all honesty, my overwhelming feeling was one of relief. The pressure of running as leader I could handle, but the emotional energy needed to fight off the personal attacks and the stress of shielding my family from the heat was beyond draining.

I'd been at Jeffrey's side during his scandal, but this had been my first taste of being the subject of one myself and it was about as horrible as you might imagine. Was Westminster still a place I wanted to be? I wasn't sure anymore. Part of me felt very depressed by all the sordid machinations of recent weeks. I knew how and why it had all happened but it felt pretty dirty to have been in the fight. I wanted to walk away and have a normal life with my wife and kids. Another part of me felt like I was in a hugely privileged position. I was, after all, still chancellor. We had twenty-four months to demonstrate to the country we could provide an economic strategy that would deliver for the people, and in the end I decided this was more important than my own hurt feelings.

While the backstabbing during the contest had been unpleasant, my biggest worry was that it wasn't happening in a bubble. The race was becoming a cheap spectator sport, and the press and the public had revelled in the drama. The nation was watching and people were understandably extremely disappointed with the party's behaviour. We weren't the Kardashians; we were meant to be running a civilised nation. People were waking up in the morning worrying about their schools, their jobs, their kids and their parents, then looking at the division in our party and wondering what business we had being in charge. It was absolutely poisonous.

After I'd been knocked out of the race, I'd felt it was Liz Truss's fight to lose. She had a good understanding of the party and a team of decent people around her. If her main opponent, Rishi Sunak, did beat her, I didn't imagine he'd keep me on as chancellor. The Treasury was his domain and I knew he'd want to look after it himself. In the wake of the race, I was actually quite happy with the idea of returning to the backbenches or even building something new, outside of politics, instead. At fifty-five, I felt I still had room for one more career and maybe now would be the right time. But perhaps these thoughts were just pride? Perhaps I was just mentally preparing for the worst? As luck would have it, I didn't have to find out. When voters go to the polls, the candidate able to define the question they'll be asking themselves is the one most likely to win. In this instance, the voters were not the public but the Conservative Party membership. By telling them we needed to move away from our reluctant acceptance of anaemic growth, Liz secured nearly 60 per cent of their vote.

Rishi had been a bright and well-respected chancellor in the war cabinet, so many people wondered how he had been beaten by a less high-profile, seemingly less confident Liz Truss. If I understood anything about human psychology, I imagine he was slightly traumatised by how much he'd spent on Covid. For this reason, I think he tried to overcompensate with an extremely fiscally cautious campaign, which proved less popular with members. But he had another, even bigger obstacle to contend with: for many members, he was the guy who'd killed the king. While the Twittersphere was incensed by Boris and what they saw as his questionable moral code, a good half of the membership still considered him their hero. Outside of the London intelligentsia, who had a visceral hatred of him, the BBC struggled to get clips of anyone saying they thought he should have gone. Boris had a huge mandate – many members saw Rishi's resignation and the crisis it triggered as a betrayal, and he struggled to get round that issue. Despite how capable he was as a politician, he started the race for the leadership on the back foot.

On 5 September, Liz was declared the new leader. Kwasi Kwarteng stepped into my shoes as her new chancellor and I shifted into the role of chancellor of the Duchy of Lancaster in the new cabinet.

CHAPTER 26

LONDON BRIDGE

FOR QUEEN & COUNTRY

The chancellor of the Duchy of Lancaster is technically the second most powerful position in cabinet, but if you asked most people on the street, they'd have no idea who holds the post or what that person does. In short, the CDL is COO of government and so, when Liz was appointed PM and offered me the role in her new cabinet, I said yes without hesitation: it was hands down one of the best jobs in the world. As well as overseeing national security, COBRA and the Union, and being the minister for equalities, it was my responsibility to make sure every secretary of state delivered on their priorities, especially the big spenders. In addition, I got to indulge my love of geopolitics with a seat on the National Security Council. The heads of MI5, MI6, GCHQ, the defence secretary, the Foreign Office permanent secretary, the deputy PM, the PM and I sat in a secure room; it was pretty incredible stuff and about as close as I was ever going to get to playing Bond. Sadly, my time in office only lasted as long as Liz's premiership, which was brief, to put it mildly.

Even so, those six weeks of my life coincided with some of the most important events in British social history, because the final responsibility within my remit as CDL was the 'Bridges Programme' – the unofficial name given to the strategy around how the death of a monarch would be handled by government. We'd already had Operation Forth Bridge in 2021 with the funeral of Prince Philip, but the wonderful London Bridge was still standing. If Queen Elizabeth died during my time in office, however, her funeral would become my responsibility. At ninety-six, the Queen was considerably more frail than she'd been in recent years and it was clear to everyone that she was slowly winding down, so I knew I'd need to be prepared for a big announcement. I had no idea it would come two days after I started my new job.

With a change of British leader, the Queen would traditionally receive the departing and incoming prime ministers at Buckingham Palace, but on this occasion the decision was taken that both Liz Truss and Boris would fly to Balmoral for their meetings. The main impact of this trip was that the formation of the new cabinet was delayed and some departments didn't have their ministers in place until 10.30 that evening. Consequently, my 'second' day on the job as CDL was really only my first. Later that afternoon, the new cabinet arrived at 70 Whitehall to be given the seal of office as privy councillors. Just as during Covid, this was to be done virtually rather than face to face, and we gathered in briefing room B to await Her Majesty's appearance. It came as something of a shock when we got word the Privy Council was being cancelled. In all my time in government and all my dealings with the Palace, the Queen had never, ever been late. Everyone thought this meant something was amiss and I went to bed that day with a heavy heart.

The following morning I was introduced to a woman called Sarah Healy – the permanent secretary at the Department of Culture, Media & Sport and senior responsible officer for the Bridges team. Sarah – I would come to learn – was a brilliant, no-nonsense powerhouse who'd prove a great partner to work with in the days that followed. In early 2021, she'd been appointed as the lead civil servant on a team overseeing royal funerals. Three weeks into the job she'd been tasked with organising Operation Forth Bridge, so I knew she was no novice. In short, she was an expert facilitator, but that did nothing to diminish the weight of responsibility about to be put onto her shoulders now.

Midway through our morning briefing we got news that the Palace would be putting out a statement to say they had concerns for Her Majesty's health. Sarah and I went straight to the Houses of Parliament to track down cabinet secretary Simon Case, who was holed up in the PM's office along with Liz's brand new team of advisors. Other than the PM herself, no one in the chamber that day knew the Queen was unwell, and although she would undoubtedly have been expecting an announcement, the PM was now on her feet in the Commons delivering her energy speech. When the statement from the Palace came out on the wires, we knew she'd be the only one in the room without access to a mobile and the only one, therefore, not to see it. We couldn't leave her on the back foot like this, so Simon drafted her a note and I went into the chamber to pass it on.

Doing my best to be discreet, I squeezed between her and Kwasi on the frontbench and whispered the news into the PM's ear. No sooner was I back in her office with the team than it was decided we'd also need to tell Keir Starmer, who was by now up on *his* feet responding to the PM. From the other side of the Speaker's chair I beckoned the deputy leader of the Labour Party, Angela Rayner, who ducked out to collect the note and took it to pass on to Keir. In the event, by the time the statement was released by the Palace, Liz was back in her office and it was left to the Speaker, Lindsay Hoyle, to deliver the news to the House.

When Liz returned to her room and was given the news by Simon, she was incredibly calm. This was a huge constitutional issue and she'd been in the job less than twenty-four hours, but whatever she might have been thinking privately, she was, I thought, impressively unflapped. This seemed to go a long way to setting the tone for her new team, who were by now looking pretty bloody petrified. Going forward, the PM's steer was to step back and let it happen. Her advice to her team was, don't faff around or try and interfere or put yourself in a difficult position where you might be accused of having tried to influence things for political gain. Just let the civil service do what they do best; they had it all under control.

My job – just as with the vaccine – was to protect that team from the noise and ensure safe delivery of the project. The Queen was much loved in Westminster and everyone wanted to be a part of the process. A big part of my role was fending off any clever ideas anyone might have about how they thought things should be done. However well intentioned, it was just an additional distraction for the team. More to the point, it was obvious the machine was beautifully well oiled. Preparations made over many years meant all they really need do was flick a switch and turn it on.

That afternoon we received word that Her Majesty had passed away. The second-longest reign in global history had come to an end and Britain had a king for the first time in seventy years. The BBC would announce her death at 6.30 p.m. as part of the evening's news. Huw Edwards would don his black tie and Operation London Bridge would formally be triggered as the world looked on. A significant part of the Britain I'd arrived in forty-three years earlier was gone forever.

For those two hours until the public announcement, it felt like we were in no man's land. Just as when I'd heard about the UK's first lockdown, I watched as people in Westminster went about their day oblivious to what we now knew and wondered whether they, like me, would find themselves alone in a room in tears when they did eventually hear the news.

The emotion of that day was something I'd have expected but what really struck me was people's behaviour. It was one of those really impressive moments in government where everybody pulled together. For anyone outside the central team it was pretty obvious something serious was afoot, but everyone just got on and helped. No one asked questions, because they realised it would put anyone who *did* have the answers in an awkward spot. In extraordinary circumstances, people calmly and discreetly got on with their jobs. The fact nothing leaked out was testament to both the civil service and the PM's measured leadership.

The moment a monarch dies, there's a detailed list of people to be informed and a very fixed cascade that's triggered to ensure everyone with a role in managing from the centre is engaged as quickly as possible. As soon as the announcement was made, plans began for a COBRA meeting, and when you entered the room you were met by an incredibly impressive hive of activity. Every person there knew exactly where they should be and wordlessly began organising themselves to handle their responsibilities. It was a flawless division of labour. They'd worked so hard to be ready that, when it finally happened, it was like watching a perfectly choreographed ballet.

Late that evening, the PM chaired the first COBRA meeting on Bridges before handing over to me to manage operations going forward. For the twelve days that followed, Sarah would effectively be reporting to me and not her own secretary of state. Just as with the pandemic, I did my best to make myself useful, protect my team, to allow them to do their work, and make sure we were fully coordinated across government and the Palace. Sarah would tell you she was just there in case something went wrong, but it was obvious from one meeting she had an ironclad grasp on plans because she'd been the one who'd spent the past eighteen months making them. All I really needed to do now was back her up.

Despite this, the unpredictable nature of the subject matter itself meant it was still a bit like putting on the Olympics with less than two weeks' notice – a completely extraordinary operation. For each of the eleven days between the Queen's death and her funeral, the Bridges team met daily at noon, and parliamentary and home life paused for everyone involved. Sarah and her team – especially the excellent Ellen Atkinson – would brief me and I'd chair the meetings, and we quickly got into the rhythm of our new temporary life. Lana got used to eating alone with the boys and Mia knew Daddy was doing something so important he wouldn't be home in time for a goodnight kiss. It was the same for everyone involved. Falling as it did in early September, mums and dads missed first days of school and university as they holed up in town for the sake of their monarch. No one complained; everyone stayed focused. That was what working for your country meant sometimes.

THE QUEUE

The team were clear with me from the start that the riskiest part of the whole programme would be the queue for the lying in state. While the expectation was that many, many people would want to pay their respects, it was still fundamentally very unpredictable and high numbers would mean people waiting for a very, very long time. Modelling something with so many moving parts was incredibly complicated and we knew managing it would be problematic too but we didn't expect it to go quite so bonkers or have its own autonomous, viral presence. We have Michelle Donelan, secretary of state at the DCMS, and her team to thank for its delivery.

The route largely followed the river going east. Three miles of winding barriers were put up in Southwark Park to accommodate the thousands joining the queue to pay their respects. It quickly became a worldwide phenomenon and its success in part was thanks to the hundreds of volunteers who helped steward the operation. Brits did what Brits did best and stepped up to help. Cultural institutions stayed open all night along the South Bank, and staff clapped and cheered as mourners came in for loo breaks and coffees in the middle of a long night. To make doubly sure things were going to plan, I secretly sent out my chief of staff, James Price, on a 'Mystery Shopper' mission on the first night to flag up any on-the-ground concerns – most of which centred round loos and the frequency of their distribution. In fact, there was only one tricky day when we reached capacity and were forced to close the queue, and even then, people self-regulated and formed their own queue for the queue to wait. Happily this was the same day David Beckham had chosen to queue for twelve hours, helpfully taking the spotlight off us in the process.

In all, around 250,000 to 300,000 mourners filed past the Queen. It was the first state funeral to take place in the UK since the death of Churchill in 1965. There were all sorts of exaggerated stories that 320,000 people had filed past *his* coffin but, having managed this operation myself, I don't see how that would have been mathematically possible. Privately, I thought this meant she was even more beloved by the nation.

As with all the best royal events, there was a huge amount of pageantry around the funeral. Dignitaries from all over the world arrived in their finery and hundreds of years of British history were encapsulated in one day. But there were also moments of heart-warming human nature on show too. We sung 'God Save the King' in the chapel and I, like many others, had another cry when the Queen's grandchildren walked into the abbey. I was extremely moved to be a small part of something so momentous.

But my favourite reminder that we are all the same under our clothes came the evening before the funeral at a reception hosted by the new King in the gallery rooms at Buckingham Palace. On the surface, things didn't get much grander. It was the greatest gathering of monarchs and world leaders at short notice in history and an awe-inspiring turnout. Despite being a sombre, pre-funeral drinks' evening, take away the champagne and waiters and it was basically the UN General Assembly on steroids. It wasn't every day the President of Botswana could saunter up to Joe Biden and ask what he thought of the canapés, so making sure everyone who needed to have conversations had them without offending anyone else was an operational nightmare. Early in the proceedings, I was discreetly made aware that President Macron and his wife Brigitte had arrived but were on the 'wrong' side of the room. The new King and Queen were just about to enter on the 'right' side, and the Foreign Office was determined the two couples should have proper time to talk. Getting the Macrons across the floor without snubbing anyone in the process would be like trying to cross the North Circular with a stack of Ming vases: a very delicate operation.

I knew that if anyone would know how to handle this kind of tricky socio-political etiquette it would be his wife, so I went direct to Macron HQ for advice. I have no idea what magic she whispered in his ear but within seconds he'd extricated himself from a conversation about Afro-Franco relations and we sailed through the crowds unimpeded. Thanks to Brigitte, our journey across the waters was a logistical triumph.

No sooner had we hit our mark than the same civil servant reappeared to tell me that, once again, the Macrons were on the 'wrong' side of the room because Charles and Camilla were now due to enter through the opposite door. Just as I was wondering how to avoid a diplomatic incident, I spotted Biden ducking into a side room where some of the even bigger cheeses were penned up. I knew this was the King's ultimate destination and decided it was better to leave the Macrons there *pro tem* rather than attempt to go back. I guided them through the arch and waited for His Majesty to arrive.

The moment he appeared, a surge of world leaders clamoured to shake his hand and offer their condolences or, in some instances, throw their arms around him if they were sufficiently close. The emotion of the moment meant the idea of an orderly queue was entirely abandoned. It was a no-holds-barred scrabble for the top slot, and the King and Queen of the Netherlands led the charge. Waiting behind them was the King of Bahrain. Behind him were the King and Queen of Spain – who are probably two of the most beautiful human beings ever to have walked the earth – and behind them, the Crown Prince of Kuwait. Behind Kuwait was Biden and behind *him*, finally, the Macrons. I could see there was no point trying to control the situation so stood back instead and waited for natural selection to do its work. I was quite enjoying the show when I turned to see the humblest-looking man I'd ever encountered in real life patiently waiting his turn. 'Hello,' he said, in a gentle voice, 'I'm the Emperor of Japan. Nice to meet you.' This beautifully dignified man was a god in his own country, with citizens forbidden to look him directly in the eye, and here he was, lining up with everyone else as if he were queuing for a burger and chips before the game at Old Trafford. It was the greatest display of human nature I'd ever seen. I only wish I'd taken a photograph.

D-DAY

The most wonderfully serendipitous thing about the Queen having died at Balmoral was that she'd be travelling to Edinburgh first before returning to England. Even in her death she did the nation a great, great favour. Privately, I like to think this was not accidental; that in fact, when she knew the end was near, she made sure she was in Scotland and would have to make that journey. I believe the Queen was, privately, like me, a deeply committed Unionist. When the helicopters tracked what was effectively her funeral cortege from Balmoral to Edinburgh, the world got to see Scotland's full beauty and the Scottish people got to see their queen.

When she eventually arrived at Westminster Abbey she was met by nearly 2,500 mourners. As well as foreign dignitaries, many more invitations went out to people recognised in the Queen's Birthday Honours earlier in the year: ordinary people who'd done extraordinary things for their community. It was exactly the sort of thing the Queen would have done herself. She'd dedicated her entire life to her people.

The Met and the mayor of London had planned for 149,000 people in Hyde Park on the day of the funeral, but in the end, agreed to extend capacity to a quarter of a million. It was the biggest security operation the UK had ever seen and the largest policing operation in the history of the Met. To help manage such huge numbers, a formal ceremonial footprint was put in place – setting out where the action would happen and the viewing areas around it. To ensure we could safely disperse the crowds, we restricted entry to the footprint to four places. That way, we could monitor how many people had entered and, when it got to capacity, shut the 'gates'.

On the morning of the funeral itself, the teams who'd coordinated the operation battled through the growing crowds to see the culmination of their efforts come to fruition. For the first time since Her Majesty's death, there'd be no need for me to chair COBRA to check on our state of readiness. Instead, the armed forces, the police, the royal family and thousands of members of the public were in place to say goodbye to their queen. By 10 a.m. the stalwarts who'd camped out overnight had been joined by such numbers that we closed the 'doors' to our footprint.

Sarah refused to attend the ceremony in person and instead stayed with the team to watch it on the big telly in the operations room. She knew that if something went wrong, every senior member of the government would be unreachable in the abbey and so refused to leave her colleagues alone. It was typical of her selfless nature.

I took my seat next to Brandon Lewis and the woman the world would come to know as sword-bearer extraordinaire, Penny Mordaunt, and did my best to relax despite knowing the eyes of the world were upon us. London Bridge had been planned on paper since the 1960s but, just as with the rollout, we didn't know whether it was going to work until we put it into action. We'd planned and planned and planned again; all we could do now was cross our fingers and hope the threads of our work wove together to make the final picture we'd envisaged. All in all, I was incredibly proud of what we created in the Queen's honour. The world saw the best of Britain during the funeral, and whatever else I do in my career, I feel incredibly privileged to have served my country in this way.

The day after the funeral we met for one last time at COBRA. It was oddly bittersweet. We were a group of people pulled together under the saddest of circumstances, but I think we all felt there was something remarkable about having been part of the team. Although my term as chancellor had been almost record-breakingly short, I'd been the last one sworn in by Her Majesty. I'd gone to Windsor to receive the seal of office and she'd chatted a little, as she always did; ever ready with a pertinent question or comment. She was a woman who'd dedicated her entire life to her country. It seemed unlikely we'd ever see her kind again.

CHAPTER 27

BRITAIN'S SHORTEST-SERVING PRIME MINISTER

BACK TO WHERE WE'D STARTED

The parliamentary party, sadly, were never united behind the new PM and the backbiting that had been going on prior to Boris's resignation continued apace. The campaigning and undermining from within never stopped. It was like *Game of Thrones*. I knew that unless we could close the divisions within the party we'd be paralysed, and I resented how much time we seemed to be wasting dealing with what I considered to be unnecessary noise. It was clear that if we couldn't come together for the good of the party and the country, we'd have to get used to sitting on the opposition benches. I wanted everyone to put on their jerseys and get back out on the pitch, but it was not to be.

A few weeks later, after the now infamous mini-budget, the back-garden barbecue of discontent around Liz Truss became a forest fire and swept through parliament, destroying everything in its path. As much as I knew Liz and Kwasi to be good, decent people, what they failed to appreciate was how much institutions matter. Whether it's the civil service, the Bank of England or the BBC, these things are important lynchpins in our society. Human beings organise themselves around them. I have to admit, I was completely blindsided by her determination to smash up rather than reform some of the cornerstones of our political and financial landscape. I didn't disagree with the need for growth, but the mini-budget was too much, too soon and, coupled with a range of other existing factors in the market, managed to pull the rug out from under everyone's feet. Liz's great strength as a politician was her decisiveness, but in this instance it proved to be her undoing.

Why they acted as they did was still something of a mystery to me, but I could have made an informed guess. Oddly enough, I think it was the death of the Queen that altered their planned course of events. On the day it was announced, Liz was in the Commons delivering her energy speech setting out the assistance package for the public that had been prepared in the Treasury. Had it not been for the subsequent period of mourning, I imagine she and Kwasi might have stuck with that. As it was, those eleven days gave Liz more time to push her new chancellor to expand on their original offering. Ordinarily, a cabinet would see a mini-budget only hours before the chancellor gets to his feet at the despatch box. In No. 10 that day, Kwasi had taken us through his announcements, saying he'd be returning to each secretary of state after the mini-budget to identify cost savings in their departments to pay for his proposed tax cuts in order to demonstrate to the markets we were being fiscally responsible. But none of that made it into his speech. If you asked me why not, the honest answer is, I don't know, but I think potentially they wanted to show the Office for Budget Responsibility that they could do this without them. Whatever their reasoning, it was a rash move. I knew that the one person in cabinet who could not afford a single misstep was the chancellor. If you occupied that seat, every word, breath and utterance you made could move markets, and as Thatcher once said, you can't buck the market. It will destroy you. Even during the political turbulence of Boris's departure, as the waves crashed against the rocks, the most important thing for me to demonstrate to the world at the Mansion House speech was the strength and security of our financial institutions. During my time as chancellor, I made sure I spent regular time in the City and knew how much they valued stability. As Liz and Kwasi would quickly come to find, being spooked was the one thing they really did not like.

What really set the cat among the pigeons was Kwasi's appearance on Laura Kuenssberg's show during the media round the Sunday after the mini-budget. Watching the interview in bed with my wife that morning, it was easy to see that when Laura asked Kwasi what else he was planning, it was a landmine, and he, unfortunately, stepped right on it. When he effectively told her that he and Liz were just getting started, I turned to my wife and said, 'Just watch the markets on Monday.' In that one throwaway remark, Kwasi had implied more tax cuts lay ahead, and the markets went bonkers trying to work out how we were going to pay for them. By Monday, he was a dead man walking and it was clear Liz was probably going to be making that journey with him.

Liz and Kwasi almost certainly had other advisors, but the mistake they made was not so much the initiatives on growth as the sequencing and insular nature of their plans; they underestimated the place of confidence in an equation such as this and, as a result, they failed to carry the markets with them.

I was in Dubai on my way to Singapore for a cyber security conference when things reached peak velocity, and I texted Liz to say, 'Stay strong.' For all her public awkwardness, the Liz I worked with was a very decent human being and I felt for her on a personal level. There was now an insane amount of backbiting, so I put a note out on the MPs' WhatsApp group saying that colleagues would do well to remember that when you have the initials MP after your name and the media asks you for an opinion, you're a participant not a commentator. When you opine how terrible your government is, the media won't congratulate you on your incisive commentary; they'll splash 'Conservative split' all over the front pages. As far as the press were concerned, there was only one thing better than opposing parties attacking one another and that was a party attacking itself – ideally the one in power. But things had gone too far. My text fell on deaf ears and Liz called me to ask if I'd come back for what I felt was a bit of moral support. My plane landed the next morning.

At Wednesday's PMQs, Keir Starmer failed to put the ball in the back of the net despite the PM's goal being wide open. At a time when the whole country was worried about the cost of living and he could have silenced the chamber with a Corbyn-esque 'I've had an email from Mrs Jones who tells me she's just lost her house ...', Keir decided instead to open with a joke, missed the mark entirely and thereby bought Liz a temporary reprieve.

On 19 October, roughly six weeks after her appointment as PM, Labour put forward a motion linking a vote on fracking to taking control of the order paper. It was effectively a confidence vote in the government and a very clever motion; any Conservative colleague who'd campaigned against fracking in their constituency was going to be shaky on supporting the government now. We tweaked the wording of the legislation a little to try and get round the issue and make it more palatable, and the whip sent out an email first thing in the morning to say it was a three-line whip and a confidence vote. Everyone – including cabinet – had to back it. Disobey at your peril.

Having spent that day working on my national security brief in the Cabinet Office, I was unaware of the drama that had broken out over the road in the chamber. I arrived at 7 p.m. for the vote to hear a backbencher question the minister speaking about whether this was indeed a confidence vote. When the minister replied that it wasn't, he undermined the chief whip, and consequently the government's position, and caused chaos to break out in the chamber. Apparently, the minister had been going on information from someone in No. 10 but they had not thought to verify things with the chief whip. Had it been me on such an incredibly sensitive issue on such a difficult day, I'd probably have checked in with the PM herself; there was, after all, only one boss. As the division bell rang and we left the chamber to vote, the murmurings of confusion became a 7.9-magnitude earthquake and the lobby was positively febrile. In twelve years in parliament I'd never seen a prime minister trying to stop a chief whip or deputy chief whip from resigning their role in the middle of a vote. It was clear from the room that Liz had lost the party, and she knew it. It was game over. It was an extraordinary way to try and govern, and my honest feeling was, we're done for.

Liz later told me that when her husband suggested she'd have to put up taxes because of the turmoil in the markets, she knew she'd have to go; doing that would have gone against everything she believed in and she couldn't bring herself to do it. The following day she called Graham Brady MP, the chairman of the 1922 Committee, to say she'd be stepping down, making her Britain's shortest-serving prime minister. It was another instalment of an already very, very bizarre story, and I honestly had no idea what would happen next.

The one thing you could bank on, though, was that the moment Liz resigned, the question of Boris would resurface. On the Thursday, he called me from his holiday in the Dominican Republic to say he was indeed thinking of running and would I back him? Given the fact I'd asked him to resign less than four months earlier, I understood why some people might have thought it absurd to be considering supporting him now, but for me, the decision was a simple one: Boris was the only candidate with a mandate. The fact he'd ended his last PMQs with the words 'Hasta la vista' should tell you he'd never truly let go of the idea he should be leading the charge, so it was no surprise to me that he wanted to try again now. Had we kept his name off the ballot paper, what would that have said to our members and the millions who'd voted for him? This wasn't the politburo. Some wouldn't care, but many were still very loyal to him. If Boris was going to stand aside in a situation like this, the decision would need to be his own.

On the morning of Sunday 23 October, he called again to ask if I'd publicly declare my support for his bid, knowing it might encourage other senior members of the party to do the same. I told him I wanted to wait until the morning, but he turned on the charm. If Boris's superpower/kryptonite was loyalty, we had that in common; I was acutely aware of what he'd done for me and my career. I did feel there were things he could have handled better, but the reason I'd asked him to resign the previous July was not because of Partygate. I'd asked him to go because the noise around him made forming a government impossible and that was damaging our ability to lead the country. But we'd now lurched forward to another fork in the road and it was time to decide what to do. Over breakfast, I made up my mind, pulled the trigger and tweeted my support for his bid. My phone blew up immediately. By the evening, we'd got him past the threshold of 100 set by the 1922 Committee, but of the 102 votes he had gathered, only 55 of those MPs were prepared to publicly declare their backing. Technically he did have the required numbers, but he was scraping the barrel. The old Boris would have gone to a members' ballot and probably won. This would have created chaos in the party because he wouldn't have had the confidence of the parliamentary party, who were largely behind Rishi, and *that* would have made governing impossible. Again.

Later that day I travelled to Chequers for Liz's farewell party. I spent most of the afternoon finessing an article in support of Boris 2.0 due to appear that evening online in the *Telegraph* and the Monday morning paper. Knowing the 'fluidity' of these kinds of situations, my chief of staff, James, repeatedly checked in with Boris's team to ensure he hadn't changed his mind about running. Repeatedly reassured that he had not, James pushed the button and the article made its way through the ether to the *Telegraph*. We were all set.

At 8.58 that evening, Steven Swinford at *The Times* tweeted the news of Boris's decision to pull out. Two minutes later, our article went live online. In our telephone call that evening, Boris told me he knew he didn't have the resounding support of the parliamentary party and apologised for having put me in such an awkward position. It had been an 'eventful' day to say the least but, whether by accident or design, we'd arrived at a good place. The membership were able to see Boris step back of his own accord and that allowed room for a legitimate rival to take his place.

As soon as Boris removed himself from the equation, I got another call. This time it was Rishi, who very magnanimously asked that I be on his team. With the mandate question out of the way, I didn't need to think about my answer. He was clearly best placed now to bring the party back together, which was all I'd really wanted from the start.

CHAPTER 28

NOTES ON A SCANDAL

A FALL FROM GRACE

Approximately six weeks after Liz had been appointed, we'd ended up back where we'd begun and had now appointed our third prime minister in as many months. Meanwhile, talk in the press around my tax affairs had not stopped since it had started. In fact, if anything, it had intensified. When Rishi took over in October 2022 he appointed me party chairman and I again went through the induction process with PET, just as I had done when I'd been made chancellor and CDL. When they asked whether anything had changed with my taxes, I said, no, things were still the same as when I'd been asked by the team before I was appointed CDL. By January 2023, however, the noise around my tax affairs had reached sufficient volume that Rishi understandably felt he had to act. He instructed his ethics advisor, Sir Laurie Magnus, to carry out an investigation into matters surrounding the issue prior to making a decision about my future in cabinet. We were due to meet on Wednesday 25 January and reporters camped outside my house in the days leading up to it. By Sunday night the press intrusion was so loud it was making it virtually impossible to do my job. I was also keenly aware of how all this was affecting Lana and the kids. I will always defend the right of our media to scrutinise powerful people – coming from a police state, the free press is something I cherish – but what upset me about their coverage of the situation was the language they used. In January, the *Independent* ran another piece on me under the headline: 'Zahawi Tax Storm: The Noose Tightens'. Given there are unhinged people who'd take a statement like that as just cause for their actions, I did feel very uncomfortable at what seemed an unnecessarily salacious caption. As an MP, the only time I'd ever had police protection was as chancellor and CDL – and even then that did not include protection for my family. Less than eighteen months earlier, David Amess had been stabbed in his constituency surgery, and six years before that, Jo Cox had been shot and stabbed outside hers. This fundamentally changed the way MPs conducted their surgeries. Today, we are given a budget to have what amounts to a security guard to sit in on each and every meeting. In the face of these facts, I do find the violent rhetoric used in the press irresponsible at times.

At home that night, with all this in mind, we talked about whether I should resign, but Lana told me I should fight my case; that Sir Laurie's investigation would be a chance to set the record straight, and I agreed to hold on.

THE MEETING

When I met with Sir Laurie later that week we agreed the faster we could get things done, the better. We discussed my version of events and I accepted I should have done more to correct the public record around the HMRC investigation. I agreed to give him direct access to my account with HMRC to investigate further and he finished what was billed as an introductory meeting by saying we'd convene again, when I'd be able to present a detailed account of my position. He agreed to send the transcript of our meeting for my approval and assured me I'd have the right to reply before any conclusions were sent to the PM. I was relieved to be able to present the facts rather than rely on a trial by media and was pleased I'd hung on.

Later that afternoon, I received an email asking me to approve the transcript of that first meeting and a request for my authority for Sir Laurie to liaise with HMRC, which I duly gave. Since the following day would be spent at a cabinet meeting at Chequers and the one after that in my constituency, we agreed I could look at the transcript over the weekend. It felt good to be getting to the bottom of things. My chief of staff began work on a detailed timeline of events to present at my next meeting with Sir Laurie.

The following day, I presented what I'd been doing as chairman at Central Office to the political cabinet at Chequers. I talked about our plans to raise £100 million for the party, and how there was a narrow and steep path to victory in 2024. Our guest speaker for the evening was William Hague, who sympathetically put his arm around my shoulder and told me how much I'd achieved and that I'd endured far worse under Saddam Hussein; I'd get through whatever was being thrown at me now, he said. As I was leaving I thanked Rishi for allowing me the space to set the record straight with Sir Laurie. I felt broadly positive. The next day, however, the papers dissected events at Chequers, concluding that, not only was the PM livid with me, there were three other people auditioning for my job. Perhaps I was being naive but I'd felt the day had gone well, even though the onslaught had been pretty relentless, and I now felt uncharacteristically fed up. I realised from the headlines that someone had been briefing the papers and that minds had evidently already been made up.

Back in London on the Saturday night, I got a call from the No. 10 switchboard. It was Sir Laurie and he did not have good news. He told me my ministerial declarations had fallen short of the standards expected and that he would be writing to the PM that evening with his findings. I officially started to panic. I thought I'd have the following week to go over the evidence. I'd been told the meeting we'd had was an introductory one. I tried to press home that I had evidence I'd not yet had the opportunity to present, which supported my claim that I'd informed PET of the situation. But it was all too late, the decision had already been made. I was furious this was happening before I'd had the chance to defend myself.

I was totally floored, my mouth too dry to swallow. As I left the bedroom, Lana passed me on the stairs and asked if everything was okay. I didn't want to frighten her and told her it was, even though I knew then the die had already been cast. I spent the night kidding myself I'd be able to sleep before finally giving in and getting back up at 6 a.m. At seven, I decided if I wasn't going to be given the right to reply, at the very least I'd now send Sir Laurie the additional evidence by text. If I was going down, I wanted to have this on the record.

At 8 a.m. I got the call I'd been dreading from No. 10. 'Minister, I've got the prime minister and the chief whip on the line for you.' I prepared for my execution. Rishi told me he'd had the letter from Sir Laurie. I told him I'd not had a proper opportunity to present all the facts. I threw everything I could at him to try and prevent him saying what I knew he was inevitably about to say. 'I'm sorry it had to end like this, Nadhim.' I told him I was sorry too and we both put the phone down. That was it. A thirty-minute conversation to defend myself and my work as chairman was concluded. My time in cabinet over. Why would anyone think I'd have bothered to put myself and my family through this ordeal if I hadn't believed my position to be defensible? I'd watched Jeffrey and my father wait for the truth to smash into them and knew how much worse it had made things. I did not, however, believe this was the situation I was in. I felt like I'd not had a chance to present it.

There was a horrible pause in which I felt like my stomach had been slashed open and I was just waiting for my guts to tumble onto the floor and the end to kick in. I'd come into government to try and make a difference. I'd hoped to be a memorable footnote in political history. I guess now I really would be.

CHAPTER 29

THE GREAT ESCAPE

A SENSE OF PERSPECTIVE

There was no time for reflection or self-pity. I knew I had minutes to react. The second the PM's letter hit the wires, my house would be surrounded and I'd either be trapped inside or forced to make an appearance. I knew from my days with Jeffrey that this was something I wanted no part of. In public scandals, the bit I hated most was the fallen politician forced to react in front of the cameras, like a bear being baited in a pit. I had no intention of giving the press the satisfaction of catching me at my worst. I'd gone to bed that night without saying anything more to my wife but I couldn't put it off now. I went back upstairs to wake her and break the news: 'Rishi's made the decision to get rid of me; there's gonna be mayhem.' She was up like a rocket and straight into action. Still in my shorts and T-shirt, I sat on the edge of the bed and scrambled to get my trainers done up. Lana found my keys and wallet and trusty baseball cap. There was no time to change or for a proper conversation; every second now meant a head start outside. From behind the bedroom curtains Lana said she could only see one reporter. One was better than ten. I'd risk it. He must have been a novice or thought it was too early, though, because as I came out of the house, he'd walked away round the square, giving me just enough time to duck out the front door and into my car.

I drove down through Chelsea and across Albert Bridge, and followed the river. I had no idea where I was heading but the car took me towards my old council seat in West Putney, past my first flat on Portsmouth Road, and Ross Court, where I'd lived with Jihan and my parents when Dad lost his money. This was where my career had begun and I knew the streets well enough to drive on autopilot. I kept going, onto the A3 and out to Esher. I didn't want to be anywhere near the house.

I called my chief of staff to tell him we were done. No. 10 sent over a draft of a reply to the PM's letter for my approval, so I pulled over in an empty car park on an industrial estate and James and I tweaked the text together over the phone.

I knew I couldn't keep driving forever. It was Sunday, which typically meant lunch somewhere with the family. Since Broosk had an underground car park in his block of flats, that seemed like the safest place to go, and I made my way back to Battersea. Broosk was uncharacteristically gentle with me, but I imagined he'd berate me later for not paying more attention to the paperwork when things weren't quite so raw. The news was on the TV in the background and my story dominated every programme. Jihan texted to say I must have done something good for the country if they were bothering to give me this much airtime. I could always rely on her to try and protect me. For a moment I felt safe with my family, but I knew I couldn't stay at Broosk's forever. My son booked me a ticket out of London and, after lunch dwindled to an end, I left the children with Broosk. Lana drove me to Heathrow, where we said a fleeting goodbye in the drop-off zone. At 10 p.m. I must have looked like a tourist heading to the sun as I sat in the departure lounge still in my shorts and T-shirt, drinking my way through three vodka tonics. One of my councillors in Stratford-on-Avon texted to say there was a helicopter over my house. Good luck to them, I thought, as I walked towards passport control. Despite my cap lowered over my eyes, one of the security guards asked if he could shake my hand to thank me for what I'd done on the vaccine. Oddly, it just made me feel sad.

As I boarded my flight, I didn't feel upset or worried, just heartbroken. I knew why Rishi had done it. I knew there were people around him who'd have said the longer I stayed, the worse it would be for him. To his credit he did try and stand by me, but when the voices got too loud there was no way to stop them other than find a way to kill the story. I knew from experience it was nigh on impossible to run a government when media noise was driving the agenda. So it was time for me to go. It was what I'd asked Boris to do only months before. Now it was me being pushed out the door. It's a brutal game but anyone playing knows the rules.

I landed in Dubai the next morning and got a taxi to the city. I showered and shaved for the first time since the Friday and made my way down to the beach, where I sat on the sand staring out to sea until sunset. There was nothing to do and no one to talk to. It was the closest I could get to being back up in Mum and Dad's narenj tree. I wasn't hidden among the leaves, but being out of the bubble of Westminster made me feel invisible for a few hours, which was exactly what I needed to think clearly.

My immediate instinct was not to react. A knee-jerk emotional response is never a good idea. If you can step back for a second, things are rarely as bad as they first seem. In every crisis I've ever had, if I've been able to take a deep breath and not react in the moment, it's always been the best decision. Even now, the dozens of requests from journalists wanting an interview from that day remain unopened on my phone. I wanted to take time to make sense of what had happened myself before I opened my mouth to answer.

I sat on the sand and ran through the events leading up to that point. When I'd started working on this book, my story was about a boy from Baghdad who'd fled a dictatorship, arrived in the UK with no English and went on to become the country's education secretary. Events over the past seven months had pushed all that up into one corner. More had happened to me in my political career since July than in the previous decade. Unlike those first eight years in Westminster, this last year had moved at breakneck speed, with no time to digest the ramifications. Despite the pitfalls, I still loved it. I was the guy who leapt out of bed in the morning, clapped my hands and said, 'This is gonna be a great day!' The thought of no longer being in cabinet was upsetting, not because of power or money but because it meant not being able to do my job. If anything had kept me going over the past twenty-four hours it was the messages from the teams I'd worked with saying I was a good leader and a decent human being, but they were as poignant as they were comforting. If the world outside thought I was a monster, I was grateful to have people I knew say different. Even so, I felt totally battered.

Alone with my thoughts, I began to doubt myself, questioning why I'd taken the job with Rishi in the first place. After all, I hadn't backed him in the leadership race. I did admire Rishi – he was bright, smart, efficient and talented – but we were a different intake and weren't close, and both he and I knew he was never 'my guy'. Had that played any part in my demise? I began to question it now. Perhaps my first instincts had been right and I should have just said a polite 'no thank you' when he'd asked me to be chairman. The personal attacks during the leadership race had made me feel it was time for a change of career. Perhaps I should have listened to my gut.

So why *did* I agree to take the job? Had I just been flattered to be asked? That was definitely a part of it. Rishi had sold it to me beautifully. He was going to hand over the mechanics of a party I'd been a part of since that day at the students' union during Freshers' Week almost forty years earlier. I was going to get it working again. That was music to my ears. I loved a challenge. It was just like that first dinner with Pete and Jonny; there were things I knew I could fix and I wanted to get involved.

And then there was the question of Sir Laurie. Would he have come to a different conclusion had I been given the chance to submit all the evidence? Or was I just damaged goods? I was, after all, a guy with a past outside parliament, which made me both good at my job but likewise 'tainted' by a life in business. I was 'unclean' in a way others weren't. Had that had something to do with it? It was impossible to say.

One day of navel-gazing, however, was more than enough. Fitter friends are constantly telling me about the power of exercise for mental health, and I decided there was no better test of that maxim than now. I rented a mountain bike and got pedalling. I did the same route every day for a week: 21 kilometres from A to Z. My own bike is gathering dust in our shed at home so the circuit nearly killed me at first, but it was a great distraction. Something to master. And it was true. These rides did do wonders for my sanity. Half term came and Lana arrived with Mia. It felt like a little piece of normality. I started to feel a renewed sense of equilibrium. We sat together in tears on the sofa as we watched *The Swimmers* about the two Syrian girls who flee Damascus. Despite the crisis, I felt like I could start enjoying my own life again and realised I'd normalised the scale of magnification on us. Lana said we were finally free: from the shackles of constantly worrying about what was happening in London and from the restrictions on when we could be together. It felt good to get out from under the microscope. When I'd come home and relay the events of the day in parliament, she'd often tell me, 'There's more to life than politics, Nadhim.' All she wanted to know was whether I'd helped Mia with her homework or talked through interview techniques and CVs with Ahmad and Jaafar. The world, she'd often say, is bigger than Westminster; not everything revolved around its corridors and conversations.

Two days later a 7.8-magnitude earthquake tore through Turkey and Syria. Everything I'd been churning over for the past week suddenly seemed pathetically trivial and insular. No one cared about Westminster here. I looked at the photograph of the man holding his daughter's hand trapped under the rubble, and wondered how he'd ever gain the strength to let go and get up and leave her. That was a real human crisis.

We drew breath and returned home, ready to face the world again. My little team. My family. With the pressures of cabinet removed, I answered the phone to my wife and kids when they called; I helped Mia fix the amp for her electric guitar so she could play 'Orange Crush' at her school concert; I made plans to go to sports day. It felt something like old times when the boys were small and all we really had to worry about was whose turn it was to be pushed on the swing.

A week is a long time in politics. In the space of seven days, everything I'd done over the course of my career had been cancelled. It was a brutal game, but oddly, I felt liberated. As much as I loved my job, it could be a straitjacket at times. From the backbenches I felt like I was seeing the world again. There was little I could do to change people's minds about me – at least not the minds of strangers. I'd have to hope that those who knew me still trusted me to do a good job, be a good friend and make the right choices. There was nothing left to do but get on with another day.

Four weeks later and the paparazzi had given up on my house and the front pages were dedicated to something or someone else. That's how we do politics in this country. The feeding frenzy is part of the political culture, but once they've got their scalp they move on. The decision about my departure was not just made by Rishi; it was made by the press in the court of public opinion. By popular demand. The weight of the story was too heavy to carry any longer. In the end, it would have crushed him too. So I got it. It didn't mean I liked it. The beautiful irony of it all was that YouGov had been the first to come out with a poll saying the public wanted me to step down. I had to laugh at the elegance of it: hoist with my own petard. It was Shakespearean.

After thirteen years as an MP, I'd had a chance to do quite a few jobs on the way up. I'd seen the big offices with the shiny doors but I also knew how to sweep the floors. The journey to the top had been an interesting one, but I don't believe my principles ever really changed on the way: surround yourself with talent, listen to what they have to say and do your best to make the kind of judgements that allow you to sleep easily at night. What I realise now was, whether I was working from the front or backbenches, it made little difference. It was still my job to get people into a room together to try and work things out. Whether that was sending an officious note on the Portcullis letterhead to help a guy get his driving licence back or preparing the energy package in Treasury to help the nation through a crisis, it was really the same thing when you reduced it down to the bare bones. The only difference was whether you were working at a granular level or scaling up, and I was very happy doing either. It was just like Thatcher had once said: there was no point coming into government unless you wanted to help people. How you did that didn't really matter, as long as you got it done.

In the end, Mum had been absolutely right: anything could happen here. I was just incredibly lucky that it had.

ACKNOWLEDGEMENTS

First and foremost, I want to thank my wife Lana and our children Ahmad, Jaafar and Mia for allowing me to publish such a personal account of my life, even though they are inherently very private people. For putting up with the hours of our evenings and weekends I should have spent with them but have instead devoted to working on this book. For being the epicentre of my world, running our lives and keeping me grounded. Thank you.

To my mum, dad and sister, who have all shared their memories of our lives together and allowed me to write about them here with total honesty. To my dad for passing on to me his skill and passion for business, and my mum for giving me the balance and thoughtfulness to use those things with care and compassion. And a special thanks to my dad who, even though memories have sadly failed with age, has tried so hard to help me tell my story. To my sister for doing her best to protect and guide me despite my best efforts to go off the rails. While the decision to come to the UK was born out of necessity, I will never be able to thank my parents sufficiently for bringing me to the place I now call home, and giving me the opportunity to be a part of its democratic framework.

I could not have produced this book without the support of a wonderful network of colleagues, friends and family – some of whom have given hours of their time reading and rereading to help me get things right; making sure I didn't blunder into an ill-thought-out conversation or a full-blown diplomatic incident.

In particular, I'd like to thank my brother-in-law, Broosk, for his help piecing together my childhood memories of Iraq and our trip to Kurdistan. I must also thank Jeffrey Archer – not only for his tireless support of my career, but for allowing me to write about him, warts and all, without allowing his ego to get in the way of what I hope is a sympathetic but realistic account of a man I consider to be a significant part of my life. To Jesse Norman for encouraging me to stand up and be counted in my early years as a politician; to Stephan Shakespeare for his integrity, intellect and partnership; and the late Neil Bruce-Copp for believing in us both and backing our venture. To Peter Dubens and Jonny Sieff for the start they gave me. To Kate Bingham, Emily Lawson and Ruth Todd not only for their commitment to their work but for taking the time to read and fill in the gaps in their parts of my story. To Brandon Lewis for his unswerving support and friendship, and James Price for always having the right answer somewhere in his pocket. To my long suffering PA, Katie Payne, who has supported me in my political career for twelve years and taken time out of her private life to read the manuscript and point out all the glaring errors. To Neil Blair and Rory Scarfe at The Blair Partnership, thank you for encouraging me to step into the abyss. Finally, to Charlie Redmayne at HarperCollins for giving me the chance to write my story in the style I wanted, and Imogen Gordon Clark for the more difficult task of taking it through to the printed page.

To describe the writing of this book as a rollercoaster would be an understatement. Coinciding, as it has, with the most turbulent period of my career to date, it's been an interesting journey. For helping me navigate the waters, I have to thank my collaborator,

ACKNOWLEDGEMENTS

Charlotte Sones. Over the course of eighteen months she listened to what I wanted to say and helped me find a voice with which to say it. I have loved the process of looking back over my life – finding accidental patterns and themes hidden where I least expected – and retracing my steps to the present day. Charlotte has been on hand every step of the way, helping me curate that story.

As we talked, what began as the tale of an immigrant boy who became the UK's education secretary slowly morphed into one about my values and the roots of my morality. A good 30 per cent of this story took place *after* we'd begun work on the book, and the ending that presented itself out of the confusion was not the one I'd originally envisaged. I hadn't intended to leave cabinet under a black cloud when we started, but the process of putting the story down on paper allowed me to evaluate my strengths and weaknesses. I hope what I have arrived at is an open and authentic account of how I came to the place I am now.

Over the course of my life I have done my best to surround myself with talented individuals and listen to what they have to say. There are many more people not mentioned in the pages you've read here to whom this mantra applies, but whom I must nonetheless thank for their part in my journey: Peter Kellner, Peter Bazalgette, Roger Parry, Sir Ben Elliot, Stefan Kaszubowski, Kate Tabram, Theresa Parker, James Holloway, Commander John Mankatee, Gerry Matthews, Mark Segalov, Mark Fullbrook, Sir Robbie Gibb, Nick Finegold, Richard Sharp, Adam Levinson, Sir Mohamed Mansour, Wafic and Khalid Said, James Archer, Jonnie Goodwin, Gary Eldon, Jón Ferrier, Sajid Javid, Lord Richard Harrington, David Meller, Lord Nicholas Soames and Sami Zouari. Last but certainly not least, all my great friends in the Middle East and across the world.

I realise I've taken a punt in writing a book like this – that I may be criticised for not having written a traditional political memoir – but I stand by my choice to try and give a different view of the life of a sitting MP. Many will question why I've chosen to write in so much detail about my years learning to read via the pages of the *Sun* or the tracksuit I wore as a football fanatic rather than taking time to go into greater depth about my years as a politician. Maybe one day I will write a more detailed, formal account of my political life, but for now I wanted to show that there are no superhumans in government. That, whatever you think of the people you see on the television or in the news, there's usually a pretty normal person behind that public persona and they're probably not so very different to you.

PICTURE CREDITS

While every effort has been made to trace the owners of copyright material reproduced herein and secure permissions, the publishers would like to apologise for any omissions and will be pleased to incorporate missing acknowledgements in any future edition of this book.

All photographs are courtesy of the author, with the following exceptions:

p. 1 (middle) Dellal (née Hafidh) McDonald
p.4 (top) 'The Simple Truth', produced by Tony Hollingsworth

p.5 (top) Geoff Robinson/Masons Pictures/SWNS

p.5 (bottom left) Avalon.red

p.6 (top) Broosk Saib

p.7 (top left, middle left, middle right) Simon Dawson/No. 10 Downing Street

p.7 (top right) Tom Nicholson/Pool/AFP via Getty Images

p.7 (bottom left) Andrew Parsons

p.7 (bottom right) Gareth Cattermole/Getty Images